Is God an Economist?

Also by Sigmund Wagner-Tsukamoto

HUMAN NATURE AND ORGANIZATION THEORY

UNDERSTANDING GREEN CONSUMER BEHAVIOUR

Is God an Economist?

An Institutional Economic Reconstruction of the Old Testament

Sigmund Wagner-Tsukamoto
School of Management, University of Leicester, UK

First published 2009 by
PALGRAVE MACMILLAN

Palgrave Macmillan in the UK is an imprint of Macmillan Publishers Limited, registered in England, company number 785998, of Houndmills, Basingstoke, Hampshire RG21 6XS.

Palgrave Macmillan in the US is a division of St Martin's Press LLC, 175 Fifth Avenue, New York, NY 10010.

Palgrave Macmillan is the global academic imprint of the above companies and has companies and representatives throughout the world.

Palgrave® and Macmillan® are registered trademarks in the United States, the United Kingdom, Europe and other countries.

ISBN-13: 978-0-230-22222-9   hardback
ISBN-10: 0-230-22222-6   hardback

This book is printed on paper suitable for recycling and made from fully managed and sustained forest sources. Logging, pulping and manufacturing processes are expected to conform to the environmental regulations of the country of origin.

A catalogue record for this book is available from the British Library.

A catalog record for this book is available from the Library of Congress.

10 9 8 7 6 5 4 3 2 1
18 17 16 15 14 13 12 11 10 09

Printed and bound in Great Britain by
CPI Antony Rowe, Chippenham and Eastbourne

To M., M. and N.

Contents

Figures

xii

Preface

In *Is God an Economist?* I introduce a fundamentally new way of looking
at the Old Testament. I reconstruct stories of the Old Testament, especially of Genesis and Exodus, in institutional and constitutional economic terms. Ultimately, this book is about truth and moral guidance
but a different kind of truth and moral guidance as is conventionally
associated by theology, moral philosophy or a religious economics with
the Old Testament. The emerging key thesis is that the stories of the
Bible fulfil a rational, institutional and constitutional economic function when it comes to questions of the societal contract, nation-building
and international cooperation. The search is on for a radical, economic
humanism in the Old Testament. This gives the Old Testament a highly
relevant and contemporary role for organizing life in modern society in
a rational, scientific manner.

I argue in this book that the Old Testament, in considerable degrees,
anticipated advances in modern constitutional and institutional economics, as it was pioneered, for instance, by F. Hayek, R. Coase,
J. Buchanan, G. Brennan, D. North, O. Williamson or V. Vanberg. In
the present book, I introduce theoretical concepts slowly, on a step-
by-step basis. This allows even readers who are initially not acquainted
with constitutional and institutional economics to follow my economic
reconstruction of the Old Testament. The intended audience of the
book ranges from scholars and professionals in the fields of economics,
philosophy, theology, sociology and the scientific study of religion to
students, laymen and anybody who shares an interest in, and is intellectually curious about, modern interpretations of the Bible.

The present book focuses on stories such as the Paradise story, the
stories involving Jacob, the Joseph stories and the stories surrounding
the Exodus. I argue that these stories reveal a conceptual structure that
mirrors and anticipates, in considerable degrees, a modern institutional
and constitutional economic approach and ideas such as governance
structures (incentive structures, property rights arrangements, the
constitutional contract), capital exchange, mutual gains, the model of
economic man (even opportunism and predation behaviour) and the
idea of an economic dilemma structure (the prisoner's dilemma, the
commons dilemma). I pay special attention to dilemmatic interaction
conditions of scarcity, on the one hand, and pluralism, ethnic diversity,

moral disagreement, even value decay, on the other. Such conditions characterize most Old Testament stories; for instance, when cooperation problems among tribes and nations are discussed with regard to the desert problem and the related scarcity in water or fertile land or when we meet interaction scenarios of a multicultural nature, for instance, Israel's and Egypt's interactions.

Key theses developed by the book are a climax thesis for the Joseph story of Genesis and a hero thesis for Joseph as well as a decline thesis for the stories that follow Genesis, and here in particular a non-hero thesis for Moses. I justify these theses in an enlightened, moral philosophical manner, specifically on the basis of a radical, economic humanism that can be attributed to the Joseph story of Genesis.

The resulting economic reconstruction of the Old Testament rivals theological, philosophical, sociological or psychological interpretations, among others. The book demonstrates that the Old Testament reveals a deeply economic ethos, even a radical, economic humanism. This fresh, new look at the Old Testament will lead to a good deal of constructive discussion with other disciplines.

Acknowledgements

This book began its life towards the end of 1999 when I started writing two articles on the economic interpretation of the Old Testament, which were initially published as Discussion Papers by the University of Leicester. They later appeared in 2001 in the *Journal of Interdisciplinary Economics* and in 2008 in the *Scandinavian Journal of the Old Testament*. These articles were initially inspired by my realization, when working on another book project at the time, *Human Nature and Organization Theory* (published by Edward Elgar, 2003), that the claimed dark image of human nature by economics – the model of economic man – has striking parallels with some of the characters in the Paradise story of the Old Testament. From here it is only a small step to critically and comprehensively challenge conventional interpretations of the Old Testament. The 2001 article then basically set out a research agenda for a modern, institutional and constitutional economic reconstruction of the Old Testament, which the present book followed up. Work seriously began on this book project in 2003 and it developed, step-by-step, into its present, final format over the next couple of years.

I am very grateful that I could write this book with the academic support of my peers but, of course, most of all, I would like to thank my family, and above all my wife and sons, for encouraging me to undertake this intellectually fascinating journey.

Copyright Acknowledgements

The author is grateful for the following permissions:
All scripture quotations, in this publication are from the Holy Bible, New International Version®. NIV®. Copyright © 1973, 1978, 1984 by International Bible Society. All rights reserved worldwide. Used by permission of Hodder & Stoughton Publishers, a member of the Hachette Livre UK Group. All rights reserved. 'NIV' is a registered trademark of International Bible Society. UK trademark number 1448790.

With kind permission of A. B. Academic Publishers, excerpts selectively taken from Sigmund Wagner-Tsukamoto (2001), 'Economics of Genesis: On the Institutional Economic Deciphering and Reconstruction of the Legends of the Bible', *Journal of Interdisciplinary Economics*, 12 (3), 249–87.

With kind permission of Edward Elgar Publishing, excerpts selectively taken from Sigmund Wagner-Tsukamoto (2003), *Human Nature and Organization Theory: On the Economic Approach to Institutional Organization*, Cheltenham, UK and Northampton, MA, USA.

With kind permission of Springer Science Media and Business Media, Figure 1 taken from Sigmund Wagner-Tsukamoto (2005), 'An Economic Approach to Business Ethics: Moral Agency of the Firm and the Enabling and Constraining Effects of Economic Institutions and Interactions in a Market Economy', *Journal of Business Ethics*, 60 (1), 75–89.

With kind permission of Taylor and Francis Publishers, excerpts selectively taken from Sigmund Wagner-Tsukamoto (2008), 'An Economic Reading of the Exodus: An Institutional Economic Reconstruction of Biblical Cooperation Failures', *Scandinavian Journal of the Old Testament*, 22 (1), 114–34 (see also http://www.informaworld.com).

With kind permission of the University of Chicago Press, Copyright © 1975 by the University of Chicago, excerpts (up to 750 words) taken from James M. Buchanan (1975), *The Limits of Liberty: Between Anarchy and Leviathan*, Chicago, USA and London, UK.

Introduction

Has the Old Testament anything to say to man today –
man living in a world of revolutions, automation, nuclear
weapons, with a materialistic philosophy that implicitly or
explicitly denies religious values?

(Fromm 1967: 3)

The Bible is one of the oldest and most widely read documents of man-kind's cultural heritage. Its existence raises questions regarding its ration-ale, purpose and relevance. It is full of symbolic meaning: 'The outwardly meaningless narrative may reveal inward truth and light. Before that truth and light can be received, the veil of allegory must be lifted and the symbols interpreted' (Hodson 1967: 8). Theology here lifts spiritual and metaphysical veils of meaning, referring to a spiritual motivation behind the Bible and issues such as the nature of God, the godly identity and nature of human beings, the holy nature of the world, the sacred history of Israel and related questions concerning the meaning of life and the human condition (e.g. Gräb 2002: 281–2, 289–90; Rogerson and Davies 1989: 116; Childs 1985: 43–50, 97–8; Tullock 1981: 1–3, 39–41; Bruce 1979: 390–1; Lace 1972: 103–6, 115–18; Hodson 1967: 114–16; von Rad 1963: 16). Gilkey (1962: 153) and Kaiser (2001: 81) clearly stated in this connection that for understanding the Old Testament the ques-tion that has to be examined is, what 'biblical authors meant to say' – and from here they move on, in a theological tradition, to spiritual and metaphysical issues. Now and then, theology related the relevance of the Old Testament to issues of belief and moral guidance (Kaiser 2001: 184–4). Early key examples of Old Testament theologies which take the Old Testament as the revelation of God, of the relationship of humans with God, etc. are the ones of Eichrodt or von Rad (Spriggs 1974: 7).

1

Besides spiritual purposes, one can think of secular motivations and worldlier, symbolic meanings of the Bible, especially in relation to the handling of social conflict within a society and among nations. A key thesis of the present book is that the Old Testament analyses the resolution of *economic conflict* in social interactions, specifically social interactions that concern nation-building and international relations in a multicultural, pluralistic context. The book argues that the question of the societal contract looms large in biblical texts. The present book applies in this respect ideas of constitutional and institutional economics to analyse these issues. This reflects the lifting of rather different veils of allegory and the interpretation of different symbols and meanings than spiritual and metaphysical ones.

The approach I pursue is an essentially non-metaphysical one. Ultimately, even the idea of God is reconstructed through concepts that lie at the heart of institutional and constitutional economics, for example, God being a partner in constitutional contracting among humans, such as a sovereign whose primary duty is to enforce laws and who is bound by agreements made by humans. I thus explore the scope for an economic humanism in the Old Testament. A quote from Buchanan well captures the purpose and direction of institutional and constitutional economic reconstruction the present study pursues:

> If man could but design a God who would punish for violations of man-determined rules, and would, at the same time, constrain his own impulse to power, stability and progress in social order might be insured. ... Only then could we think of social order as a game in which the umpire is neither himself among the players nor a potential seeker in the winnings. ... But faith cannot follow design; the man who might imagine such a God could not himself faithfully abide by the precepts. Shivering man must rely on his own resources to pull himself from and stay out of the Hobbesian war. ... Man cannot design a God, and man will not universally abide by the promises he makes. The world is neither Christian nor Kantian [nor Jewish, Islamic, Buddhist, etc.], although Christians and Kantians [and Jews, Moslems, Buddhists, etc.] inhabit it alongside their heathen and amoral brethren. The necessity for law enforcement must be squarely faced, regardless of our romantic yearnings for an imaginary paradise.
> (Buchanan 1975: 130–1, words in brackets added)

Of course, the idea of God is widely present in the Old Testament. But this presence as such does not immediately imply that the Old Testament were of a metaphysical nature, with humans relying on spiritual, godly interference and inspiration to resolve problems of social order. Buchanan discussed such problems with reference to the Hobbesian war. Rather, one can examine how far the texts of the Old Testament allow for a non-metaphysical, economic deconstruction and reconstruction of the very idea 'God'. Thus, I discuss how far, even for a text like the Old Testament, 'shivering man can rely on his own resources to pull himself from and stay out of the Hobbesian war'. In particular, I search in the Old Testament text for ideas and arguments that support an economic reconstruction of the Old Testament with respect to issues of social order and societal contracting. In this way, I unearth a deeply economic ethos, even a radical, economic humanism for the Old Testament.

Based on the works of pre-eminent economic scholars like J. Buchanan, G. Brennan, R. Coase, F. Hayek, G. Hodgson, K. Homann, D. North, V. Vanberg or O. Williamson, to name a few, institutional and constitutional economics has rapidly gained in significance and influence over the past decades. It is now one of the most promising and influential domains within economic research. Economics in general, and constitutional and institutional economics in particular, are especially strong when it comes to analysing questions of the societal contract, interest conflicts, cooperation dilemmas – and also pluralistic interaction conditions, as this book argues and unearths for the text 'Old Testament'.

Drawing on the constitutional and institutional economic approach, the present book reconstructs some of the most important stories of the Old Testament, such as the Paradise story, the stories involving Jacob, the Joseph stories, the stories surrounding and following the Exodus of the Israelites from Egypt and here, in particular, Moses' role. A key thesis in this respect is that an economic reconstruction of Old Testament stories provides better explanations and a more coherent and more integrative account than previous religious economic analysis of the Old Testament. The present book thus lives up to Paris' (1998: 42) call for a coherent Old Testament economics. By bringing a systematic approach to Old Testament research, the present research also competes with theological research on the Old Testament, which has been accused of ad hoc theorizing, lacking theoretical coherence and integration and random, arbitrary or metaphysical interpretations (Iannaccone 1995: 78).

The present study aims to enlighten scholars, laymen and anybody who shares an interest and curiosity about one of the oldest and most fascinating pieces of literature of mankind. The academic audience of the book ranges from the fields of economics, theology, philosophy, the sociology of religion and the economics of religion to the fields of the scientific study of religion. In addition, the book aims at students, laymen and a public audience who come without a prior or profound knowledge about the Bible. The economic ideas and concepts I apply in this book are introduced step-by-step, and technical, conceptual explanations are developed slowly. Also, I have recapitulated important concepts and ideas throughout the book where necessary. I interpret the economic approach along a set of five key ideas. In theoretical perspective, I draw on the idea of incentive structures, or 'governance structures' in Williamson's (1985) terms. They provide an institutional regulative for social exchange and societal contracting. Another theoretical idea is the one of capital contribution–distribution interactions as model of social exchange. In practical, normative perspective, I apply the idea of mutuality of gains as desirable interaction outcome. In instrumental, methodical perspective, I draw on an interest–conflict model of social exchange – the idea of a dilemma structure or the 'war of all' as Hobbes figuratively called it. A final methodical idea is the model of economic man – the self-interested maximizer of own gain ('homo economicus'). On this basis, I develop the constitutional and institutional economic analysis and reconstruction of Old Testament stories. These ideas allow for a particular economic conceptualization of the 'societal contract': how a group of people can develop and maintain productive and cooperative interactions. Special strengths of the framework applied are its conciseness and conceptual coherence. Chapter 1 has further details, but already at this early stage it is worthwhile stressing that a social conflict model is of paramount importance to the analysis conducted by the present book. Such a conflict model lies at the heart of institutional and constitutional economic analysis:

> If there is no conflict among separate persons, there is no basis for social contract; there is no need for law, as such. By the same token, however, there is no need for ethics; there is no function of a moral code. In the strict no-conflict setting, pure anarchy remains ideal without tempering. When conflict does emerge, however, anarchy in its pure form fails, and the value of order suggests either some social contract, some system of formal law, *or* some generally accepted set of ethical-moral precepts.
>
> (Buchanan 1975: 117, emphasis as in original)

As it becomes very quickly clear in an analysis of the Old Testament, social conflict is an ever-present topic. For instance, Brams (1980: 78) noted, the Old Testament reflects 'conflict piled upon conflict, with battles, war, and family feuds [as] the norm rather than the exception' (see also Childs 1985: 74–7). Apparently, what Buchanan (1975) referred to as 'Hobbesian anarchy' and the 'Hobbesian jungle,' is all the time encountered in the Old Testament, with interaction and cooperation problems abundant in the society depicted in the Old Testament. This society was mostly still engaged in conquering its own land, in nation-building and in developing stable relations with other nations, with legal–political and economic institutions largely undefined and still emerging. Miller (1993a) discussed a nation-building purpose from a legal–economic perspective for some of the early stories of Genesis. The present study extends on this theme, by means of constitutional and institutional economic reconstruction. I argue that the key purpose and relevance of the Old Testament lies in addressing modern interaction conflicts in the context of nation-building and in developing international relations, with societal contracts still emerging. The idea of the 'modern' is here roughly interpreted as pluralistic interaction contexts where competing tribes and people did not share same values and beliefs, where moral disagreement was high and possibly even value decay raged within a society.

In this connection, I pick up Fromm's (1967: 4) critical comments on much previous analysis of the Old Testament, that 'the Old Testament is believed to express exclusively the principles of justice and revenge … and that it is believed to have been written exclusively in a spirit of narrow nationalism and to contain nothing about supranational universalism.' Like Fromm, I challenge such conventional beliefs but in difference to his liberatory, humanist philosophical approach I do so from an economic perspective, and from here I make suggestions on how the Old Testament can be projected to questions of economically inspired societal contracts in pluralistic, international settings. The interaction conditions of pluralism and moral disagreement among agents imply that from the two routes outlined by Buchanan (1975: 117) to overcome social conflict, as quoted above, social contract is likely to be the one that dominates the analysis of social conflict in the Old Testament since the presence of pluralism – of ethnic diversity, moral disagreement, even value decay among parties – implies that 'some generally accepted set of ethical-moral precepts' is both difficult to negotiate and more costly to maintain than economic order. In the Old Testament, social conflict was played out in a complex, multicultural interaction setting, Israel even facing pluralism, diversity and moral disagreement among its own tribes besides seeing itself confronted with powerful neighbouring tribes and states, for example, Egypt, Assyria, Persia or Babylon, which did not share the values and beliefs of Israel. Considering these types of problems and interaction conditions, the relevance of the Old Testament for contemporary social problems, not only in the Near or Middle East, becomes easily apparent, especially – so this book argues – when the Old Testament is interpreted through the ideas of constitutional and institutional economics. Of course, in the stories of the Old Testament, other interaction conditions further aggravate the analysis and resolution of social problems, specifically the special socio-geographical and geopolitical conditions of the Near or Middle East they are located in. The desert problem and the threat of dilemmatic scarcities, poverty, famine and starvation are ever looming in the social scenarios depicted in the Old Testament.

The present book derives its originality by bringing a new approach to Old Testament interpretation, namely concepts from constitutional and institutional economics, which were not available to previous Old Testament studies. This allows for a radical, non-metaphysical, humanist economic interpretation and reconstruction of the Old Testament. Although Fromm did not favour the economic approach, he early on argued for the appropriateness of a radical approach to the Old Testament: 'Perhaps, paradoxically enough, one of the oldest books of Western culture can be best understood by those who are least fettered by tradition and most aware of the radical nature of the process of liberation going on at the present time' (Fromm 1967: 7). Buber (1982: 4–5) argued along similar lines. Based on the institutional and constitutional economic approach, the present study lifts a new 'veil of allegory' for understanding the Bible and it advances a new radical view on what the Bible tells us about human conflict handling.

It is especially the new approach of constitutional and institutional economics that allows me to make claims to original findings. I do not want to claim that this approach can explain 'everything' in the Old Testament but I am convinced that it gets at least a step or two closer to holding a 'magic key' for unlocking some of the mysteries of the Bible than previous books. Brams (1980: 177) was in this respect rather self-critical regarding his economic, game-theoretical analysis of the Old Testament. In my view, the economic analysis developed by the present book on the Old Testament and how Old Testament stories interrelate is unrivalled regarding explanatory power and conceptual coherence. In general, a behavioural approach to economics and ethics, such as a religious economics, has significant theoretical and practical deficits when conditions of pluralism, moral disagreement and competition are considered (Wagner-Tsukamoto 2003: 204–6; see also Wagner-Tsukamoto 2008c, 2008d, 2007a, 2007b, 2005). The non-behavioural economic interpretation of the Old Testament developed in the present book is in this regard an advance since it clearly shows that the old dualism of economics and theology (and philosophy in general), on which most ethics approaches are built, is historically and systematically not justified. This implies some very significant progress in interdisciplinary debate, as Karl Homann's stated (see book cover).

When deconstructing the ideas of the Old Testament in economic terms, I follow a so-called *source-critical* approach to Old Testament research. This approach rejects the so-called *literalist* thesis, specifically the idea that the Bible is a holy text, reflecting the word of God. For instance, Bruce (1979: 387) claimed that the 'Old Testament retains its independent quality of divine revelation.' In contrast, the source-critical approach I follow attests to the so-called documentary hypothesis, which suggests that the Bible is a purely man-made text (Paris 1998: 39–40). My research also finds no problem to subscribe to other ideas which have gained increasing acceptance in theological research on the Old Testament, namely that a kind of narrative-art impulse drives Bible stories, and related hereto, that the Old Testament reflects a rational text, being purposefully organized but being not a 'haphazard compilation of archaic texts' (Paris 1998: 41; see also Wagner-Tsukamoto 2001a: 279; 2008a). The 'narrative-art' impulse my research identifies in the Old Testament is the constitutional and institutional economic approach. This also connects back to the idea of searching for a 'new' veil of meaning and a different kind of truth and humanism in the Old Testament as compared with theology and religious economics.

The key questions of the book are:

- Can economic concepts and ideas be found in the Old Testament, in particular ideas that reflect constitutional and institutional economic thought?
- Is the Old Testament interested in cooperation problems? Are cooperation problems resolved in relation to the idea of mutual gains?
- Is succeeding/failing cooperation analysed in relation to the human condition (values or moral precepts held by the individual) or in relation to situational conditions (institutions such as incentive structures, property rights arrangements, constitutional contracts, economically understood)?
- Does the Old Testament predominantly draw on value structures ('behavioural institutions') or incentive structures ('economic institutions', e.g. governance structures) to resolve interaction conflict?
- Does social exchange reflect a capital contribution–distribution model?

- Do biblical interactions reflect a dilemma structure, as abstractly illustrated by the prisoner's dilemma or the commons dilemma?
- Do biblical characters reflect the model of economic man?
- What models of the societal contract can be found in the Old Testament: value-based, behavioural ones and/or economically inspired, non-behavioural ones?
- How far are interaction conditions like the desert problem and pluralism a topic in Bible stories and how does their presence affect the resolution of interaction problems?
- Do the stories of the Old Testament have implications for modern cooperation problems regarding constitutional contract, nation-building, international relations and/or the multicultural, global society?
- How far can the idea of God be deconstructed in economic terms, for example, as economic cooperation principles and economic, ethical ideals, such as the wealth of nations (mutual gains)?

Through addressing these questions, I deconstruct and reconstruct Old Testament stories in economic terms and ultimately reflect upon the question, 'whether God is an economist'. Chapters 2 to 5 deal with the economic reconstruction of Old Testament stories as such. Indirectly, this already hints at a non-metaphysical deconstruction of the idea of God in Bible stories. Besides addressing the question whether God is an economist in such an indirect way, a more direct approach is sought in Chapter 6, which is of a more reflective nature in comparison to previous chapters. Specifically, the chapters of the book proceed as follows:

Chapter 1 outlines key ideas of the constitutional and institutional economic approach which I apply to the analysis of the Old Testament. It specifies differences of my economic reconstruction in comparison to theological research and previous, religious economic research on the Old Testament, which frequently was grounded in theology. I also reflect in Chapter 1 on the question of the permissibility of scientific, economic research on the stories of the Old Testament.

Chapter 2 takes a closer look at the first story of Genesis which discusses social conflict – the Paradise story. The chapter argues that, above all, the Paradise story has to be read in methodical, heuristic perspective when it comes to the analysis of subsequent Bible stories. The Paradise story seemingly models a dilemma structure of rationally foolish behaviour, which heuristically drives later stories of the Old Testament. A key message of the Paradise story is that 'defective' incentive structures have to be focused on in order to resolve social conflict, ensure cooperation, a stable, productive societal contract and outcomes such as mutual gains.

Subsequently, so I argue in later chapters of this book, the Joseph story and the Moses story reflect ultimate, positive and negative examples of how the Eden dilemma was respectively resolved or not resolved.

Chapter 3 focuses on the institutional economic analysis of Genesis, especially the Joseph story, which is one of the longest and richest stories of the Old Testament. The story is interpreted as the culmination of successful institutional and constitutional economic problem-solving in the Bible. Then, the skilful intervention of the Israelite Joseph at the top of Egypt's industrial hierarchy mastered interaction conditions such as dilemmatic desert problems and pluralism among interaction partners. I critically examine and discount conventional characterizations of Joseph as an anti-hero or non-hero. Implications for international cooperation are derived from Egypt and Israel's successful interactions.

Chapter 4 discusses the apparent counter-story to the Joseph story: the Exodus story and the interactions between Moses and Egypt's pharaoh. I analyse failing cooperation and escalating conflict between Egypt and Israel as an unresolved economic dilemma structure, for which the 'rulers' of Egypt and Israel, but also an interventionist God, were to blame. Interaction outcomes resulted which can be assessed as rationally foolish since both sides lost despite the possibility that both could have won – if only cooperation had succeeded (as demonstrated in the final stories of Genesis).

Chapter 5 extends the economic reconstruction of Bible stories beyond the books of Genesis and Exodus. For the other books of the Old Testament, I advance the claim that they can be interpreted in economic terms, too. The chapter is structured into two parts, dealing, first, with the Exodus journey and, second, with the resettlement phase. Frequently, in these stories religious crusades and zero-sum games are described which aimed to exterminate other tribes and conquer their land. Some rather painful conclusions emerge in this respect regarding the breakdown of the societal contract. An exception is king Solomon's reign when successful economic ordering made Israel a powerful and wealthy nation, which succeeded to maintain stable relations with its neighbours.

Chapter 6 subjects the idea of God to an economic interpretation. At different levels of abstraction, I raise the question of how the idea of God can be deconstructed in constitutional and institutional economic terms. At the most concrete, I interpret God as an interaction agent who joins humans in social interactions. Still at the rather concrete, 'God' is thought of as a contracting host, a sovereign or 'ruler'. In a more abstract perspective, I discuss 'God' as (an economic/non-economic) principle of social ordering. At the most abstract, the book analyses 'God' as an (economic/non-economic) meta-variable of the Unexplained in general. I derive implications regarding wider questions, such as the meaning of life, the question of God and schisms between economics and theology / religion an economic reconstruction might create – or reduce. The chapter argues that, on the one hand, constitutional and institutional economics, properly understood, can help to reduce schisms between economics and religious studies of the Bible and religion in general. On the other hand, economic reconstruction and the secular, rational approach it implies necessitates a theological reformulation of certain questions, such as the one regarding the specific nature of God.

Chapter 7 summarizes the key findings of an institutional economic reconstruction of the Old Testament. It discusses the question of how far the Old Testament can provide role models for societal contracts, international relations and nation-building. I comment on concepts of an economic reconstruction of the Old Testament, especially the model of economic man and dilemma structures as well as organization structures. The chapter also reviews environmental conditions, such as scarcity and pluralism as interaction conditions of Old Testament storytelling. Revisiting Max Weber's work, I argue for a potentially capitalist ethic of the Old Testament. Finally, the chapter returns to the question of whether God is an economist.

1
The Economic Approach to Reconstructing the Bible

There is nothing new under the sun. Is there anything of which one can say, 'Look! This is something new'? It was here already, long ago; it was here before our time.

(Ecclesiastes 1: 9–10)

This chapter prepares the economic reconstruction of the stories of the Old Testament. The key thesis I advance is that the Old Testament aims at economic questions of societal contracting, nation-building, international relations and constitutional and institutional ordering in general. The resolution of social conflict and cooperation problems is seemingly the goal. From here, one can derive modern principles from the Old Testament for solving cooperation problems in contemporary settings of social conflict, such as the multicultural society or the international community.

Economists, like Hayek, Coase, Buchanan, Brennan, North, Vanberg or Williamson, for example, may have pioneered the constitutional and so-called new institutional economic approach only over the past half-century or so. However, as it will become apparent in subsequent chapters of this book, basic ideas and principles that compare to this economic approach can already be found in the Old Testament. And in this respect, this book holds up the thesis that there has been 'nothing new under the sun' for the past 2000–3000 years for addressing social problems of societal contracting, nation-building and international relations. Here, the key thesis emerges that both on historical and conceptual grounds, the old dualism and widely claimed dichotomy between economics, on the one hand, and theology, religion, philosophy and ethics, on the other, may have to be very critically re-examined. A deeply capitalist ethic seems to organize the Old Testament. A related thesis is that the Old Testament has a high contemporary relevance. From a constitutional and institutional economic point of view, I here critically question Meeks' (1989) theological, religious economic analysis of the Bible which asserted that 'there is, of course, no scientific economic theory in the modern sense in the Bible. ... The Bible cannot solve any technical problems facing us today' (Meeks 1989: 3).

In the following, first, I outline key ideas of the institutional and constitutional economic approach (section 1.1). Mostly, from now on, I will use in this book the notion of 'institutional economics' only since it is the potentially broader concept, covering constitutional economics as well. However, when I am dealing with constitutional economic works in particular, for instance, of Buchanan, Brennan or Vanberg, I will use the more specific term of 'constitutional economics'. Second, this chapter distinguishes the institutional economic approach from theological and religious economic research on the Old Testament (section 1.2). Third, I address the question of whether a text like the Old Testament should be and could be analysed from a rational, scientific point of view (section 1.3).

1.1   How to read Old Testament stories in institutional economic terms

In the following, I introduce a framework of institutional economics that distinguishes so-called theoretical, practical concepts, which are open to empirical testing, from heuristic, methodical ones, which are of a pre-empirical nature and thus are beyond empirical testing. To the empirical category belong ideas like 'incentive structures', 'interest equilibration', 'capital contribution–distribution interactions' and 'mutuality of gains as interaction outcome'. The latter idea is potentially also of a normative nature when it comes to practical intervention in the course of institutional design. Heuristic, methodical ideas are the model of 'economic man' and the idea of the 'dilemma structure', as illustrated by the prisoner's dilemma. All these ideas form the backbone of my economic reconstruction of the Old Testament. Before introducing and discussing these ideas, I briefly explain the textual, non-redactional, non-historiographical approach taken by the present study.

On the textual nature of Old Testament deconstruction

In my analysis of the Old Testament, I focus on the books of Genesis and Exodus but Chapter 5 extends the discussion to the other books of the Torah and the Deuteronomic history (i.e. up to the books of Kings).

Reasons of relevance and economy justify this focus. Also, as far as the composition of the Old Testament is concerned, biblical interpretation in the various books of the Old Testament is an ongoing process, as Kugel (1997: 556–7) noted, with later books of the Old Testament interpreting earlier ones. By focusing on the Old Testament's earliest books (up to the ones of the Deuteronomic history), I cut short this problem of interpreting interpretations.

The deconstruction of Old Testament stories in this book is purely historical–textual in nature, meaning, my deconstruction follows the storyline laid out in the Old Testament. I treat the Old Testament as mere text (see also Clines 1998: 29–31, 43–4). By 'textual analysis' I mean the analytic interpretation – through economic reconstruction – of the Old Testament text as it presents itself to us today. Economic theory is applied to unravel plot construction of the Old Testament and to better our understanding of economic elements of a fictional situation; 'literary exegesis' is conducted (see also Brams 1994: 33, 35, 46). My book leaves aside the question of the actual historicity or historiography of the Old Testament, whether it reflected a witness statement of Israel, a multilayered account of what happened or actual, non-legendary events in space-time that are depicted in narrative–historical prose (Kaiser 2001: chapters 4–6; Rogerson and Davies 1989: 91, 116; Childs 1985: 16; Cazelles 1979). Feinman (1991: 29–31) or Kaiser (2001) argued along these lines for the actual historicity of events depicted in the Old Testament. In contrast, others have argued as follows:

> In order to discover the … wisdom of the … scriptures we must divest ourselves from the notion that they were conceived and written entirely as chronologically and historically authentic accounts of actual events. Rather are they to be read as blends of history, metaphor and revelations of occult and mystic lore.
>
> (Hodson 1967: 35)

Especially for the stories that precede the books of Kings in the Old Testament, it has been argued that the question of historicity needs to be left aside. Historical reconstruction is, up to this point, difficult and questionable (Rogerson and Davies 1989: 133; Thompson 1974: 2–5; similarly Plaut 1981: 1015). As Armstrong noted for the book of Genesis:

> The authors of Genesis do not give us historical information about life in Palestine during the second millennium BC. In fact, as scholars have shown us, they knew nothing about the period. … Our authors

are not interested in historical accuracy. Instead they bring to the reader's attention important truths about the *human predicament* that still reverberates today.

(Armstrong 1996: 7, emphasis changed)

Similarly Lemche (2005: 210) argued with regard to the work of critical scholars in theology on the historicity of events depicted in the books of Genesis and Exodus. Hence, the literary treatment of the Old Testament appears important in this respect. Accordingly, I interpret religion, religious events and God as depicted in the Old Testament in mere textual perspective, specifically as aspects of a textual, interconnected *economic* reality. This reflects economic reductionism. Its purpose is the institutional economic reconstruction of the Old Testament, creating a better – economic – understanding of the apparent 'human predicament' that is analysed in the Old Testament. Some theological researchers lament this – Childs (1985: 25) does so regarding the sociological approach – but then scientific reductionism is the hallmark of scientific research and the growth of scientific knowledge (Wagner-Tsukamoto 2003). Other theological researchers have been more enlightened in this respect; for instance, Schmidt (1989: 129) acknowledged that a sociological reading of the Bible does not 'involve the evaluation of the truth, historicity, or veracity of the [biblical] text'. The same claim can be made for an economic reconstruction of the Old Testament.

As Childs (1985: 15–16) noted, there is no one correct way to interpret the stories of the Old Testament. The introduction of categories for interpretation – systematic ones, historical ones, theological, sociological or economics ones or others – depends on the quality of insights generated. The present study makes claims to original insights that a textual, economic approach to Bible stories yields. I guess Brett's (2000) discussion of methodological pluralism for the study of Genesis would support this argument too.

Regarding its general approach, my reconstruction of the Old Testament proceeds in rational, institutional economic terms. This is compatible, in degrees, with so-called revisionist theological approaches to Old Testament studies. Revisionist, theological studies identify narrative art as the foundation of biblical storytelling. Basically, the present study applies institutional economics as 'narrative art' to the Old Testament (see also Brett 2000: 58). Ideas of research heuristics and of research approach come close to what a more literature-oriented genre terms narrative impulse or narrative art (Wagner-Tsukamoto 2003; Wagner 1997).

On a related point, the research focus of the present study is non-redactional, that means it differs from the focus of so-called redactional, 'authorship' research, which is conducted by theology (e.g. Briend 2000; Westermann 1987, 1986, 1984; Clements 1979; Eissfeldt 1974). This type of research dissects the Old Testament in relation to the question of who wrote different bits and pieces of the Old Testament. It identifies, at times right down to the level of individual verses, words and even letters, different authors. Theology has spent much time and effort in this way to dissect the Old Testament according to different sources of authors, and various hypotheses have been proposed in this regard, such as the documentary hypothesis for Genesis, the fragmentary hypothesis, the supplementary hypothesis, etc. (Weiser 1961: 75–7, 80–1; see also Mayes 1983: 1–21, 39). Basically, these theses reflect that the Old Testament initially evolved over many centuries through a redaction process in which various authors and schools of authors participated. One kind of secular implication of this type of source-critical research is – one with which I can agree – that the Old Testament is a man-made text, which in metaphysical perspective at best reflects the revelation of the Word of God through humans but not directly the Word of God.

Despite centuries of redactional research on the authorship question, theology has not produced conclusive findings on this issue. Weiser noted with regard to literary, redactional research on the Old Testament and the results it has yielded:

> In view of the widely differing attempts to dissect the sources of the Pentateuch further, it is hard to resist the impression that the method of literary criticism for identifying the sources down to the individual wording has reached its limit and has sometimes exceeded it.
> (Weiser 1961: 80)

As stated, there is much debate in the theological community on how and when the compilation of different texts into the single piece of literary work, that is, the Old Testament happened and which authors were involved (for a review, see, for example, Gilboa 1998: 13–14). The lack of conclusive findings on the authorship question may indicate that it is as such comparatively irrelevant for understanding the nature and questions of the Old Testament. If one follows Miller (1993a) who points towards an oral tradition of emerging Bible stories, the authorship question appears even more futile to address. Also, I fully agree with Valiquette (1999: 65) that meaning predominantly resides in texts not in verses, sentences, words or even letters. Hence, for the interpretations developed in this book, the question of authorship and redactional processes was intentionally sidelined: The author who had the 'last word' on the writing of the Old Testament, as reflected by the way the Old Testament presents itself to us today, provides the implicit reference point for questions of authorship. Regarding this 'last word' approach, I connect to Fromm's (1967: 8) approach that suggested:

> The Hebrew Bible ... can be read as *one* book, in spite of the fact that it was compiled from many sources. It has become *one* book, not only through the work of the different editors but also through the fact that it has been read and understood as one book for the last two thousand years.
>
> (Emphasis as in original; see also Fromm 1967: 24)

Pfeiffer (1948: 29) similarly commented on this process that led to the composition of the Old Testament as one piece of literary work as follows: 'Out of single stories ..., the Hebrew storytellers created cycles of tales or novels.... Eventually outstanding literary men wove folk tales, sagas, and legends into the great national epics recounting the heroic age of ancient Israel.' Regarding the 'last word' approach, Brett (2000: 58) found that narratological analysis of the Old Testament proceeds similarly. Kaiser (2001: 48–9) affirms in this respect that a high consensus has emerged in the field of Old Testament studies regarding the textual soundness of the Old Testament. Similarly, Vanderkam (1994: 122–5) noted that the copying of the Old Testament through time (before printing press was invented) was conducted with high diligence, yielding only surprisingly little variations from times as far back as a couple of centuries before Christ through to the middle ages. Also, for the books one and two of the Bible, Genesis and Exodus, which the present study focuses on in Chapters 2 to 4, there have been comparatively few disputes regarding authorship. It is generally acknowledged that they belong to the oldest parts of the Old Testament. The same applies for the other books of the Torah as well as books of the Deuteronomic history that are focused on in Chapter 5 of this study. Therefore, the present study sidelines the authorship question and the question of redactional research.

A possible dialectic in the Old Testament between 'behavioural economics' and conventional ('non-behavioural', 'situational') economics, as it is unearthed in Chapter 3 of this book, can be explored with regard to questions of authorship of the Bible. Such questions are debated in the theological literature regarding different groups of authors: avowed economically oriented Yahwists and avowed spiritually oriented Elohists (Gordon 1994: 19–21). In this respect, I examine whether Elohists were as 'non-economically' oriented as claimed: They may have pursued 'at least' a behavioural economics. In general, my institutional economic analysis of the Old Testament can shed new light on questions of authorship by focusing first on the *why* of authorship, asking what basic problems motivated the writing of the Bible before the *who* of authorship is re-examined. Possibly, theology has paid too much attention to the question of authorship in its own right. As noted, the absence of conclusive findings on questions of authorship despite centuries of theological research seem to underline this point.

Also, it is very clear that I am not interested in textual criticism in the sense subscribed to by Holmes (1989: 53), who traced and found through 'textual analysis' the earliest and original composition and transmission of the texts of the Bible. Rather, my 'textual' analysis treats the Old Testament as one piece of literary work. I focus on substantive issues when it comes to Old Testament analysis, namely the textual analysis of social conflict through the institutional economic approach. In this way, I assessed contents and context issues for Old Testament stories. The book builds its textual analysis on a standard version of the Bible, as it is available today (*The Holy Bible*, Hodder & Stoughton, New International Version, Copyright by the International Bible Society). In this respect, I assume some canonical agreement regarding what constitutes the text 'Old Testament'. I subscribe to the hypothesis that the Old Testament was composed as a whole and has to be read as a whole. I follow the 'last word' approach, as it was referred to above (see also Brett 2000: 55–6; Gilboa 1998: 223; Valiquette 1999: 49–50). I agree with Otzen et al. (1980: 47) that 'the most important thing is to understand the [Old Testament] narrative in its final form'. In this connection, I largely followed Gilboa's key assumptions on the textual analysis of the Old Testament, although I did not follow her mythically inclined approach but an economic approach. Specifically, I agree with Gilboa (1998: 28): The textual analysis of the Old Testament has to focus on the 'current traditional manuscript'; the Old Testament (and here especially the Torah as focused on by the present study) is regarded 'as having been written by one author who is responsible for the final version of the text'; the Old Testament is to be examined as a 'secular narrative', free from metaphysical assumptions, and 'therefore, God is but a literary persona in it'; concepts from the social sciences can be applied to the analysis of the Old Testament (instead of Gilboa's psychological–mythical motifs, I apply economic ideas); 'all suggested interpretations ... have to be grounded in the text and the text alone.'

To sum up, rather than by focusing on the authorship question, the present study is driven by the question of which specific purpose the Old Testament was written for, and here I focus on institutional economic ones. As indicated, this approach is supported by the absence of conclusive findings of theological, authorship research and redaction research on the Old Testament. Especially in view of the dissatisfying results authorship research has yielded, a basic reorientation of research on the text 'Old Testament' is advisable. I seek this reorientation by means of non-redactional, institutional economic reconstruction. In the following, I now introduce the key concepts of institutional economic reconstruction.

Incentive structures and the societal contract

Institutional economics analyses interaction conflict through concep-tualizing a special type of institution: *incentive structures*. They reflect the 'rules of the game' and have to be strictly distinguished from the 'moves of the games' made by agents and even more so from the agents themselves (Hodgson 2006: 9). This understanding of 'institutions' is compatible with a more general understanding of institutions which defines institutions as 'systems of established and prevalent social rules that structure social interactions.' (Hodgson 2006: 2; North 1990: 3–5) However, the kind of social rules this study is mainly interested in are *economic institutions*, which could be said to be 'prevailing rule structures that provide incentives and constraints for individual action.' (Hodgson 2006: 6) I would further specify this understanding of economic institu-tions with regard to an economic *inter*action model rather than a mere model of individual action. This is done below, especially when I discuss the idea of the dilemma structure. Examples of economic institutions this study is interested in are basically *governance structures* in the way Williamson (1985, 1975) linked them to the economic approach.

I will reconstruct contractual arrangements (which set out payment rules, property rights allocations, etc.), organizational structures (such as pay systems, hierarchical decision rights systems, promotion sys-tems, etc.) and laws as economic institutions, specifically as incentive structures. Incentive structures specify decision-making rights of agents as well as capital contribution arrangements and capital distribu-tion arrangements. Incentive structures sanction choice behaviour of agents by linking different capital gains and capital losses (or 'costs')

of 'central authority' and constitutionalism arises here immediately – of who is going to design economic institutions. In this respect, Buchanan's, North's or Williamson's underlying research question is how cooperation can be encouraged to emerge from interaction conflict in a world of economic men *with the support of a central authority*, which intervenes with governance structures, to use Williamson's terminology. Of course, the issue of central authority is widely present in the Old Testament, for instance in relation to the idea of God and how God intervenes in the organization of human interactions. But worldly players and rulers too perform a huge part in the Old Testament when it comes to conflict handling. The present study will show in this respect that the apparent pre-eminence of central authority in the Old Testament lends a higher relevance to governance-oriented institutional economics for analysing the Old Testament as compared with an evolutionary economics. The key research question of Axelrod's (1984: 3) evolutionary economics, for instance, is: 'Under what conditions will cooperation emerge in a world of egoists *without central authority*?' (emphasis added; see also North and Taylor 2004: 1). As noted, this approach is likely to be less relevant for Old Testament analysis than an institutional economic one which involves the question of 'central authority'.

I link my economic analysis of the institutional problem to the problem of *societal contracting*: of how to avoid war-like anarchy in a society or organization and ensure cooperation among interacting members of a society or organization. The key means the present study applies for analysing social conflict and related societal contracting are incentive structures. In my economic analysis of the Old Testament, the concept of the 'covenant' and what it exactly stipulated between God and the people is in this connection of high importance. It explicitly enables us to analyse societal contracting in the Old Testament and I will do so from a conventionally non-behavioural, economic perspective, mostly a constitutional economic one. As Fromm (1967: 24–9) noted, the nature of a contract ('covenant') between God and the people changes throughout the Old Testament – and the present study analyses such changes regarding supposed societal contracting in economic perspective through the ideas depicted by Figure 1.1.

Social philosophy has conceptualized and discussed the idea of societal contracting at least since Hobbes. Buchanan (1975) essentially reconstructed such social philosophy in a non-behavioural, economic manner, with explicit reference to concepts such as economic institutions, mutual gains and dilemma structures (e.g. Buchanan 1975: 23–8, 130–46). The key analytical question here is: 'Might existing institutions conceptually have emerged from contractual behaviour of men?' (Buchanan 1975: ix) And Buchanan (1975: 130) focused especially on the question of how, without relying on God in the first place, 'shivering man must rely on his own resources to pull himself from and stay out of the Hobbesian war.' Societal contracting, as set out by the contractarian, constitutional economic paradigm, then tests alternative sets of incentive rules for organizing social order:

> Whether the contractarian paradigm is applied at the level of simple exchange, within the constraints of well-defined rules, or at the most basic constitutional level where institutions themselves are the objects upon which agreement must be reached, or at any intermediate level, the emergent results of the trading process are properly summarized as a set of optimal solutions, each one of which represents a possible outcome and none one of which dominates any other in the set.
>
> (Buchanan 1977: 239)

Practical, normative institutional economic analysis has to generate mutually acceptable rules or 'institutions' that can efficiently (speak: in a pareto-superior manner) govern social exchange through a social contract model. Its purpose is to analyse 'alternative institutions on which members of the community of rational individuals might agree jointly' (Buchanan and Tullock 1962: 316). Importantly, institutional rules, as they set out societal contracting,

> are, and must be, selected at a different level and via a different process than the decisions made within those rules ... and conceptual agreement among individuals provides the only benchmark against which to evaluate observed rules and actions taken within those rules.
>
> (Buchanan 1977: 11; also Buchanan 1975: ix)

Buchanan (1975: 31) here specified that from an anarchic, war-like, *'natural distribution state'*, in which no cooperative gains are realized by interacting parties, a constitutional contract has to be negotiated that allows interacting parties to better their respective welfare positions. This happens as a matter of *'disarmament contracts'* through which interacting parties agree to reduce investment efforts in predatory and defence activities, as they characterize the natural distribution state. Once a constitutional contract has been reached, so-called post-constitutional contracting becomes possible both regarding private-goods exchanges and regarding public-goods exchanges.

The present study will argue that institutional problems of societal contracting are an ever-present issue in the Old Testament and that the Old Testament proceeded in very considerable degrees in an essentially non-behavioural, institutional economic way, without necessarily relying on a metaphysical entity in the first place, to address and resolve problems of societal contracting. The idea of God is in this respect deconstructed in non-metaphysical terms.

From positive to normative institutional economics: Analysing and achieving mutual gains

The institutional economic framework I apply projects theoretical analysis in practical, normative perspective by advising on the (re)design of incentive structures. Positive institutional economics analyses succeeding/failing cooperation in relation to *existing* incentive structures and *existing* societal contracts in general. Such analysis is subsequently transcended in practical, normative perspective and questions of central authority arise here quickly. Insights from positive analysis are used to treat interaction problems as a systemic, situational condition, namely in relation to the (re)design of incentive structures – the 'rules of the game' or 'rules structures' or 'governance structures' – in order to encourage cooperation (if desired). '[T]he rules of certain social "games" must be changed whenever it is inherent in the *game situation* that the players, in pursuing their own ends, will be forced into a socially undesirable position.' (Luce and Raiffa 1957: 97, emphasis added). The studies of Homann (1997: 16–17, 23, 1990: 17–20), Buchanan (1995: 142, 146–7, 1987a: 21–32, 51–63, 1987b: 243, 1975) or Williamson (1985: 28–9, 33–4, 72–9) provide details on this issue. Stigler and Becker (1977: 76) and early on Neumann and Morgenstern (1947: 44, 49) too hinted at this issue.

Successful (failing) cooperation is strictly treated as a problem of *incentive-compatible* (incentive-*in*compatible) institutional structures, understood as incentive structures of one kind or another (see also Wagner-Tsukamoto 2003; Vanberg 1994): Incentive-compatibility implies that incentive structures realign and '*equilibrate*' (Williamson 1998: 34, 76) individual (self-)interests of interacting choice makers so that '*mutuality of gains*' (Buchanan and Tullock 1962: 19; Buchanan 1960: 122) results as interaction outcome. 'Pareto-superior' results have to be generated leaving all parties, involved in social exchange, better off, as Buchanan (1975) constantly reminds us. Similarly, unresolved conflict and a breakdown of cooperation is analysed as a problem of 'defective', incentive-*in*compatible incentive structures, which do not realign interests of (potentially merely) self-interested agents and thus yield mutual loss as interaction outcome, or 'rational foolishness', as Sen (1990: 35–7) formulated in behaviouristic terms. Thus, the institutional problems of societal contracting, nation-building, governance of a firm, etc. are not treated by institutional economics *by* interfering with human nature or 'the human condition', as theology (e.g. Tullock 1981: 42–3, Otzen et al. 1980: 53) and behavioural sciences do and as is, at times, implied by behavioural economists (e.g. Sen 1990, in degrees even by Williamson, e.g. Williamson 1998: 1–2, 10, 15–17, 1985: 6, 30–2, 64–7, 391, 1975: 26–30). The (institutional) economic research programme, conventionally understood, is likely to be abandoned if the institutional problem were theoretically analysed in relation to the 'behavioural make-up' of the individual, for example, preferences, tastes, values, moral precepts, etc. In practical, normative perspective, a behavioural approach implies intervention with behavioural institutions and intervention techniques such as value education, communicative techniques, social conditioning, conscience training, religious therapy, moral appeal or preaching, which are not associated with economics, understood in a conventional, non-behavioural way (see also Iannaccone 1995: 81–2, 86; Stigler and Becker 1977: 76).

With regard to intervention focus, a key thesis of my institutional economic reconstruction of Old Testament stories is that a systemic condition of 'defective' incentive structures of one kind or another is to be (or should be) dealt with to successfully handle social problems but not a claimed human condition. A discussion of contracting over rules that are embodied in incentives structures reflects the kind of non-behavioural approach followed in this book. Specific design criteria for intervening with incentive structures in order to ensure mutual gains are the generation of mutual gains *for some time* ('stability') and *at low cost* ('efficiency'). So, incentive-compatible incentive structures are to efficiently produce a pareto-superior equilibrium in contribution–distribution interactions for some time (for details, see Wagner-Tsukamoto 2005, 2003: Chapter 2, 2001a). These goals of institutional economic ordering reflect that interacting individuals – despite being (potentially merely) self-interested – succeed in cooperating. This was already implied by Mandeville's maxim of 'private vices, public good' and Smith's maxim of the 'wealth of nations'. In this respect, a key advantage of an economic approach over a behavioural approach to handling cooperation problems is that it tolerates value pluralism, even moral disagreement and value decay in social interactions, and can still induce socially desirable interaction outcomes. Thus, economics conceptually and practically accommodates the 'condition of modernity' (value pluralism, ethnic diversity, moral disagreement, value decay, etc.) without having to overcome it in order to solve the institutional problem (for details, see Wagner-Tsukamoto 2008a, 2008c, 2005, 2003, 2000a).

Interactions over capital contributions and capital distributions

Generally spoken, as outlined above, the institutional problem can be understood as the problem of how to ensure cooperation in social interaction settings where conflict looms, or in brief, where problems of societal contracting and social ordering arise. This thesis already hints that it is, above all, one specific type of social exchange that an economic reconstruction of the Old Testament is interested in: Institutional economics analyses social exchange as *inter*action – how one agent's choices affect and interrelate with choices made by other agents (Brennan and Buchanan 1985). Interactions are likely to be conflict-laden, as Simon (1945: Chapter 6) had already hinted by drawing on Barnard (1938) (see Wagner-Tsukamoto 2003). Above all, institutional economics is interested in analysing and resolving interaction *conflict* (Buchanan 1975: 117) and cooperation dilemmas (see below). Similarly, North (1993b: 260) noted: 'Institutional theory focuses on the critical problems of human organization and the problems of achieving cooperative solutions to human interactions.' The idea of the interaction implies that agents co-determine outcomes of social exchange (discussed below in more detail when the idea of the dilemma structure is introduced). An interaction model can be detailed regarding capital contributions that agents have to make to the interaction and capital distributions they receive from the interaction. Special contingency features of capital and capital utilization processes specify the institutional economic analysis of and intervention with interaction processes. Williamson speaks of 'transaction attributes' (1985: 41–2, 387–8) or Hesterly et al. (1990: 403–4) of 'inherent characteristics of the exchange'. The more complex and 'asset specific' (Wagner-Tsukamoto 2003: 32) contingency features are, the more sophisticated techniques (i.e. incentive structures) are required to steer interaction processes towards cooperative solutions.

A key issue in modelling interactions and interaction conflict is the conceptualization of *interdependence* among the choices made by individual agents. This is discussed below when the idea of the dilemma structure is reviewed. A critical consideration is that individuals participating in social exchange ultimately co-determine through their individual choices – unavoidably, intentionally or unintentionally – outcomes for each individual but also for the group as a whole. It is especially the consideration of interdependence that makes the conceptualization and resolution of social conflict a non-trivial problem. Early on, game theory discussed this issue in detail (Luce and Raiffa 1957, Neumann and Morgenstern 1947).

A key thesis here for institutional economic reconstruction is that the stories of the Old Testament reflect patterns of decision-making and social exchange that go beyond the simple exchange or action model. Interdependence and interaction analysis imply complex patterns of capital contribution–distribution arrangements that are embedded in (societal) contracts. It will become apparent later that Old Testament stories such as the Paradise story, the Jacob stories, the Joseph story or the stories involving Moses reflect such complex interdependence patterns of institutional ordering and contracting.

Dilemma structures and economic man and intervention with the incentive compatibility of the situation

Institutional economic theory and its practical, normative programme are methodically instructed, like any scientific research programme, by heuristic concepts. They map out an 'axiomatic' – sub-theoretical, pre-empirical, quasi-tautological – problem formulation and problem-solving apparatus (Wagner-Tsukamoto 2003; see also Penrose 1989: 135–7, 538, 558; Hofstadter 1979: 17–20, 183; Popper 1978: 67; Lakatos 1970: 132–7, 1978: 4, 47–52, 148). Weiser's (1961: 150, 171) suggestions on the structure of the Old Testament, which he made for the book of Judges, can be projected with regard to research heuristics, too. He pointed out that a certain 'stereotyped scheme of theological pragmatism' combined with framework elements sets up the book of Judges. The next chapter develops a similar argument for the Paradise story, proposing that this story heuristically sets up storytelling in the Old Testament.

Two key heuristics of institutional economics are the ideas 'dilemma structure' and 'economic man' (see elements 1 and 2 of Figure 1.1). Simply expressed, the model of economic man (the 'homo economicus') is a situatively geared calculus of self-interested choice. The idea of the dilemma structure suggests that interacting agents simultaneously encounter common interests – to cooperate in order to reap socially desirable outcomes such as mutual gains – and conflicting interests – to organize contributions to and distributions from the interaction to one's own advantage and to the disadvantage of other agents (in detail, Homann 1999a, 1999b, 1997, 1994; also Buchanan 1975: 26–8).

Institutional economics models cooperation dilemmas as a *nonzero-sum* game, that means it models a scenario in which all agents lose because of self-interested choice, despite the possibility that all could gain if only cooperation succeeded. In a dilemma structure, self-interested, rational choice of the individual seems to maximize own gains but actually results, because of the rational choice reaction of others, in mutual loss. The prisoner's dilemma and the commons dilemma are classic illustrations (Hardin 1968: 1244–6; Luce and Raiffa 1957: 94–7; see also Wagner-Tsukamoto 2003; Hardin 1996; Maskin 1994; Libecap 1989; Brennan and Buchanan 1985). Williamson (1985: 32–4, 42, 1975: 135–6) speaks of the 'contracting dilemma', Buchanan (1975: 117, 130–46, 167, 180) of a social conflict model and the 'punishment dilemma' or behavioural economics of 'rational foolishness' (Sen 1990: 43). In general, dilemma analysis has a long history in philosophy and in the social sciences. Otherwise, if social conflict were negated, most moral philosophy and political economy could be shelved and forgotten. Unless the resolution of social conflict is taken for granted, social research needs to (heuristically) invoke a dilemma model. Nussbaum (1986) hinted at this for the modelling of tragic conflict in Greek philosophy; or, the model of the 'war of all' predominantly served Hobbes as a tool to discuss the prevention of war (Homann and Suchanek 1989; Buchanan 1977, 1975; Mintz 1962). And as Chapter 2 of this book outlines, the Old Testament's concept of the original sin can be similarly interpreted (see also Wagner-Tsukamoto 2001a).

With the concepts 'dilemma structure' and 'economic man', institutional economics analyses cooperation problems as a situational condition of 'defective', incentive-*in*compatible incentive structures. 'Dilemma structure' and 'economic man' instruct theoretical analysis and practical intervention that enable 'even' merely self-interested agents to escape from dilemmatic conflict and reap socially beneficial outcomes. Only for heuristic, instrumental purposes, agents are modelled as economic men and social interactions as dilemma structures (in detail, Wagner-Tsukamoto 2003: 33–43; see also Homann and Suchanek 2000: 32–40; Homann 1999a, 1999b, 1997, 1994; Brennan 1996: 256–7; Persky 1995: 223–4, 230; Suchanek 1994, 1993; Becker 1993: 402, 1976: 5, 13–14; Buchanan 1987b: 51–63; Brennan and Buchanan 1985: Chapter 4; Machlup 1978: 292–9, 1967: 7, 11; Buchanan and Tullock 1962: 3–4, 17–21). The functional nature of 'dilemma structure' and 'economic man' can be well illustrated through the analogy of the car crash test (see Wagner-Tsukamoto 2003).

Hence, (institutional) economics attributes 'rational foolishness' *not* to the human condition, such as deficits in rationality, compassion or benevolence and it does *not* favour pedagogic intervention with behavioural institutions, as behavioural economics does (e.g. Simon 1997, 1993, 1976; Hollis 1994; Sen 1990; Etzioni 1988; Margolis 1982; in degrees even Williamson 1998: 1–2, 10, 15–17, 1985: 6, 30–2, 64–7, 391, 1975: 26–30). Theological research has similarly interpreted the model of economic man in empirical, behavioural terms, for example, Hopkins (1996: 133). For reasons of problem dependence, economics – understood in a conventional, non-behavioural tradition – abstracts from the human condition, which is 'non est disputandum' (Stigler and Becker 1977: 76). Only for behavioural research, the concepts of an economic dilemma structure and of economic man can be rejected – on grounds of problem dependence but not on grounds of being unrealistic or immoral (in an empirical, behavioural or normative, behavioural sense). Of course, behavioural economists (and behavioural researchers in general) here frequently but unjustifiably advance unrealism and immorality claims regarding 'economic man'.

In this regard a key thesis of the present study is that especially under interaction conditions of pluralism, cultural and ethnic diversity, moral disagreement and even value decay – which the present book later unearths as key interaction conditions in the Old Testament – institutional economics, heuristically grounded in the ideas 'dilemma structure' and 'economic man', is more effective, more efficient and even more moral than behavioural approaches (Wagner-Tsukamoto 2003: Chapter 8). Chapter 2 further introduces the heuristic concepts 'dilemma structure' and 'economic man' when discussing the Paradise story. Then, some of the key theses of this book are presented, namely that the stories of the Old Testament are grounded in heuristic models of social conflict and human nature, which mirror the economic approach, such as the prisoner's dilemma and the model of economic man.

1.2   Differences to previous economic and theological research on the Old Testament

In the following, first, I outline the theological approach through a comparable schema as developed above for the economic approach. I discuss key differences between a theological and an economic reconstruction of the Old Testament. Of course, it is beyond the scope of the book to outline in detail the different types of theological interpretations available in the field (for reviews, see Kugel 1997, Childs 1985). The section also assesses differences between religious economics, which is grounded in theology, and the non-behavioural understanding of the institutional economic approach I presented previously.

The theological approach to understanding the Bible

As hinted above, the Old Testament is likely to reflect an early documented attempt to analyse and solve the institutional problem – of how to ensure cooperation in social interaction settings where conflict looms – or, in brief, to solve problems of societal contracting and social ordering. The identification of such a suggested interest in the institutional problem does not (yet) differentiate an economic interpretation of the Bible from a theological one. Indeed, theological research on human nature, the nature of God and the nature of social life frequently seems to be at least implicitly geared towards advising on the institutional problem, too. However, what differentiates a theological interpretation of biblical thought from an economic one is its different approach, namely the heuristic, theoretical and normative ideas it brings to research on the Bible. Especially its theoretical variables tend to be anchored in non-empirical, metaphysical concepts.

At the level of institutional rules that are meant to guide behaviour, theology draws on value-based, ethical rules, which the individual has to internalize through religious practice. The human condition and value structures held by the individual (i.e. behavioural institutions) are intervened with for solving social problems. For an Old Testament-based religion, the Ten Commandments are a key example (see elements 3 and 4 of Figure 1.2). This approach compares to a behavioural, socio-psychological research programme. Once group members have homogeneously internalized ethical rules, the problem of social conflict is resolved. Grounded in a value consensus, harmony or 'peace' is expected to emerge in social exchange and social problems are to disappear (see element 5 of Figure 1.2). Hodson (1967: 11) speaks of 'harmonious human relationships' as the goal. Childs' (1985: 97–9, Chapter 17) discussion of humanity touches upon this issue, too, although his discussion remains focused on the individual rather than a social entity.

In general, theology aims to overcome social conflict and foster humanity as a matter of treating the human condition, for example, lacking religious belief. The successful resolution of social conflict is related to the metaphysical entity 'God', to the revelation of God to man, as Childs (1985: Chapter 4) puts it. Schenker poignantly summarized theology's idea of the realization of humanity in social exchange, through the example of biblical legislation on debt slavery and the release of slaves:

> The Covenant Code and Deuteronomy try to limit debt slavery, and Deuteronomy interrupts the accumulation of debts. ... It is a

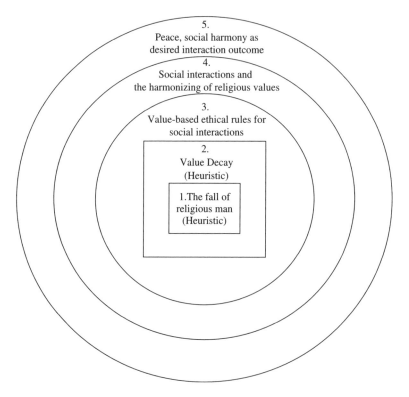

Figure 1.2   The theological approach

periodical eschatology and a periodical purification of human society from the distortions of life and bad luck. When the world is close to creation and to the Creator, then it is close to being a humane world.

(Schenker 1998: 37)

Of course, as Kugel (1997) or Reventlow (1985) review, there is a huge variation in how the humane revelation of God to mankind in the Old Testament has been interpreted in religious terms since ancient times. This approach, which is anchored in the revelation of God to humans in order to ensure humanity or 'peace' in social life, implies that in theoretical perspective Old Testament theology aims to uncover '*homines religiosi*' (Eissfeldt 1974: 45). *Homines religiosi* provide – religious – role models for human beings to overcome social problems. Elements three and four of Figure 1.2 reflect this behavioural approach to solving the institutional problem. However, a religious model of human nature is, of course, not the only theoretical (and/or heuristic) model of human nature that can be identified and reconstructed for Old Testament stories: For example, economic man, sociological man or psychological man are alternatives for analysing the modelling of human nature in the Old Testament. This tends to be underestimated by theology (see also Wagner-Tsukamoto 2003: section 1.2 and Chapter 3, especially section 3.4).

In addition to these stark differences at a theoretical, practical and normative level, theological research further deviates from economics in heuristic perspective. Besides entertaining a theoretical model of human nature as such, which provides the focus for practical intervention by theology and by behavioural research programmes in general, theology *also* invokes a heuristic model of human nature. Its heuristic model of human nature reflects 'fallen religious man' or 'fallen theological man' – the potentially sinful human being who strives for godly wisdom and belief but is tested and tempted by dark forces to deviate from the religious path (see element 1 of Figure 1.2). Theology's heuristic model of social conflict is complementary to this heuristic model of human nature. Social conflict is approached as value diversity and even value decay, as exemplified by the idea of the original sin in Old Testament-based religion (see element 2 of Figure 1.2). This has implications in practical, normative perspective. If individual belief systems are not harmonized and a value consensus is not reached, the sinful condition of humans undermines the effectiveness of religious practice. Besides constructive attempts, such as preaching, missionary, etc., less admirable practices can be applied to remedy this situation, for example, religious crusades. Old Testament theology here seems to have no problem with events such as the destruction of Sodom and Gomorrah or the destruction of Egypt in the Exodus story. In these stories, problems arising from value diversity and value decay were 'remedied' in an arguably forceful and non-pluralistic manner.

In order to generate peace and harmony in social relations (element 5 of Figure 1.2), theology needs to promote the sharing of same, value-based rules (i.e. behavioural institutions) among interacting agents (element 4 of Figure 1.2). If such sharing cannot be achieved through peaceful preaching or missionary, certain, harsher intervention may follow. As noted, economics, conventionally understood in a non-behavioural manner, has less of a problem to handle conditions of pluralism, ethnic diversity, moral disagreement or even value decay. Its approach tolerates such social conditions since heuristically and theoretically it does not rely on value sharing and behavioural institutions to solve the institutional problem. This tolerance is a by-product of its non-behavioural, but situational, systemic approach to solving social conflict – by focusing on incentive structures rather than the human condition as such.

As indicated above in section 1.1, the present book shares certain sympathy with source-critical theological research on the Old Testament. As much as the present study and source-critical theological research handle questions of authorship, similarly, an economic interpretation of biblical thought as developed in this book still differs considerably from redactional, source-critical theology, namely with regard to the methodical and theoretical, practical interpretation of the substance of biblical thought. A comparison of Figures 1.1 and 1.2 reveals this quickly.

The religious economic approach to Bible studies

Hybrid approaches comprising both theological and economic components have been developed. They linked in different ways and degrees metaphysical ideas on God and godly wisdom to economic research. Such approaches are unsatisfactory for a rational, scientific explanation of the Old Testament when the idea of the 'rational' is linked to ideals of the Enlightenment. A key thesis here is that institutional economic reconstruction, building on a rational, non-metaphysical approach, as outlined above, develops a highly coherent, economic analysis of the Old Testament. A conceptually integrated Old Testament economics emerges which easily rivals the few previous economic attempts in the field that built on mixed, religious economic approaches, connecting to theology, on the one hand, and to behavioural economics or socio-economics, on the other.

In general, the institutional economic analysis of biblical thought pursued in this book moves in its direction and scope away from microeconomic studies of religious behaviour, for example, an economics of believing, charitable behaviour, church attendance behaviour, conversion behaviour, etc. (e.g. Smith 1999, Iannaccone 1998, 1995, Benner, 1997, Ensminger 1997, Hardin 1997, Raskovich 1996, or Kuran 1994). Although at least some of these studies were of a rational, scientific nature, they are of comparatively little interest to the present study since these studies did not analyse *inter*action problems in the context of biblical *textual* analysis. More important for the present study are previous economic analyses of Bible stories which directly or indirectly aimed at the institutional problem, such as game theoretical analysis (Brams 2002, 1994, 1980), scarcity-based research (Gordon 1994, 1989, also Paris 1998), legal–economic analysis of Bible stories (Miller 1994, 1993a, 1993b), Paris' (1998) more general attempt at an Old Testament economics, and, to a lesser degree, Meeks' (1989) theological work on political economy, which partly covered the Old Testament. These studies touched upon issues that can be viewed as methodical and/or theoretical fragments of the institutional economic reconstruction of Old Testament stories pursued in this book. They provide valuable source material and reference points to indicate the different type of economic analysis pursued by the present study and what different insights were generated. The present study suggests that an institutional economic reconstruction, as outlined above, can accommodate and put into perspective Gordon's (1994, 1989) hypothesis that the Bible analysed the problem of scarcity in human choice behaviour; Brams' (1994, 1980) hypothesis that biblical characters, including God, were rational economic game players; Miller's (1994, 1993a, 1993b) hypotheses that the Old Testament analysed economic aspects of animal sacrifices and of practices of oral contracting in the context of nation-building; or Paris' (1998) research on Old Testament economics. For the present study, Gordon's work is especially interesting regarding interaction conditions, such as the desert problem; Brams' work is interesting because of its explicit treatment of game theory for Bible studies, which I, however, mainly draw upon heuristically for Old Testament economics; Miller's work is interesting because of its references to nation-building, which more or less directly refers to the institutional problem and related issues of societal contracting; Paris' work is interesting in various respects since he investigated different parts of the Old Testament in economic terms.

However, differences remain between these previous studies and the present one, mainly regarding approach and interaction conditions considered. Firstly, in terms of general approach, the present study explores differently the idea that the Old Testament is rational than envisaged by Paris (1998: 42), who favours a literalist, theological approach. He interpreted the Old Testament as the word of God and thus explored economic issues through metaphysical ideas of godly wisdom, faith and belief (also favoured by Gordon 1994, 1989; Meeks 1989). This approach lacks the application of rational economic theory, which Paris otherwise complained about (Paris 1998: 44–5). Also, Paris drew in a rather eclectic manner on economic theory when exploring the Old Testament. No coherent single approach can be made out. In contrast, the present book explores the idea that the Old Testament is rational and secular solely through one 'abstract' economic theory, namely institutional economic reconstruction (as outlined above and summarized through Figure 1.1). Miller (1993a: 19–20) similarly favoured a secular approach to Bible studies, namely a legal–economic one. A secular approach draws on the hypothesis that the Bible is a man-made text rather than the word of God. My research, like Miller's, is in certain respects compatible with redactional, source-critical research of theology.

Secondly, the present study approaches social problems as a situational condition that is caused by 'defective' incentive structures or 'defective' incentive signals of societal contracts in a wider sense. I explicitly exit from a behaviourally grounded, religious economics to which Brams (2002, 1980), Paris (1998), Gordon (1994, 1989), Miller (1993b) and Meeks (1989) can be said to subscribe. A behavioural economics or socio-economics that aims to conceptually integrate with theology looms in these studies. They related social problems – in a behavioural research tradition – to the human condition, for example, individual character failures, such as psychological deficits, lacking belief, greediness, etc. In contrast, the present book coherently reconstructs social problems depicted in Bible stories in non-behavioural, institutional economic terms: as a reflection of the institutional problem understood as a capital contribution–distribution conflict that is induced by incentive-*in*compatible governance structures. Thus, social problems are reconstructed as a situational condition but *not* as a reflection of the human condition. This also implies a very different vision of the societal contract as such and how to establish and maintain a societal contract from an economic point of view.

Thirdly, the present study strictly models *inter*action behaviour through a *capital exchange* model whereby successful capital exchange requires the pareto-superior (mutually advantageous) equilibration of interests among agents regarding contributions made to and distributions received from the interaction. Previous research now and then touched upon elements of such a capital model; for example, Gordon (1994, 1989) examined scarce time capital for the Paradise scenario and Paris (1998), connecting to Brams, also discussed scarce capital for the Paradise story. On a related point, I dispute Miller's (1993a) thesis on the simple contract model, even for the early Old Testament stories, which Miller focused on, for example, the Jacob-Esau exchanges. The present book demonstrates that what Miller termed 'simple' contracts, oral and written ones, were embedded in larger, complex social *inter*actions, which at times involved more than half a dozen interaction steps regarding capital exchange (Chapter 3 follows up). Thus, the present study applies an interaction model rather than an action model to analyse social conflict. Meeks (1989: 33–7), at least implicitly, also subscribed to an action model in his attempt to read a Trinitarian God into economy and economic theory and to interpret Bible stories through a religiously grounded, economic household theory (applying the idea of a 'household of faith' to the Bible; Meeks 1989: 33).

Fourthly, and related to the previous points of a situational approach and a capital contribution–distribution model, the present study draws on game theory and rational choice theory, for example, the ideas of the dilemma structure and economic man, predominantly in *methodical, heuristic* perspective but not in a theoretical and/or empirical, behavioural sense. The latter is explicitly done by Brams (1980) and Paris (1998: 45), and implicitly by Miller (1993a) and Gordon (1994, 1989). Miller (1993a: 24), for example, complained that the apparently greedy and unfair character of Jacob, who so closely resembles economic man, has dismayed much theology. Or, Paris (1998: 43, 55) explicitly stated that cooperation problems directly reflected the human condition, and hence should be resolved through the behavioural internalization of principles such as 'man must honestly cooperate with man and God'. This, to a large degree, may just assume away the problem of social conflict within a community. This approach has even less to say when different communities interact, which do not share an understanding of 'honesty', 'human nature' or 'God', that means when pluralism, ethnic diversity or moral disagreement are met as interaction conditions of social exchange.

Fifthly, in practical, normative perspective, the present book reconstructs the resolution of social conflict with regard to the idea of mutuality of gains ('pareto-superiority', see Buchanan 1975: 39; Buchanan and Tullock 1962: 172–4, 189–90; Buchanan 1960: 123) – the 'wealth of a community of nations', as Genesis (35: 11, 48: 4, 19) referred to. Previous economic studies of the Bible did not analyse this issue. Such a cooperation principle and further, ethical principles derived hereof are not too far away from religious ideals of sharing, solidarity and social justice, although an institutional economics in the rational scientific tradition of the Enlightenment obviously proceeds conceptually in a rather different way than theology or a theologically grounded, behaviourally oriented economics. In this connection, the idea of mutual gains has a high potential to clarify theological teaching on wealth, poverty and wealth distribution. As Kaiser (2001: 156) noted: 'Current teaching on the biblical view of wealth is confusing to say the least.'

Sixthly, the interaction conditions focused on in this study are the ones of pluralism, ethnic diversity, moral disagreement and even value decay, as they can be identified for the non-archaic society or the multicultural society of today. As Old Testament stories unfold, they seem to increasingly and quite explicitly deal with such modern conditions, especially so the stories from Jacob onwards. Previous Old Testament studies frequently neglected these conditions or focused on the archaic society.

Miller (1993a: 16, 18, 21, 44, 1993b: 477) or Paris (1998: 43) did explicitly the latter. A further interaction condition considered in this book is the one of the 'desert problem', namely the socio-geographic scarcities it reflects and the social, dilemmatic implications regarding the management and distribution of scarce resources it implies. Specifically, I analyse the desert problem as a dilemmatic interaction scenario caused by scarcities in certain commodities that are to be shared by a group. In this interpretation, the desert problem is related to interaction conditions encountered in the commons dilemma (e.g. Hardin 1968), where overgrazing and overpopulation threaten to exhaust scarce resources and drive interacting agents into poverty. Gordon's scarcity-based interpretations or Paris' (1998: 54–5) population management problems touched upon this condition. In this connection, the present study has little interest in the actual historicity of events depicted in the Bible: I purely analyse the Old Testament and the scarcities depicted there in textual perspective. I argue that the analysis of scarcities and the interaction dilemmas it instigates are a key issue in the Old Testament. This is in stark contrast to Meeks' (1989) theologically based approach to a biblical economics which explicitly denied that scarcity presented a problem in biblical storytelling *once* humans followed God's word (Meeks 1989: 12). I will discount this claim in Chapters 2 and 3, even for the Paradise story and the interactions between Abraham and Lot, that is for stories in which God still was heavily involved as 'central authority' for resolving the institutional problem.

Seventhly, regarding its substantive research focus, the present book looks at the stories of Genesis and Exodus and here especially the Paradise story, the stories involving Jacob, the Joseph story and the Exodus stories. The Torah is basically focused on by the present study. I reconstruct these stories in institutional economic terms and, importantly, I *interrelate* the stories in institutional economic terms. Such a focus and coherent interrelation of stories distinguishes the present study from previous religious economic work in the field, which were more selective, less comprehensive and less integrative. This focus also reflects the analysis of the interaction conditions described above.

Finally, a theologically grounded economics conceptualizes God as a metaphysical entity: as an omnipresent and omnipotent personal God, who intervenes with the resolution of the institutional problem (e.g. Paris 1998: 42, 50, 71; Meeks 1989: 1, 33, 75, 181). Meeks (1989: 75) explicitly stated in this connection that he did not intend to reconstruct the idea 'God' in relation to concepts of democratic capitalism: 'The divine metaphor Economist should be ruled by the naming of God in the biblical traditions.' In contrast, my rational, scientific economic analysis of the Old Testament ultimately deciphers and reconstructs the idea of God (as far as it relates to issues of societal contracting and social ordering) in non-metaphysical, non-spiritual terms; for example, 'God' is interpreted as the Bible's reference to an economic principle of ensuring public good in social interactions. Even more generally, the idea of God could be interpreted as a principle of social ordering. Hodson (1967: 93) pointed out that the original Hebrew term used for 'God' in Genesis (*Elohim*) refers to 'order of creative, evolutionary intelligence' but not to a personal God as many later translations and interpretations of the Bible imply. If one abstracts such an understanding of 'God' further, it can be linked to principles of organized and self-organizing social order as it permeates the writings of an institutional economics (and institutional studies in general). Chapter 6 follows this up.

This issue of how to conceptualize the idea of God in an economic analysis of Bible stories leads to possibly contentious, but for an economics of religion, important methodical and theoretical questions. In an economics of religion, the idea 'God' may have to be differently approached than by a theologically grounded economics, which ontologically interprets 'God' as a given, metaphysical entity, and treats the stories of the Old Testament as a 'religious, holy reality', as done by Brams (1980: 3–5, 169–70, 173), Gordon (1994: 22, 39, also 1989), Meeks (1989: 1, 33–7, 75, 181) and Paris (1998: 42), and, of course, by much theological research (see Tullock 1981: 2, Spriggs 1972: 7, Hodson 1967: 4, 9, Anderson 1966: 6). In particular, the present book questions suggestions, such as the ones put forward by Paris (1998: 42), namely that a coherent economic analysis of Bible stories had to be grounded in a 'literalist' theological approach, treating the Old Testament as a holy text that directly reflected the word of God.

The present book suggests that institutional economics can reconceptualize metaphysical ideas without the a priori postulation of certain pre-scientific concepts. They are deciphered and reconstructed through the very methodical and theoretical elements that make up the institutional economic approach (see Figure 1.1; see also Wagner-Tsukamoto 2003: Chapter 8). A metaphysical conceptualization of the idea of God and of God's role in resolving social conflict is probably only of interest to theology (and behavioural, theologically grounded sciences, such as religious economics). However, such conceptualizations appear methodically and theoretically difficult to reconcile with a scientific research tradition (see also Hayek 1976: 170; Buchanan 1975: 130–1). Such a tradition aims at conflict resolution through means of human intervention (in the case of economics, with incentive structures) but not by waiting for and relying on an omnipotent and omnipresent metaphysical entity to intervene as problem solver, as suggested by theology (e.g. Cohn 1981: 1; Lace 1972: 115–17; see also Kaiser 2001). Thus, an economic analysis of the Bible, as outlined above, can enquire rather differently about the basic nature and purpose of the Bible.

1.3   On the permissibility of economic and other scientific research on the Bible

There is certain unease among economic researchers when it comes to the economic analysis of Bible stories. This reflects the perception that the Bible may represent a holy text that is beyond scientific research. Different responses to such unease can be observed. Some economic researchers follow a theological path, entering a religious economics and analysing Bible stories under the prerogatives and assumptions of theology, for example, Paris (1998: 42) and similarly Gordon (1994, 1989). Other economists sought consultation with theologians regarding the acceptability of economic research on the Bible. Miller (1993a, 1993b) and Brams (2002, 1980) seemingly chose this way. The following discusses this issue in more detail: why and how economists may be at unease when it comes to economic research on the Bible and what response strategies can be taken.

Economic research on the Bible: Ontological issues or a matter of approach?

It is generally accepted that Bible stories need interpretation and theologians frankly admit that there is much debate even within theology on how to study and interpret the Bible. They admit that the field of biblical studies reflects an 'inexact, debate-ridden field of exegesis' (Schmidt 1989: 115; similarly Hurst 1989: 134–48). Nevertheless, historically, theology has fought hard on ontological, literalist grounds to prevent sciences from interpreting its claimed subject matter. For instance, physicists and biologists faced stern opposition and confrontation once they began to analyse the origin of the world and the origin of life in a way that was incompatible with theological and biblical thought of the time. Over the centuries, theology seems to have at least implicitly acknowledged that such ontological claims made to and derived from the Bible are untenable. This is reflected by its acceptance that physical or biological theories, for example, on the origin of the world or the evolution of life, are compatible with the Bible – although, as the present study implies, the Old Testament may not be really interested in physical and biological problems of creation in the first place but institutional problems of social conflict and societal contracting.

An ontological understanding of scientific, philosophical or theological research may be helpful for illustrating simply what a research programme is about, for example, the fall of stones could be said to be the physicist's, markets could be said to be the economist's, role behaviour could be said to be the sociologist's, God could be said to be the theologian's etc. An ontological understanding, however, is likely to be unhelpful for understanding the basic nature of research. In one way or another, the various social sciences, philosophy and theology all research the same subject matter. For instance, a phenomenon like marriage has been successfully conceptualized and analysed in the terms of theology, philosophy, psychology, sociology or economics. The same could be suggested with regard to the institutional problem. What seemingly distinguishes different research programmes may not be different subject matter as such but different *ways of looking* at the subject matter, reflecting methodical differences of 'approach' (Becker 1993: 385, 402, 1976: 5; implied by Friedman 1953). Such an understanding of research is in the first place *methodically* grounded rather than ontologically or phenomenologically. Leibniz and Kant pointed at such a methodical understanding of research early on, and the philosophies of science of Popper (1978) and Lakatos (1978) detailed such an interpretation (Wagner-Tsukamoto 2003: section 1.1, Suchanek 1994, Homann and Suchanek 1989: 72–3, 81; also Cassirer 1962: 4–5, 532–3). On these grounds, findings from different research programmes become compatible, that is, once they are transcended for methodical differences of approach. In this respect, an economic interpretation of Bible stories does not directly compete with theological research and theologically grounded economic research on the Bible, in particular a theological interpretation of God as an omnipresent and omnipotent personal God. To some extent, questions regarding the ontological status of the idea 'God' in biblical thought could even be said to be irrelevant to the present study. I interpret the idea 'God' as a mere conceptual component of the text 'Bible', abstracting this idea in different respects (see Chapter 6).

In addition to issues concerning matters of approach, institutional economic research on the Bible can be justified from another direction, too. There is an impressive body of research in the philosophy of religion, the sociological study of religion and in the sociological study of the Bible (e.g. Schmidt 1989: 117; Gottwald 1980; Stolz 1974: 36; also Best 1983). Also, the body of works in a religious economics (See, for instance, publications in the Journal *Faith & Economics*) is impressive. Hence, the question regarding the permissibility of social science research on religion in general, and on the Bible in particular, already seems to be answered. However, as indicated, there are few, 'pure' economic studies of the Old Testament. Even more so, there is a scarcity of economic research on the Bible which proceeds in a scientific, rational tradition. And obvious difficulties exist between economists and theologians to understand each other's research approach – turmoil, even hooliganism was reported from one of the first conferences that was shared by theologians and economists (Brennan and Waterman 1994: 3–4). The reasons for such turmoil may largely reflect the misunderstanding that economics was a claimed immoral science, which promoted self-interest and egoism related to the model of economic man (see also below). But similar communication problems and a similarly difficult debate exists even within theology, between so-called literalist interpreters of the Bible, who read the Bible as a holy text, and so-called source-critical readers, who approach the Bible as a purely man-made text (see also above); for instance, Gilboa (1998: 223) intentionally left aside the question whether the Bible is a holy book. As stated, to resolve such communication problems between economics and (Old Testament) theology, differences of approach have to be made explicit.

Regarding its general outlook on research approach, I repeatedly stressed that the present study is closer to source-critical, theological research rather than to literalist interpretations. I agree with Fromm (1967: 7) that the Old Testament does not reflect the 'word of God' but is 'a book written by men' – and *for humans*, I would add here. I argue that it derives a worldly purpose regarding the understanding and resolution of cooperation problems among human beings: the institutional problem and related problems of societal contracting. Still, key differences of approach exist between the present study and a source-critical Old Testament theology. They are captured by Figures 1.1 and 1.2. Once such differences of approach are understood and accepted, different readings of the Old Testament by different disciplines are just a matter of acceptance and tolerance. And from here constructive dialogue can emerge. As discussed, this requires a conceptual understanding of what economics is about and what it is not about.

Does economics entertain an unrealistic and dark image of human nature?

In the debate whether economic research on the Bible is permissible, it is one particular aspect of what economics stands for and does not stand for that needs to be clarified. The research heuristics of economics – 'dilemma structure' and 'economic man' – may attract empirical and moral criticism regarding a claimed unrealistic, dark worldview and a dismal image of human nature.

It has been suggested that economics is a 'dismal', 'dehumanized' science since it projects, so it is claimed, a negative image of human nature and of social life. Even renowned economists like Hodgson (1988: 51–116), Williamson (1998: 1–2, 10, 15–17, 1985: 6, 30–2, 64–7, 391, 1975: 26–30), Simon (1976: xxi) or Sen (1990: 25) voice such concern at times. It can be suggested (Wagner-Tsukamoto 2003: sections 2.3, 2.4; Homann and Suchanek 1989: 75, 79, 84) that this reflects a misunderstanding of the economic approach, mostly a misunderstanding of the *methods* of economic research as a reflection of an image of human nature and a worldview, of 'real people' and 'real life'. Theology could in this respect only take issue with an economic reconstruction of Bible stories if the status of economics as a moral science is questioned.

Also, there are stark and dismal scenarios of failing human interactions and fallen human nature in the Old Testament. Indeed, the Bible is full of it – Adam and Eve stealing from God, Cain killing Abel, Jacob cheating Esau, Joseph being sold by his brothers and so on. It can be claimed that the Old Testament invokes such 'fallen' characters and dismal scenarios for normative purposes, for discussing how they can be prevented – by solving the institutional problem anew and (re-)establishing cooperative societal contracts anew. Models of these characters and scenarios would thus function as instrumental tools, comparable to 'economic man' and 'dilemma structure' in economics. Indeed, in *generic* heuristic perspective there are likely to be little differences among social sciences, philosophy and theology when it comes to 'dark' models of human nature and of human interactions at a very basic, heuristic, methodical level (Wagner-Tsukamoto 2003: 199).

Rather than in relation to its heuristic, methodical tools, such as 'dilemma structure' and 'economic man', economics' world view and image of human nature, and its moral status as a social science has to be better assessed by focusing on its approach to theory-building and practical intervention – which are open to empirical and moral scrutiny (Wagner-Tsukamoto 2003: Chapter 8). In general, the moral status of (institutional) economics appears difficult to question: It advises on solving social problems *to the mutual advantages of all interacting decision makers*. Normative goals like mutual gains, mutual prosperity, 'pareto-superiority' and increases in the wealth of nation*s*, as Adam Smith put it, but not merely the increase of individual welfare, is aimed at. This reflects moral values like social justice, solidarity or fraternity

(Wagner-Tsukamoto 2008b, 2008c, 2008d, 2007b, 2005, 2003: section 8.1, 2001b). Indeed, if economics were not a moral science, which aimed at the generation of socially desirable outcomes, it would be difficult to comprehend why the moral philosopher Adam Smith, after decades of research in a behavioural moral philosophy, ultimately should have favoured the economic approach, conventionally understood in a non-behavioural tradition, to analyse social problems of modern society (Homann 1990: 4–5; see also Iannaccone 1998: 1465). This suggestion is reinforced by the present book by outlining that biblical stories can be reconstructed as a body of thought which examines – for moral reasons, so I argue – problems in social behaviour *in economic terms*. A deeply capitalist ethos and a radical, economic humanism will here become visible for the Old Testament. A reconstruction of biblical thought in economic terms thus may also encourage a re-evaluation of economics' status as a moral science.

1.4   Concluding remarks

There appears to be ample room for interpreting Bible stories in non-behavioural, institutional economic terms with reference to ideas like economic interactions, capital contribution–distribution conflicts, mutuality of gains as interaction outcome, incentive structures as institutional regulative and the heuristic ideas of dilemma structure and economic man. Such an analysis of the Bible has hardly begun. The few existing economic interpretations of the Bible are either microeconomically oriented, applying the theoretical approach of rational choice theory, or they analyse Bible stories through a religious, theologically grounded economics rather than an economics of religion.

A lack of coherent approach is seen in the previous studies on the Old Testament, for example, as mentioned by Paris (1998: 44–5). The present study closes such a gap. Also, the economic concepts applied by this study to the Old Testament avoid the pitfalls of previous scientific research on the Bible of being either too general and too vague or too complex and too oversubscribed by variables, as complained by Schmidt (1989: 121–2). The model depicted by Figure 1.1 is well suited for a precise, conclusive, meaningful economic analysis of the Old Testament.

The chapter outlined an understanding of the institutional economic approach which easily rivals in terms of coherence, integration and scope of analysis the previous research on the Bible and other organization research in general (for the latter claim, see Wagner-Tsukamoto 2003). Institutional economics, as outlined in this book, enables a different, more integrated and more fundamental economic analysis of Bible stories: It examines in theoretical and practical perspective how far the Old Testament positively and normatively handles the institutional problem as an interactive capital contribution–distribution conflict in relation to incentive structures and methodically grounds such analysis in the idea of conflict-laden interactions (the idea of a dilemma structure) and the idea of self-interested choice behaviour (the model of economic man). Findings of such an economic reconstruction of the Bible compare in considerable degrees to Adam Smith's *Inquiry into the Wealth of Nations* – making the more plausible why the moral philosopher Adam Smith ultimately switched from a behavioural ethics to a non-behavioural ethics, that is, economics, for investigating social problems of modern society.

The chapter discounted reservations of theology regarding an institutional economic reconstruction of Bible stories, both on ontological, methodological and on moral grounds. Ontologically, the Bible does not 'belong' to any specific scientific research programme. Historically theology may have been the first discipline to research the Bible but that does not give rise to exclusiveness claims. This suggestion rests on the understanding that research is 'defined' by approaches rather than subject matter. Also, I clarified that ideas like 'economic man' and 'dilemma structure' and comparable ideas in other research programmes, for example, the sinfulness of man in theological research, should be understood as heuristic fictions that theoretical analysis and practical intervention apply in order to ultimately generate socially desirable outcomes. From here, research programmes such as theology and economics can make considerable yet different moral claims.

This book makes claims that an institutional economic reconstruction gets closer to holding a 'magic key' to some of the mysteries of the Bible, at least more so than theological studies and previous, religious economic studies: Brams (1980: 177) concluded that his game theoretical analysis did not yield such a 'magic key'. The present study points in this respect towards the lacking understanding of the heuristic nature of game theory in Brams' analysis. As outlined, the present study differs in various respects from previous, economic studies of the Old Testament which largely connected to a religious economics. The present study differs from such previous research regarding its specific research focus and its vision and understanding of the economic approach, including the demarcation of economics from theology. The book coherently and comprehensively brings Old Testament stories under a scientific, economic scheme of analysis. The approach followed is grounded in an *economics of religion* rather than a religious, theologically grounded economics. The latter followed in the footsteps of theology and tried to integrate economic analysis with theological concepts. For instance, it would view the idea of God as a given metaphysical concept which should be beyond an economic conceptualization, as suggested by Paris (1998: 42). In contrast, an (institutional) economics of religion deconstructs and reconstructs, in the tradition of the Enlightenment, metaphysical ideas. Such an economic interpretation might attract criticism from theology and a theologically oriented economics (and here the more so from orthodox, literalist, theological researchers) since it rethinks basic prerogatives, assumptions and conceptualizations of theology, for instance, the analytical nature and status of ideas like 'God', 'original sin', the 'wickedness of humans', etc.

As a result of the approach chosen, the present book gains, as stressed by Karl Homann (and quoted on the cover of this book) a very special profile in the debate on economics, theology and ethics. Its approach very clearly distinguishes it from theological and other combined approaches to economics and theology both regarding the clearly spelled out research approach and regarding research method. The book intentionally does not follow a behavioural approach to economics and theology but a non-behavioural, institutional-theoretical economic approach. It is highly necessary to discuss in theology and ethics research such alternatives to a behavioural approach. This is the more important since a behavioural approach to economics and ethics has significant theoretical and practical deficits when conditions of pluralism and competition are considered. The economic interpretation of the Old Testament, as presented in this book, is here a special treat since it clearly shows that the old dualism of economics and theology/philosophy, on which most ethics approaches are built, is historically and systematically not justified. This reveals some very significant progress in interdisciplinary debate.

2
The Eden Story and Dilemma Analysis – A Paradise Lost?

*You must not eat fruit from the tree that is in the middle of
the garden, and you must not touch it, or you will die.*
(Genesis 3: 2)

The chapter reconstructs the original sin in economic terms as the Old
Testament's idea of a dilemma structure. I compare the fall of humans
in Paradise to the prisoner's dilemma and the tragedy of the commons –
concepts which have been well researched in the economic literature.
The functioning/ill-functioning of interactions between God and Adam
& Eve are discussed in relation to capital contribution–distribution
arrangements and incentive structures as they existed in Paradise. In
particular, Adam and Eve's theft from the tree of knowledge is analysed
in relation to 'defective', incentive-*in*compatible incentive structures
and related, incomplete contractual arrangements. On this economic
basis, the nature and scope for succeeding and failing cooperation
between God and Adam & Eve can be better understood.

The subsequent first discusses the idea of the dilemma structure in
more detail (section 2.1) before it moves on to analyse dilemmatic interaction conflict in the Paradise scenario (section 2.2). Finally, I stress the
heuristic, methodical role of the model of economic man in an economic
reconstruction of the Paradise scenario (section 2.3).

2.1 The heuristic role of the commons dilemma and the prisoner's dilemma in institutional economic reconstruction

The following details the concept of dilemma analysis in institutional
economics. Institutional economics as well as most other social sciences

and social philosophy do not take for granted interaction outcomes such as cooperation. As Brennan (1996: 256–7) noted: 'To assume at the outset that the actor is motivated directly by a desire to promote the collective interest simply subverts the analytical exercise.' Brennan's reference to 'analytical exercise' points towards the heuristic nature of certain research concepts that are needed for guiding research in theoretical, practical and normative perspectives.

Here, institutional economics analyses incentive structures, such as constitutional contracts, governance structures, property rights arrangements or pay systems, in order to advise on their reorganization and ensure cooperative outcomes of interactions (or non-cooperative ones, if desired). Incentive structures set out what agents are expected to contribute in one form or another to an interaction and what they can expect to receive in return. Cooperation is diagnosed if interactions yield mutual gains (see elements 3, 4 and 5 of Figure 1.1). This theoretical framework projects analysis in practical, normative perspective by advising on the (re)design of incentive structures. Incentive structures are to be designed in a way so that cooperation – mutual gains – results (if desired).

Like in any scientific research programme, heuristic concepts methodically instruct institutional economic theory and practical intervention derived hereof. Research heuristics are analytical tools of institutional economics, mapping out an 'axiomatic' – sub-theoretical, pre-empirical, quasi-tautological – problem formulation and problem-solving apparatus (Wagner-Tsukamoto 2003; see also Penrose 1989: 135–7, 538, 558; Hofstadter 1979: 17–20, 183; Popper 1978: 67; Lakatos 1970: 132–7, 1978: 4, 47–52, 148). Two key heuristics of institutional economics are the ideas 'dilemma structure' and 'economic man' (see elements 1 and 2 of Figure 1.1). Simply expressed, the model of economic man is a situatively geared calculus of self-interested choice ('homo economicus'). The idea of the dilemma structure suggests that interacting agents simultaneously encounter common interests – to cooperate in order to reap socially desirable outcomes such as mutual gains – and conflicting interests – to organize contributions to and distributions from the interaction to one's own advantage and to the disadvantage of other agents (in detail, Homann 1999a, 1999b, 1997, 1994; also Buchanan 1975: 26–8). Broadly speaking, the idea of the dilemma structures suggests that unresolved interest conflict undermines mutually advantageous interaction outcomes. As Williamson (1996: 137) summed up, in a dilemma structure 'potential *conflict* threatens to undo or upset opportunities to realize *mutual* gains' (emphasis as in original). The prisoner's dilemma and the commons dilemma are classic illustrations (Hardin 1968: 1244–6; Luce and Raiffa 1957: 94–7; see also Wagner-Tsukamoto 2005, 2003; Hardin 1996; Maskin 1994; Libecap 1989).

In game-theoretical terms, institutional economics models cooperation dilemmas as *nonzero*-sum interactions but not as zero-sum ones; that means it models a scenario in which all agents lose because of self-interested choice, despite the possibility that all could gain if only cooperation succeeded. In a dilemma structure, self-interested, rational choice of the individual seems to maximize own gains but actually results because of the rational choice reactions of others, in mutual loss. In contrast, in zero-sum interactions it is inconceivable that all players could be winners or losers *at the same time*. Neither mutual gains nor mutual loss are possible interaction outcomes. The nonzero-sum game played in the prisoner's dilemma well illustrates the idea of the dilemma structure. The specific incentive structures of the prisoner's dilemma as of comparable dilemma structures, such as the commons dilemma, instigate an interaction process that drives interacting agents, on grounds of self-interested, rational choice, to violate their own best interests. Mutual loss results for interacting individuals and for the group as a whole (Wagner-Tsukamoto 2003: section 2.3; Homann and Suchanek 2000: 36–8; Homann 1999b: 2–3, 1997: 5–11, 1994; Vanberg 1994: 91–3, 1986: 93–6; Homann and Pies 1991: 609–11; see also Lohmann 1996: 132; Nozick 1993: 50–9; Coleman 1990: 203–4; Buchanan 1987b: 42–7, 157; Schotter 1981; Hardin 1968: 1244–5; Luce and Raiffa 1957: 94–7).

The idea of the dilemma structure models individual agents as co-determining – unavoidably, intentionally or unintentionally – gains or losses for each agent. Game theory is in this respect most explicit: It details that economics conceptualizes social problems as interdependence problems in which 'every participant is influenced by the anticipated reactions of the others to his own measures' (von Neumann and Morgenstern 1947: 13; see also Vanberg 1994: 92; Buchanan 1987b: 155). For example, in the prisoner's dilemma, interdependence of individual choice behaviors is set up by the way the payout matrix is constructed. Or, in the commons dilemma a contractual arrangement of shared property rights regarding the communal asset 'meadow' sets up interdependence among individual farmers (Hardin 1968; see also Scott 2000: 44; Coleman 1990: 20–1; Nussbaum 1986: 1–3, 47–50, Chapter 12; more generally on the property rights issue, Hart 1995; Barzel 1989; Alchian and Demsetz 1973). By invoking interdependence of individual behaviors, economic analysis is developed as *inter*-action theory rather than as a theory of collective action or individual action (Homann 1999b: 3–4; Gerecke 1997: 102; Buchanan 1994: 56; Vanberg 2001, 1994: 92, 1986: 75; Becker 1993: 386). Etzioni's (1988: 3–4) critique that economics did not investigate co-determination has to be qualified in this respect.

With the concept 'dilemma structure' (and the concept 'economic man') institutional economics analyses cooperation problems as a situational condition of 'defective' incentive structures. 'Dilemma structure' and 'economic man' instruct theoretical analysis and practical intervention, thus enabling 'even' merely self-interested agents to escape from dilemmatic conflict, reap socially beneficial outcomes and ultimately solve the institutional problem and related problems of societal contracting. It is important to note that only for heuristic, instrumental purposes, agents are modelled as economic men and social interactions as dilemma structure (in detail Wagner-Tsukamoto 2003: 33–43; see also Homann and Suchanek 2000: 32–40; Homann 1999a, 1999b, 1997, 1994; Brennan 1996: 256–7; Persky 1995: 223–4, 230; Suchanek 1994, 1993; Becker 1993: 402, 1976: 5, 13–14; Buchanan 1987b: 51–63; Machlup 1978: 292–9, 1967: 7, 11). The functional nature of 'dilemma structure' and 'economic man' can be illustrated through the analogy of the car crash test, in which accidents are simulated with dummies for practical reasons (see Wagner-Tsukamoto 2003, 2001a).

For a normative institutional economics the important implication here is that only if dilemmatic conflict over capital contributions to and distributions from social exchange can be resolved, can a common interest in achieving mutual gains from cooperation be realized. Otherwise, a 'defective' incentive logic drives all interacting choice makers to behave as 'rational fools', which means each individual's (self-)interests are damaged because of self-interested choice in the face of certain, given incentive structures. Thus, institutional economics does *not* analytically attribute 'rational foolishness' to institutions of a different kind, such as a deficit in shared, social values, a deficit in religious predispositions, moral precepts, etc. ('behavioural institutions'). Such institutions could be behaviourally handled, for instance, through institutional regulatives like religiosity and practices of religion (see also Wagner-Tsukamoto 2008c). At times, even economists seem to (mis-)interpret 'rational foolishness' in a non-situational, non-systemic, non-economic, but behavioural way. Institutional economics, conventionally understood in a non-behavioural way, attributes 'rational foolishness' *not* to the human condition, such as deficits in rationality or in compassion, and it does not favour pedagogic intervention, as behavioural economics or socio-economics do (regarding the latter, see

Simon 1997, 1993, 1976; Hollis 1994; Sen 1990: 30–1, 35–7; Etzioni 1988; Margolis 1982; in degrees even Williamson 1998: 1–2, 10, 15–17, 1985: 6, 30–2, 64–7, 391, 1975: 26–30).

The critical issue in understanding why economics applies the methods 'dilemma structure' and 'economic man' is the question of the purpose of economic analysis – or problem dependence (Wagner-Tsukamoto 2003; Homann 1994, 1990; Suchanek 1994; Homann and Suchanek 1989; Popper 1978; Lakatos 1978; see also above). The ideas 'dilemma structure' and 'economic man' have to be strictly understood as methods: as tools or 'heuristics' in Lakatos' terminology. Their purpose is to analyse and solve the institutional problem *in economic terms* – with regard to the (re)design of incentive structures for improving the mutuality of gains of capital exchange. To stress this important point: The key insight which the concept of the dilemma structure and the model of economic man heuristically enable is that non-cooperation 'is inherent in the situation' (Luce and Raiffa 1957: 97). This means, cooperation problems are traced to incentive structures which did not realign self-interests of interacting decision makers.

The key thesis subsequently explored in this chapter in relation to the idea of dilemma analysis is that the fall of humans heuristically invokes in the Old Testament a dilemma scenario, which then drives biblical storytelling that follows the Paradise story. Theology proceeds similarly when it interprets the stories that follow the original sin as the means of overcoming this greedy, sinful state – but it does so in a behavioural tradition, by focusing its analysis on the human condition. In difference, the present study projects the original sin in systemic, situational perspective, as the heuristic means of economic analysis that organizes the intervention with incentive structures (and contracting over incentive structures). Thus, the original sin is interpreted as a heuristic motor that drives economic themes of conflict resolution and societal contracting in the Bible. A key thesis of the present study here is that an institutional economic reconstruction of Old Testament stories supports an economic, non-behavioural view on the original sin and its role in subsequent Old Testament storytelling.

2.2 The original sin and a rational fools' dilemma in Paradise

Of course, the Paradise story is well known for one conflict incidence: Adam and Eve committing the 'original sin'. They appropriated fruits from the tree of knowledge, which belonged to God. As a result, they were evicted from Paradise (Genesis 3: 6, 15–19). One may ask why the authors of the Old Testament chose this dramatic scenario of failing cooperation *in Paradise* to start biblical storytelling. I argue that one key purpose is to draw attention early on to *contribution–distribution conflicts* and to an emerging societal contract, which at this stage was rather frail because it was incomplete and because God initially imposed it on Adam and Eve but did not negotiate it with them, especially not under economic considerations of societal and constitutional contracting. Another key purpose of the original sin is to provide a *heuristic reference point* for subsequent Bible stories that examined 'ways out' of the original sin and the re-establishing of a stable, efficient and mutually advantageous ('pareto-superior') societal contract. Hence, the subsequent draws especially on the idea of the dilemma structure to uncover specific choice dilemmas when Adam and Eve ate from the tree of knowledge and consequently were evicted from Paradise.

Capital scarcities and capital contribution issues in Paradise

The Old Testament opens up the discussion of social conflict with one of its most famous stories, of Adam and Eve in Paradise. Seemingly they lived in a land of Cockaigne with an abundance of goods, and no apparent scarcities and conflicts over capital. But was this really the case?

It can be suggested that scarcity initially instigated dilemmatic interaction problems. Gordon (1994: 20–1, 1989: 1–3) discussed capital scarcities in Paradise, which I project to dilemmatic contribution–distribution conflicts. He analysed scarce time capital, namely in relation to the amount of work time Adam and Eve had to allocate to keeping Paradise cultivated: 'The Lord God took the man and put him in the Garden of Eden to work it and take care of it.' (Genesis 2: 15; see also Stratton 1995: 37 or Otzen et al. 1980: 41). Following God's work pattern, this implied six days of work and one day rest (Genesis 2: 2–3; also Genesis 1: 27). 'Work was man's sober destiny even in his original state [in Paradise]', as von Rad (1963: 78) put it. Gordon (1994: 25) noted: 'God is a worker....Man is made in the image of God who works.' Or, Gilboa stated (1998: 94, 97): 'Adam is put there to till and guard the garden....Idleness is not part of his life.'

Furthermore, Adam and Eve's cultivation efforts in Paradise required certain entrepreneurial skills regarding agricultural knowledge. Such – scarce – knowledge can be attributed to Adam and Eve already at this stage – and it had to be acquired, learnt and updated which further constrained their time capital. Apparently, the need to work in Paradise severely curtailed Adam and Eve's free time in various ways and this reflects a *capital contribution* problem that was encountered by Adam and Eve in Paradise.

Some scholars overlook such cultivation efforts of Adam and Eve and the economic implications this has regarding scarce time capital for keeping Paradise cultivated and for acquiring necessary cultivation skills. An example is Plaut (1981: 502) who claimed that humans were given bread in Paradise without having to toil for it. Similarly, Anderson (1992: 16) argued that Adam and Eve had to do no work in Paradise and 'consume a special type of food that required no cultivation'. However, the capital contribution issues I discussed above imply certain scarcities, although, in my further analysis I focus, like Buchanan (1975: 23), on the conceptual analysis of social conflict (that is instigated by scarcity) rather than 'scarcity' as such. In my view, social conflict is the more important concept for understanding the ultimate breakdown of cooperation in Paradise and in social interactions in general since scarcity is only a sufficient, but not a necessary, condition for social conflict to emerge.

Capital scarcities and capital distribution issues in Paradise

Questions of *capital distribution* arose in Paradise, too. In an Assyrian and Aramaic reading of the word 'Eden', abundance is specifically invoked in relation to water and fertile land (pastures) and it is more generally invoked in relation to prosperity. However, limitless, distributive abundance in the Garden of Eden would make the fall-out of Adam and Eve with God the more difficult to understand. But was this really the case that Adam and Eve were living in a land of Cockaigne, with no distributive scarcities being encountered? A careful reading of the Paradise story quickly reveals various limits to abundance in Paradise: God, for example, is referred to as 'water-controller of heaven and earth, who rains down plenty, who gives pastures and watering places to all lands, who gives prosperity (?) and … [is] water-controller of all rivers, who makes all land abound.' (Millard 1984: 105, '?' as in original) Apparently, God was in charge of certain or even most types of 'property management'. Seemingly, various capital constraints were in place in Paradise. Thus, even in the Paradise scenario some very basic capital contribution–distribution conflicts loomed. The Millard-quote already hints at this when he implicitly refers to apparent scarcities in water and fertile land and problems of prosperity distribution in Paradise. Otherwise, if there were no capital constraints, the reference to God as water-controller and the one who gives prosperity makes little sense. This already hints at economically interesting, potential, distributive conflict and the later breakdown of cooperation between God and Adam & Eve.

However, even larger distributive conflict loomed with respect to the divine trees. Regarding the harvesting of fruits from trees, the Paradise story specifies a property rights arrangement of how goods or 'capital' were distributed between the 'principal' God and the 'agent' man. Adam and Eve were allowed to make use of nearly any plant, animal and land in Paradise. They were 'only' forbidden to approach the tree of knowledge and the tree of eternal life, God threatening to kill Adam and Eve if they ate from these trees. These trees were God's (Genesis 2: 16–17, 3: 22–4). Thus, Adam and Eve could not utilize the seemingly most valuable assets of Paradise – the trees 'in the middle of the garden' (Genesis 2: 9). Being at the centre of the garden, can be read as a metaphorical reference to their high economic value.

This ban not to eat from the tree of life and the tree of knowledge clearly reflected an economic problem (see also Brams 1980: 21–33 and Paris 1998: 52). In this respect, I interpret the tree of life as a reference to scarce time capital whereas the tree of knowledge can be said to reflect scarce 'human' capital, such as knowledge and skills that go beyond the mere cultivation skills and knowledge Adam and Eve needed to keep Paradise cultivated. Gilboa (1998: 127–8) detailed such skills in particular with regard to skills that come with the spiritual autonomy of the individual, such as the ability to innovate own social rules, e.g., a code of ethics and social etiquette for constraining behaviour. This type of rule-setting behaviour is particularly interesting from the point of view of normative institutional and constitutional economics and the way it analyses social problems through alternative sets of rules and contracts for social behaviour.

In economic terms, the ban not to eat from the trees in the middle of the garden reflects a restriction of mortality, as far as the tree of life is concerned. I interpret here differently than Otzen et al. or Kugel. Otzen et al. (1980: 45, 50, 53) and similarly Kugel (1997: 69) imply that humans were prevented from achieving eternal life *as a result* of being driven out of Paradise. As I discussed, already *in* paradise Adam and Eve were forbidden to eat from the tree of eternal life: This constraint on Adam and Eve's choice behaviour reflects the very essence of the Paradise story and how the Bible conceptualized 'paradise'. Alexander (1992: 100) noted this, too, namely that the human being was denied two goods in Paradise – knowledge and eternal life.

Theological interpretations (e.g. Gilboa 1998: 96–7; Meeks 1989) generally ignore these capital contribution and capital distribution problems in Paradise and related scarcities. Meeks (1989) is here especially interesting. He claimed that scarcity is not a problem for biblical characters '*if* the righteousness of God is present' (Meeks 1989: 12, emphasis as in original). By this he meant that faithful humans who adhered to God's word would not encounter scarcity. However, this was already not the case in the Paradise story: Adam and Eve were denied to eat from the tree of life and the tree of knowledge *independent of* the issue whether they were faithful to God or not. There was no prospect whatsoever that God would grant them access to the trees in the middle of the garden in future. My critique here even upholds for a narrow, politically framed conceptualization of the idea of 'scarcity' as 'limits to *access* to livelihood' or 'limits to *access* to resources' (Meeks 1989: 72, emphasis added), rather than an understanding of scarcity as 'limits to resources' as such. As I noted above, God threatened to kill Adam and Eve if they 'accessed' the seemingly most valuable goods in Paradise – eternal life and ultimate wisdom. In this connection, Meeks (1989: 176) contradicts himself in considerable degrees when he later argued that 'the deepest scarcity of the human being comes from the scarcity created by our finitude and mortality, the scarcity of time, energy, and life.' This, of course, is the very same, biblical condition which already Adam and Eve encountered in the Paradise story.

Like Meeks, Gordon's religious economics (1994, 1989) did not identify economically meaningful constraints on choice behaviour regarding fruits from certain trees. The same criticism applies for Miller (1993b: 488) who overlooked this issue when he explicitly questioned the economic nature of the ban not to eat from the tree of life. He put forward the idea that Adam and Eve had access to an inexhaustible amount of food. Similarly argued von Rad (1963: 78) and Westermann (1984: 239) who suggested that God's ban was not oppressive and not harsh since Adam and Eve could eat from all other trees. Although they could eat from most trees, there is the undeniable fact that they could not eat from certain trees which, considering their very nature, reflected the most valuable and scarcest assets in Paradise, namely ultimate knowledge and longevity, even eternal life. Dragga's (1992) interpretation of life in Paradise as 'luxurious dependence' moves in a more appropriate direction, indicating that luxury came with certain constraints, although Dragga does not go into any details what that meant.

A constitutional economic reading of scarcity problems and interaction conflict in Paradise

The discussed capital contribution–distribution arrangements in Paradise begin to illumine why interaction problems between God and Adam & Eve could occur at all: Contribution–distribution conflicts loomed 'even' in Paradise. Indeed, they defined the paradise of Genesis. Adam and Eve did not live in a land of Cockaigne, in a limitless 'fool's paradise', as a land of Cockaigne is poignantly also referred to.

In the Garden of Eden, mutual gains that could result from interactions between God and Adam & Eve and related issues of shared prosperity were under threat. But even if Adam and Eve had lived in a place of superabundance, conflict could have still arisen, as Buchanan (1975: 23) points out for such scenarios in abstract terms. This is so because scarcity alone is not the only, and possibly not the most important, factor that gives rise to interaction conflict. As Buchanan argued, social strife and a lacking agreement over behavioural norms have to be considered here, too. These factors can undermine cooperation even in a land of Cockaigne.

Buchanan's (1975: 23–5) discussion of the 'natural distribution state' is in this connection especially interesting. It helps to further illuminate the constitutional economic, contractarian nature of the interaction conflict encountered by God and Adam & Eve regarding the distribution of goods in Paradise, especially regarding the trees in the middle of the garden. Buchanan's description of a two-person world can easily be projected to the Paradise scenario where God and Adam & Eve were interacting. In the natural distribution state described by Buchanan, all goods except one (good x) are available in abundance. For the Paradise scenario, this good x can be equated with the capital gains that resulted from the consumption of the tree of life and the tree of knowledge. In the Paradise scenario, good x was even more one-sidedly allocated to the two parties than generally envisaged by Buchanan: Adam and Eve's share was zero while God's share was 100 per cent. Economic exchange to redistribute good x between Adam & Eve and God was largely infeasible since Adam and Eve had not much to offer to God in terms of other goods that could be exchanged, the other goods being available in abundance to both parties. And, even more importantly, good x would suffer an apparent devaluation for God if God conceded exchanging it with Adam and Eve. Its value was defined in the Paradise scenario by its exclusive consumption by one party alone. Therefore, *large* conflict loomed.

In this apparently Hobbesian state of nature, as Buchanan details, each party will have an incentive to consume good x fully, or at least, in higher shares, than initially allocated: 'Each [party] would find it advantageous to invest effort, a "bad", in order to secure the good x. Physical strength, cajolery, stealth – all these … might determine the relative abilities of the individuals to secure … quantities of x' (Buchanan 1975: 24). In the Paradise scenario, this was clearly the case for Adam and Eve. They experienced an incentive to appropriate good x since their share of good x was zero and since God's only defence of his asset was a threat, namely to kill Adam and Eve if they ate from the divine trees.

Whether this was a credible threat and thus an effective defence has to be critically examined (see below). God, on the other hand, did not experience any incentive to further appropriate good x since he already fully owned good x. Thus, he may have been comparatively short-sighted and naïve in this respect, feeling wrongly safe and not realizing potential threats that could be exerted from Adam and Eve, believing good x was safely his.

The starting point of Adam and Eve's interactions with God regarding social exchange and the distribution of fruits from the tree of life and the tree of knowledge (good x) was thus an instable one. As noted, the Paradise scenario seemingly even reflects an aggravated version of the scenario described by Buchanan. Buchanan goes on to reason that in such instable natural distribution states over time a new and mutually advantageous equilibrium will emerge – for economic reasons: Both parties will agree on a fairer redistributions of good x. Such redistributions save costs, namely costs of predation and defence as they are 'paid' by both parties in the natural distribution state:

> As a result of the actual or potential conflict over the relative propor-
> tions of x to be finally consumed [by the two parties], some 'natural
> distribution' will come to be established. This cannot be properly
> classified as a structure of rights, since no formal agreement is made....
> [However], the 'natural distribution', secured upon investment of
> effort of attack and / or defense of x, serves to establish an identifica-
> tion, a definition, of the individual persons from which contractual
> agreement becomes possible. Even if all of x is secured by one party,
> both parties will be made better off if agreement can be reached.
> Trades [capital exchanges] can be arranged in the sense of agreement
> on a set of behavioural limits. Mutual gains are possible in this way.
> (Buchanan 1975: 24–5)

In Genesis, such a contractarian platform for new, explicit agreements was negotiated as a result of the Paradise story and in relation to the Paradise story – namely through new 'covenants' which involved God and Adam & Eve (and their descendants). The natural distribution state and the costly conflicts it yielded were then overcome. Agreements were then explicitly made between God and humans – through the covenants, which can be interpreted as basic, new constitutional con-tracts. The original sin and the apparent 'natural distribution' problems it describes thus drove new constitutional ordering. It can thus be read as an instrumental (heuristic) necessity for conceptualising in the

Old Testament institutional order and contractual agreements that concern God and the human being and the social ordering of interactions among humans.

But first things first. In the next section, I take a step back to analyse in more detail what actually happened in the apparently instable natural distribution state in Paradise, how a frail state of social order, which Buchanan (1975) may term 'precontract' constitutional order, collapsed. Then, the 'war of all' actually broke out between God and Adam & Eve, which left both God and Adam & Eve counting costs for the time being.

Contested 'good x' and the natural distribution state in the Paradise story

On the one hand, Adam & Eve and God had a common interest to maintain good interactions in Paradise since this benefited both with regard to improving their respective welfare positions: Adam and Eve were allowed to utilize Paradise and keep most fruits generated in the course of the cultivation of Paradise, and God got and kept earth cultivated while preserving his privileged access to the tree of knowledge and the tree of life. However, on the other hand, conflicting interests existed, too, namely regarding the specific split of capital contributions to and distributions from their interactions, especially with regard to the tree of knowledge and the tree of eternal life, which exclusively belonged to God. Scarce, contested 'good x' can here be identified, as they define the natural distribution state. They need to be protected through costly armament and defence investments in order to properly safeguard them from other parties. Otherwise, so Buchanan (1975) predicts, good x will be appropriated, stolen by the party who wants to increase its share in good x.

One has to look at these conflicting interests in order to understand why Adam and Eve ultimately ate from the tree of knowledge, stealing God's asset and defecting from a previously – solely by God – imposed arrangement regarding the sharing of assets in Paradise. God's role regarding good x is here an ambivalent one, possibly a too ambivalent one, when examined from a constitutional economic point of view. On the one hand, he was involved in what Buchanan (1975) calls post-constitutional contracting, especially private goods ownership. He acted in this respect like an owner and – an unwilling – trader in private goods, owning solely good x, the divine trees. They were clearly not public goods but very private goods, belonging to God alone. On the other hand, God was involved in potential, constitutional contracting that aimed to overcome the natural distribution state. He imposed, by exercising the function of a governmental lawmaker, a set of ownership rights and work duties on Adam and Eve, but he did so without consulting Adam and Eve in the first place. Other functions, such as policing the state of affairs in Paradise as a law-enforcement agency, can here be attributed to God, too. In these latter respects regarding constitutional ordering and the policing of ownership rights, God fulfilled the function of what Buchanan (1975: 68–70) called the 'protective state'. An enlightened political economy would here expect that the law-enforcement agency and the rule-maker of constitutional contracting be bound by agreements which would involve the subjects that are to be governed. In the Paradise scenario this was not the case. Also, from a constitutional economic point of view, God did not fulfil his job as rule-maker and law-enforcement agency, as 'referee' (Buchanan 1975: 95), very well. Especially sanctions regarding violations of ownership rights that concerned good x, the divine trees were unconvincingly set out – the questionable effectiveness of the threat to be killed is discussed below – and basically no policing of the divine trees occurred. As a result of these issues, a breakdown of constitutional order was waiting to happen. This would throw back God and humans into the natural distribution state, although an altered one as compared to the initial one since humans then had acquired parts of good x (here: ultimate wisdom and knowledge), which due to the very nature of this good could not be taken back from them.

Also, the issue of how far Adam and Eve could trust God further destabilized interactions in the Paradise scenario. God promised Adam and Eve that they could keep all fruits their cultivation efforts yielded (except the ones from the tree of knowledge and tree of life). The question can be raised whether Adam and Eve could trust the ruler 'God' regarding this promise. A problem regarding trustworthy, properly sanctioned and enforced rules exists here. North's (1993a: 14) ruler-constituent analogy is instructive (see Wagner-Tsukamoto 2008a, 2003: section 4.1, 2000b), as is Buchanan's (1975) analysis of 'predation' and attack by one party on good x which is owned by the other party in the natural distribution state. Adam and Eve's ultimate defection can in this respect even be interpreted as a pre-emptive counter-defection (see also Hardin 1968: 1244–6 on the 'self-elimination of conscience' in the commons dilemma).

When Adam and Eve's behaviour is viewed as a defection *process* there is no problem that the tree of life is only mentioned at the beginning and at the end of story about the original sin. The prospect was always there that attack and defection could be widened once a first defection (regarding the tree of knowledge) had succeeded. This yields a clarification on von Rad (1963: 76, 96) and Westermann (1984: 212–14) and others who saw a problem in the lacking treatment of the tree of life in the story of the original sin and, at times, even suggested that Adam and Eve were only banned not to eat from one tree, for instance, Stratton (1995: 134–5).

Rationally foolish interaction outcomes for God and Adam & Eve

Assessing the interaction outcomes in the Paradise story, at least in figurative terms albeit not necessarily in strict game theoretical ones, Adam & Eve and God seemingly behaved as 'rational fools': Adam and Eve suffered the eviction from Paradise and God suffered the loss of intellectual property in sole knowledge. Such an apparent loss/loss outcome can be interpreted in institutional economic terms with regard to the specific incentive structures that framed interactions in Paradise and that drove Adam & Eve and God into a prisoner's dilemma rather than helping them out of it. As further detailed below, such a substantive, theoretical interpretation of the original sin should also – and even predominantly – be projected to a methodical, heuristic purpose of the original sin in the Old Testament's analysis of social problems.

If one looks at the way incentive structures incurred gains and losses as a result of defection, Adam and Eve faced big incentives to defect and eat from the banned trees, namely to acquire privileges which came with the position of being 'God': of having superior knowledge and eternal life. Eating from the tree of knowledge would bring intellectual capital in the form of new knowledge and wisdom. And if the first attack regarding the tree of knowledge succeeded, defection could be extended to the tree of life, with the looming prospect of acquiring unlimited time capital – immortality (see also Genesis 3: 22–4). Besides gains, Adam and Eve could also expect certain losses as a result of defection. Letting Adam and Eve get away unpunished after a first defection was not a rational option to God. Otherwise, Adam and Eve could be safely expected to defect further by eating from the tree of life, thus becoming truly like God.

Thus, a rational Adam and Eve would have anticipated sanctions after a first defection, but to what extent? As Stratton (1995: 140) noted, because of their defection 'the threat of immediate death has become at worst a potential possibility, balanced by the positive aspects of the tree: beauty, sustenance, and wisdom.' This implies that death was not a forgone conclusion for Adam and Eve. Despite the threatened sanction to be killed for defecting, which would have rendered their theft valueless and yielded 'rational foolishness' (pareto-inferiority) even in strict game-theoretical terms, Adam and Eve probably could expect that killing was not a rational option to God to sanction defection: It would have implied the loss of 'human capital', and consequently devalued God's 'investments' into the creation of the earth, specifically his knowledge of good and evil since, after killing humans, nobody would be left who potentially could act in an evil manner. It would also have devalued God's sole access to unlimited time capital since a 'competitor' for time would no longer be around. Childs (1985: 45) argued in this respect that the world was created to be inhabited. A less severe sanction, like the eviction from Paradise, may thus not have come unexpected to Adam and Eve. Gilboa seems to interpret here similarly, although she did not connect to economic analysis in general and the prisoner's dilemma in particular. Rather, she suggested that God's warning to Adam and Eve of '"You may die" … does not indicate an immediate death, and might imply [only] a possibility, a warning. God, thus is a protagonist who leans on human fear of death in order to deceive.' (Gilboa 1998: 109–10, also 130) As indicated, such a suggestion of a misleading warning and a potential deceit can be well explored through the prisoner's dilemma and its possible interaction outcomes of rationally foolish behaviour, especially in relation to the defence and attack strategies chosen by interacting parties in the natural distribution state regarding a contested good x.

Thus, according to this interpretation that killing Adam and Eve was not a rational option to God, the diagnosis of rationally foolish, pareto-inferior, loss/loss outcomes for *all* interacting decision makers *depends only* on the way Adam and Eve assessed their gains and losses that resulted from their defection. God lost as a result of Adam and Eve's defection anyway, namely his privileged, exclusive access to the tree of knowledge. This means, whether defection outcomes for the Paradise scenario could be classified as 'rational foolishness' in strict game-theoretical terms (as pareto-inferiority, mutual loss), meaning that God *and* Adam & Eve lost more than they gained as a result of their choice behaviour, depends only on how Adam & Eve valued their gain from defection – ultimate knowledge and wisdom – as compared to loss resulting from defection – eviction from Paradise and other punishments occurred because of their eviction, e.g., pains in child birth for Eve, etc. In the flowery, metaphorical language of Dragga (1992: 12) this assessment can be reformulated as the comparison of a 'life of luxurious dependence inside the garden' with 'courageous maturity' and a 'life of rigorous self-sufficiency outside the garden'.

I do not want to enter in this connection a Gnostic reading of the original sin but my economic analysis is basically compatible with Gnostic ideas analysed by Alexander (1992: 100). He found that a Gnostic reading of the Paradise story views the original sin or 'fall of man' positively since it reflects an 'upward fall, necessary for human development and civilization'. Gilboa (1998: 127–8) or Fromm (1967: 121–3) argued similarly, stating that the original sin liberated the human being and gave the human being spiritual and ethical autonomy, which they viewed as an essential feature of human existence. As indicated, in game-theoretical and institutional economic terms one can agree with these statements if one carefully looks at Adam and Eve's valuation of gaining knowledge while losing access to Paradise. And regarding the issue of spiritual and ethical autonomy, the original sin opened up the possibility of new, more equal and freer constitutional contracting between God and humans and among humans in the aftermath of Adam and Eve's eviction from Paradise. The initially imposed social order by God in Paradise, which so closely resembles precontract order in the natural distribution state, could then be re-negotiated in fairer terms. And from here a derivative, conceptual and basically analytical, 'heuristic' function of the original sin in subsequent Old Testament storytelling becomes apparent.

The original sin as analytical driver of Bible stories

Most theological, philosophical and theologically grounded economic interpretations analyse the original sin in a merely literal, behavioural sense (e.g. Gilboa 1998: 100–25; Paris 1998; Gordon 1994, 1989; Tullock 1981; Otzen et al.1980). I suggested a different economic reading of this story above when drawing on ideas like the prisoner's dilemma and the natural distribution state. However, my analysis of the Paradise story does not stop there. I now follow up with a methodological interpretation, addressing the question why this story was inserted in the Old Testament at all, and why right at the beginning of the Old Testament. It can be suggested that the Old Testament, when modelling for the first time something like a social exchange, invoked the scenario of defection and of a dilemmatic breakdown of cooperation largely for analytical, methodical reasons: It heuristically enabled the Bible's subsequent analysis of the institutional problem, of serious interaction conflict in the context of evolving – economic – institutions for handling social conflict in general, and societal contracts in particular.

I suggest that the key purpose of modelling defection in Paradise and of invoking the idea of the original sin is a heuristic, methodical one.

The original sin methodically instructs the analysis of the *possibility* of defection in capital exchange – the possibility of a 'war about goods', as Genesis (14: 2, 11, 16) later details. Through the idea of the 'fallen condition of man', as theology behaviourally refers to the original sin, and a 'continuous struggle' (Gordon 1989: 1, 3), social exchange is simulated by the Old Testament as a potentially conflict-laden inter-action over capital contributions and distributions. The ever present prospect of '*if* war breaks out' (Exodus 1: 10, emphasis added) can be analysed in this way. New societal contracts needed to be negotiated to overcome this condition and to reap pareto-superior outcomes of new contract settlements. The original sin therefore 'just' provides an analytical motor, a research heuristic in the Lakatosian sense, methodi-cally instructing and organizing theory building (in the case of the Old Testament: the analysis and resolution of the institutional problem and related issues of societal contracting and resolving social conflict). In this respect, the original sin compares, both regarding its conceptual nature and regarding its methodical theory building function in institu-tional analysis, to Hobbes' idea of the war of all, or more abstractly, to the idea of the dilemma structure in institutional economics and economic organization theory (as discussed above).

Rogerson and Davies (1989: 205) hinted at such a heuristic function of the original sin when they stated that 'Genesis 3 serves to sym-bolize and dramatize ideas that *are* common in the Old Testament.' (emphasis as in original) Or, von Rad (1963: 98) noted that 'chapters 2 and 3 of Genesis are conspicuously isolated in the Old Testament.' From here it is only a small step to suggest an instrumental, heuristic interpretation of the original sin that drives subsequent storytelling in the Old Testament. Such an instrumental interpretation differs from an empirical, behavioural one, as theology (e.g. Tullock 1981: 42–3, Otzen 1980: 53) and also a behavioural, theologically grounded economics favour (e.g. Gordon 1994, 1989, also Paris 1998). They generally link the original sin to a behavioural condition of weak human nature and hence argue for behavioural 'therapy' to overcome this condition, e.g., through religious practices.

One of the final outcomes of the Paradise story also hints at an ana-lytical, heuristic purpose of the original sin. Instead of appeal, God then resorted to 'economic', institutional means to prevent Adam and Eve from a second defection with regard to eating from the tree of eternal life: God placed 'cherubim and a flaming sword' in front of the tree of eternal life (Genesis 3: 24). These new defence investments – costly 'armament investments' in Buchanan's (1975) terminology – changed the economic nature of the natural distribution state in the aftermath of Adam and Eve's first attack. Von Rad (1963: 76) and similarly Hodson (1967: 60) were here imprecise when they failed to state that only *after* the original sin the Garden of Eden was protected in this new way, by setting up new institutional structures regarding rights and punishments in relation to the tree of life. Cherubim and a flaming sword dramatically altered costs and gains with respect to eating or not eating from this tree. It implied death and thus a huge economic loss for Adam and Eve if they defected again and tried to transgress the newly imposed defence structures. Apparently God had learnt something from Adam and Eve's first defection: He now invented and tested out in a situational manner (the lack of) economic institutions that could protect his property rights regarding the tree of life from a rationally acting, self-interested Adam and Eve. God thus responded to earlier, subversive and predatory behaviour by Adam and Eve, which was encouraged by a too loosely constrained and negotiated 'precontract' state of regulating social interactions, to pick up Buchanan's (1975) terminology of precontract, constitutional and post-constitutional contract. New, additional and costly defence efforts of God are here apparent, as Buchanan (1975: 24–6, 56–8) predicts for anarchic, precontract, natural distribution states in which constitutional order has not yet been well established and where only a predation–defence equilibrium in social interactions among parties can be observed. Kugel (1997: 78) touched upon such an economic rationale when pointing out that the way to the tree of life needed to be guarded after Adam and Eve's expulsion from Paradise. But he failed to see deeper analytical reasons, as detailed by institutional and constitutional economics, of why and how such guarding was necessary and what specific heuristic purpose the Paradise story played for ultimately enabling humans to, figuratively spoken, 're-enter' Paradise in subsequent stories. This happened then when humans closed new constitutional, societal contracts with God ('covenants' in the language of the Old Testament), which then involved humans in negotiations with God in a freer and more equal manner.

To a degree, theology moves towards a heuristic interpretation of the original sin, in the tradition of Gunkel, when it views the early stories of Genesis as an 'ideal background', as a 'legend' for viewing the actual history of Israel (Kaiser 2001: 55–6). Idealism is invoked especially with regard to the creation story – but not, of course, regarding the fall of the human being in Paradise, one has to add. The latter was a hugely 'critical', non-ideal event. The question arises why the creation story and creation mythology would invoke such a critical event to discuss the human condition. Following Nussbaum's (1986) discussion of the role of conflict in Greek tragedy, again, a heuristic role of the fallen condition of the human being can be pointed out for Near Eastern mythologies. A critical, heuristic interpretation of the Paradise story, as conducted in this book, supports this view, too.

A non-behavioural, methodical answer to the question of why, right at the beginning of storytelling, the Old Testament invoked the idea of the original sin is further supported by the way Genesis (and the other books of the Old Testament) subsequently sequenced and extended interaction analysis of contribution–distribution problems. The idea of the dilemma structure is then explicitly touched upon, firstly, through the commons dilemma, in the stories of how Lot and Abraham, Isaac and Gerar and Jacob and Laban (Genesis 13: 6–9, 26: 19–24, 30: 37–43) encountered shepherding problems in relation to scarce land, livestock and water (see Chapter 3). Secondly, the prisoner's dilemma is seemingly invoked in the Joseph story, when potential conflict between Egypt and Israel was resolved, and in the story of the Exodus of the Israelites form Egypt, when conflict was not resolved and mutual suffering resulted as inter-action outcome (see Chapters 3 and 4; also Wagner-Tsukamoto 2008a, 2001a). Furthermore, a methodical interpretation of the original sin is supported by how a resolution of cooperation problems was worked out in Bible stories: not so much behaviourally in relation to the human condition (as theology might expect) but non-behaviourally in relation to a *situational* condition of defective incentive structures, advocating the changing of incentive structures, such as property rights arrangements for land and water usage. This is detailed in Chapters 3–5.

2.3   The first encounter with 'economic man' in the Paradise story: The portrayal of human nature or methodological fiction?

We know and remember Adam and Eve for their sinful, 'greedy' behaviour, when they stole fruits from the tree of knowledge. This yielded their expulsion from Paradise. Such greedy shortsightedness and apparent 'rational foolishness' (see above) seemingly implies a dark and dumb image of human nature. The subsequent section, however, here voices caution. It argues, connecting to sections 2.1 and 2.2, that the idea of economic man, as apparently introduced in the Paradise story, has to be read as a methodological fiction. The above already developed the related thesis that the dilemma scenario of the original sin basically functions as an economic research heuristic for biblical storytelling that follows the Paradise story. Through applying such methodical fictions, interaction problems can be analysed and resolved in economic terms to the mutual advantage of all interacting agents.

On the heuristic purpose of economic man

Compared to the idea of the dilemma structure, the model of economic man is a derivative heuristic of institutional economics, supporting and completing the application of the idea of the dilemma structure. As with the idea of the dilemma structure, the analytical significance and relevance of the model of economic man for economic analysis rests strictly on its methodical application (together with the idea of the dilemma structure) for analysing, in theoretical perspective, and for improving, in normative, practical perspective, incentive structures and the interactions over capital exchange they govern. In an empirical, behavioural sense, the model of economic man abstracts from human nature 'as we know it' (Wagner-Tsukamoto 2003; Iannaccone 1995: 77; Homann 1994: 387–92, 395–6, 1990: 9–13; Becker 1993, 1976; Suchanek 1993; Buchanan 1987b). Hayek's (1949) concept of 'methodological individualism' hinted at this early on.

A methodical role of a calculus of self-interest (as of the idea of the dilemma structure) in the analysis of the institutional problem can be compared to the instrumental role of the car crash dummy in the accident simulation setting of the car crash test. The car crash analogy neatly illustrates the point on the instrumental usefulness of the model of economic man (see Wagner-Tsukamoto 2007a, 2005, 2003, 2001a). Like the 'car crash dummy', economic man does not reflect an empirically too realistic portrayal of human nature. And in real life, car crash dummies are never seen driving cars on roads. They are empirically 'rare', and they are empirically 'incorrect' regarding the portrayal of 'real people' or 'human nature as we know it', to use a key phrase to which behavioural economists claim to subscribe, e.g., Sen (1990: 30–1, 35–7), Hodgson (1988: 83–93, 106–14), Simon (1976: xxi), but even Williamson (1998: 1–2, 10, 15–17, 1985: 6, 30–2, 64–7, 391), North (1993a: 14), Coase (1984: 231) or Knight (1948: 270). However, the crash dummy is rather useful for purposes of car design (but *not* for improving the driving behaviour of car drivers; this would reflect a different – behavioural – project of normative, social intervention). As the car crash dummy loses its purpose and relevance when separated from the crash test, so the model of economic man does when separated from the dilemma structure and the situational analysis of interaction problems regarding capital utilization and incentive structures. For the purpose of theology, organization psychology, institutional sociology or behavioural moral philosophy, ideas like economic man and an economic dilemma structure may be unfruitful and irrelevant research heuristics (see Figure 1.2). On grounds of problem dependence, they can be rejected for this kind of research – but *not* on grounds of being an 'unrealistic' or 'immoral' image of human nature and world view as implied by some economists and many other social scientists. It is *because of* its heuristic grounding in the ideas of economic man and of the dilemma structure that economics in the tradition of Mandeville and Smith, as probably most coherently picked up by economists of the likes of Hayek, Friedman, Machlup, Buchanan, Becker, Brennan or Homann can make considerable moral claims since these heuristics enable the non-behavioural, economic resolution of the institutional problem to the advantage of all choice makers (in detail, Wagner-Tsukamoto 2003).

Economic man in the Paradise scenario and the snake metaphor

The idea of self-interested choice plays an important role already in the very first story of Genesis. This is reflected by the splitting of assets between God and humans in Paradise, with certain assets remaining the sole property of God, namely the tree of knowledge and the tree of life (Genesis 2: 17, 22). Also, Adam and Eve met various other scarcities, namely their free time was curtailed since they had to keep Paradise cultivated (Genesis 2: 15; see above). In addition, scarcities in human capital existed, such as farming skills and other cultivation skills that were needed to keep Paradise in good condition. Without such scarcities there is less scope for economic analysis and economic man-behaviour, neither heuristically, methodologically nor even empirically. Only in a true land of Cockaigne, economic man may have no place (but see Buchanan's critical comments on this issue above).

In the story of the original sin, the snake appealed to Adam and Eve to appropriate God's assets, the tree of knowledge and the tree of life (Genesis 3: 13). The snake essentially contributed to the emergence of Adam & Eve's and God's seemingly rationally foolish behaviour. In this connection, Armstrong (1996: 27, 75, 88) or Plaut (1981: 35) explicitly associated the snake with the idea of 'guile', which Williamson's (1975, 1985) institutional economics prominently drew upon to refer to the model of economic man. North and Thomas's (1973) or Buchanan's (1975) references to economic man as a matter of 'predation behaviour' can be similarly interpreted. Other characterizations of the snake made by Old Testament scholars move it quite close to economic man, too. For example, von Rad (1963: 85) described the snake as having 'greater cleverness' than humans. Otzen et al. (1980: 52) characterized the snake as 'seducer', Dragga (1992: 6) and similarly Gilboa (1998: 130) as 'prudent' and 'cunning'. Slivniak (2003: 454) and Bloom (1982: xix) associated 'shrewdness' with the snake. As hinted, these depictions all move the metaphorical figure of the snake quite close to conventional characterizations of economic man-behaviour.

In this respect, I read the snake metaphor as one of the Bible's references to a calculus of self-interest and 'guile' – the model of economic man – which both in literal and figurative senses was frequently picked up by stories of the Old Testament that followed the Paradise story. Clearly Armstrong (1996: 29) is here mistaken when she argued that the snake never appeared again after the Paradise scenario. Armstrong here contradicts herself, even with regard to a *literal* reappearance of the snake after the Paradise story, when she explicitly states that 'Isaac accused him [Jacob] of acting "deceitfully" (*bemirah*, Genesis 27: 35), a word which derives from the same root as the adjective *arum* ("crafty") applied to the serpent' (Armstrong 1996: 75). Or, drawing on a *figurative* reading of the snake, Armstrong states that Jacob's wealth was achieved by 'the guile of the serpent' (Armstrong 1996: 88). Of course, Jacob is a key example who, in the stories that followed the Paradise event, is described as coming with 'guile' (Plaut 1981: 187). Furthermore, as much as Armstrong (1996: 27) associated the snake with the '*possibility* of evil', she did not further detail and link this insight to a heuristic test function of the snake and the methodological usefulness of the idea of guile in biblical storytelling. Although, Armstrong, in degrees, touched upon these issues when commenting:

> Eve and the serpent are both aspects of humanity. We have all experienced the inner conflict that works against our best interests. Like Eve, we are greedy for life and blessing. ... These attributes can be destructive, but they have also been responsible for some of the most admirable achievements of men and women. ... By plucking the fruit, human beings became conscious of their capacity for good as well as for evil.
>
> (Armstrong 1996: 29)

Seemingly, Armstrong's references to an 'inner conflict' and the violation of own 'best interests' link the 'greedy' snake to issues of dilemmatic interest conflicts. And Armstrong's suggestion that 'these attributes' could be both destructive but also constructive for human achievements points towards a heuristic, methodical interpretation of these ideas. However, as indicated, she did not explicate such a heuristic function.

Armstrong only implicitly hinted that the snake is ever-present in biblical storytelling, at least in a figurative sense, namely when ideas like guile, deceit etc. show up. Like Armstrong, Kugel (1997: 314) interpreted the snake too literally and did not find convincing answers to both literal and figurative presence and purpose of the snake in the Old Testament after the Paradise story.

There are many other explicit examples, apart from the ones involving Isaac and Jacob that were referred to by Armstrong, in which the snake showed up in more than a mere figurative sense of opportunistic behaviour shown by biblical characters. For instance, Joseph is said to have 'practised soothsaying from the hissing of snakes' (Plaut 1981: 278) or Aaron turned his staff into a snake for performing a miracle against the pharaoh (Exodus 7: 8–12) or Moses put up a bronze serpent to rebuke 'real' snakes (Numbers 21: 9; 2 Kings 18: 3–4; see also Kugel 1997: 480–1). These instances, which are further discussed in later sections and chapters, can be linked to the application of the snake metaphor, and related to the model of a economic man or a model of 'guile' and 'opportunism' (Williamson 1975, 1985) and 'predation' (Buchanan 1975), as institutional and constitutional economics have also referred to economic man. Westermann's (1984: 237, 255) discussion of ancient thought which viewed the serpent as bringer of prosperity, wisdom and knowledge, such as Gnostic interpretations (e.g. Alexander 1992: 97–8; also Slivniak 2003: 440, 447), allows for heuristic economic interpretations, too.

Fromm (1967: 160, emphasis as in original), similar to Armstrong, talks of humans as 'having a *striving* for evil' but he, again like Armstrong, does not follow up this idea of a 'striving' through a heuristic interpretation. Of course, as much as theology touches upon a potential test function of the snake for sorting out the human predicament, this is then followed up in non-economic terms, normatively so, through practical recommendations on improving one's religiosity. For example, Armstrong (1996: 30) linked the snake's effects on human interactions to the emergence of sin, the dissolution of community by sinfulness and the fragmentation of the soul. And from here she entered a normative discourse of healing the soul through worshiping God. Similarly, having interpreted the snake as seducer, Otzen et al. (1980: 52) did not enter an economic discussion on what possible, methodical role the snake could play in the Old Testament. Rather, they followed up with a behavioural (mis)reading of the snake as a reference to the 'human condition' (Otzen et al. 1980: 53). In particular, they did not read the snake in relation to economic man-behaviour and a test function of economic man in institutional economics, for instance, regarding the ability of governance structures to create mutual gains. Instead, they interpreted the snake as a mythological reference to the human condition. This moves their research quite close to the theological approach. In theological research, e.g., Hodson (1967: 55–7) or Kugel (1997: 72–5), the snake is generally not associated with economic man-behaviour but with 'satan'. Dragga (1992: 6) discounts such associations of the snake with Satan or a demon as 'anachronistic' but still fails to unravel a potential heuristic, economic function of the snake in biblical story-telling. A parallel behavioural (mis)interpretation could be suggested in this respect regarding a self-interested image of God, especially in relation to property rights arrangements concerning the tree of knowledge and the tree of eternal life – but this would equally miss important methodical points.

From an economic point of view, I suggest to heuristically follow up these insights that self-interested behaviour or even 'guile', 'predation' and very selfish behaviour can cause more harm than good in social life: The purpose of modelling human beings in economic analysis as self-interested, as 'snakes' that come with guile, would be to prevent such very states in human affairs where self-interest yields undesirable, social outcomes. Through proper economic analysis of, and intervention with, incentive structures, such as governance systems, self-interest is to be channelled into socially desirable states. In this regard, economic man, or figuratively the 'snake', is above all a research heuristic to alleviate the human predicament caused by self-interest, 'guile' or 'predation'. This also implies that the model of economic man or the 'snake' do not depict a negative image of human nature, which theology attributes to economic man (Wagner-Tsukamoto 2003: Chapters 2 and 3). There is clearly the danger that Adam and Eve's self-interested choice behaviour and their ultimate theft from the tree of knowledge could be misinterpreted as an image of human nature-reference, as modelling human nature as 'opportunistic' and 'self-seeking with guile', as even Williamson empirically (mis)interpreted the idea of self-interest for institutional economics (Williamson 1998: 1–2, 10, 15–17, 1985: 6, 30–2, 64–7, 391, 1975: 26–30; for a review, see Wagner-Tsukamoto 2003). However, the image of human nature of both economics and theology (and other social sciences) has to be deduced by looking at the theoretical, practical and normative outcomes of a methodological application of heuristic models of human nature and social exchange (Wagner-Tsukamoto 2003: Chapter 6).

The suggestion can be put forward that the Paradise scenario stressed the application of economic man as a research heuristic by invoking economic man in a metaphorical, figurative sense – through a *speaking* animal. It can be asked why the snake remained the only speaking animal in biblical storytelling (apart from an ass in Numbers 22: 28–30 through whom God spoke). Possibly, by invoking a speaking animal, the Bible wanted to quite explicitly prevent a behavioural (mis)interpretation of a calculus of self-interest as an empirical reference to human nature (Aesop's fables seem to proceed similarly). By projecting self-interest on a speaking animal, Genesis may have just stressed a *methodical, heuristic* role of a calculus of self-interest in institutional analysis, hinting at its empirical, behavioural irrelevance for analysing cooperation problems in general and problems of societal contracting in particular. I interpret here differently than Slivniak (2003: 452–4) who related the speaking ability of the snake to cultural advancement and contrasted this with another side of the snake as animal, namely non-rational, natural qualities. In an economic reconstruction, above all, I *heuristically* read Slivniak's (2003: 452) characterization of the snake as 'the animal side of the human being escaping rational control': namely as a reference to economic man caught up in a dilemma structure who is doomed to behave in a rationally foolish way. Equally, I do not find Gilboa's (1998: 105) suggestions on the speaking capabilities of the snake convincing. She admitted that the 'talking serpent is a strange phenomenon', but then she put forward the idea that a speaking snake posed as little an explanatory problem as a 'speaking God' in the Old Testament: If God can speak in Genesis, so she argued, why should not a snake be capable of speaking too? I think some deeper, heuristic, methodical reasons, as spelled out above, can be put forward as to why the snake remained the only speaking animal in the Old Testament.

To sum up, by hinting at a purposeful, constructive nature of the idea of self-interest in biblical storytelling, biblical statements about self-interest and 'sinfulness' can be transcended regarding a heuristic role in instructing the analysis of the institutional problem. When modelling persons as sinful, snake-like, the Old Testament may merely imply that capital contribution–distribution interactions were to be analysed under the ever-present conditions of 'if': '*if* war breaks out' (Exodus 1: 10), and related, one could add, '*if* humans behaved self-interested' ('being tempted by the snake'). Hence, when stories of the Old Testament that follow the Paradise story and the original sin discuss self-interest as evil, wickedness, sinfulness, etc. (Genesis 6: 5, 8: 21, 13: 13, 42: 22) or 'guile' (Plaut 1981: 187) or 'venality and faithlessness' (Raskovich 1996: 450), this may have to be interpreted as an instrumental, methodical application of the model of economic man – even if at times a foreground behavioural, empirical (mis)interpretation of self-interest can be found in the Bible, such as God being quoted to say that 'every inclination of his [man's] heart is evil from childhood' (Genesis 8: 21). Such statements should not be taken as an empirical, behavioural depiction of human nature. Indeed, if this were done by theology or a behavioural, theologically grounded economics, this would imply a dark and disturbing image of human nature for these research programmes. To a degree, Armstrong (1996: 36) briefly hinted at such a methodical interpretation of economic man in the Old Testament when she stated that man's 'evil inclination could be creative' or Fromm (1967: 162) implied the same when he stated: 'In the Jewish view man is born with the capacity to sin, but he can return, find himself, and redeem himself by his own effort and without an act of grace from God.' Fromm's statement is especially interesting since it opens up the way for economic analysis and intervention in order to 'redeem the human being' by means of rational, institutional economic intervention. Fromm himself, of course, had other, behavioural, spiritual ideas in mind of redeeming humans by means of repentance and forgiveness by other humans (e.g. Fromm 1967: 168–72).

2.4   Concluding remarks

There appears to be ample room and justification to interpret the Paradise story in institutional economic terms. The Paradise scenario was clearly defined by certain, contested capital contribution–distribution arrangements, God aiming to maintain exclusive access to certain goods, the tree of knowledge and the tree of life. Hence, interaction problems loomed. In dramatic fashion, the Old Testament thematically raised the issue of unresolved contribution–distribution conflicts through Adam and Eve's original sin. Destructive anarchy ultimately reigns at the paradise of Genesis. This economic conceptualization of 'paradise' as an apparently conflict-laden 'natural distribution state', to use Buchanan's (1975) terminology, subsequently drives the biblical analysis of cooperation problems – and their resolution (see the other chapters of this book.).

   In contrast to many tribal religions, the Bible is rather modern in this respect. It modelled as the starting point of a discussion of social problems, severe capital constraints on choice behaviour, with contribution–distribution conflicts arising regarding a scarcity in ultimate knowledge and wisdom and a scarcity in longevity or time. These capital constraints are central to the Bible's understanding of Paradise: Adam and Eve could only choose within a constrained decision space. They did not live in a land of Cockaigne or a 'fool's paradise', as a land of Cockaigne – a land of superabundance and unlimited choice and no constraints – is also poignantly referred to. This economic interpretation of the divine 'trees in the middle of the garden' differs from conventional ethical, intellectual, postmodern or sexual interpretations of stories that are associated with these trees (for such interpretations, see Parker 1999: 19–21; Stratton 1995; 139–40; Ward 1995: 9–11; Dragga 1992: 5–9; Westermann 1984: 211–36; Plaut 1981: 38–9).

The capital contribution–distribution conflicts played out in the Paradise scenario can be easily reconstructed through dilemma concepts such as the prisoner's dilemma and the commons dilemma. In these dilemma scenarios all interacting agents lose because of individual, rational choice that does not (cannot) take account of the choice behaviour of other agents. The overall outcome is mutual loss for all interacting agents. Such pareto-inferior outcomes characterize the natural distribution state of precontract social order. In the Paradise scenario such a seemingly 'rationally foolish', loss/loss outcome was reflected by God's loss of exclusive access to the tree of knowledge and by Adam and Eve's eviction from Paradise (assuming Adam and Eve valued access to Paradise higher than the gaining of ultimate knowledge and wisdom).

Related to the idea of a heuristic reading of the original sin, I identified the model of economic man as a research heuristic of Old Testament storytelling. In this connection, I heuristically read the snake metaphor, too, namely as a reference to economic man-behaviour. Through the snake, a calculus of self-interest was most explicitly imported into the Paradise interactions between God and Adam & Eve. In this connection, the Old Testament apparently stressed a metaphorical, heuristic role of the snake by modelling self-interest through a *speaking* animal.

The non-behavioural, institutional economic reconstruction of the Paradise story, as pursued in this chapter, made abundantly clear that the discussion of cooperation problems and societal contracts in a wider sense was a key topic from the very outset of biblical storytelling. Interaction conditions of scarcity were already present in Paradise and the more so after Adam and Eve's eviction from there. Adam and Eve then had to deal with the 'desert condition' in aggravated form. From here dilemmatic conflicts over capital contributions and capital distributions emerge in Old Testament storytelling and institutional problems of societal contracting, nation-building and developing international relations unfold.

The question remains why the Old Testament opened its discussion of human agency and social behaviour with such a dark and destructive story. The key thesis of the present book here is that the original sin provides, above all, an analytical, heuristic device for biblical storytelling: Subsequent stories of the Old Testament examine ways out of this dilemma and back into Paradise in a sense, regarding the (re-)establishing of a stable and efficient societal contract, regarding successful nation-building and state formation, and regarding the maintaining of harmonious international relations in a multicultural, pluralistic context. The present study then explores the key thesis that the Old Testament focused on the role of institutional rule-making in order to analyse the prevention of rationally foolish dilemmas. In practical, normative perspective, a heuristic reading of the original sin implies the need to prevent and resolve contribution–distribution conflicts in order to preserve Paradise and its abundance of water, fertile land, prosperity and mutual gains. How the Old Testament proceeded in this respect is examined in the following chapters.

3
On the Genesis of the Wealth
of Nations

Joseph is a fruitful vine, a fruitful vine near a spring,
whose branches climb over a wall. With bitterness archers
attacked him; they shot at him with hostility. But his bow
remained steady, his strong arms stayed supple, because
of the hand of the Mighty One of Jacob, because of the
Shepherd, the Rock of Israel, because of your father's God,
who helps you, because of the Almighty, who blesses you
...Your father's blessings are greater than the blessings of
the ancient mountains, than the bounty of the age-old
hills. Let all these rest on the head of Joseph, on the brow
of the prince among his brothers.

(Genesis 49: 22–6)

The book of Genesis starts the analysis of social conflict with the
Paradise story. Chapter 2 argued that the Paradise story heuristically
sets up the analysis of the institutional problem in the Old Testament,
that is, cooperation problems and problems of societal contracting.
This chapter critically reconstructs in economic terms some of the key
stories that follow the Paradise story. The chapter traces social conflicts,
even anarchy, in the book of Genesis that concern incentive structures,
dilemmatic interactions regarding capital contributions and distributions, mutual gains and economic man. In relation to the absence or
presence of these ideas, I examine how far behavioural, theological
models of societal contracting can be found in the Old Testament or
whether economic modes for resolving social conflict and organizing
cooperative behaviour were pursued. The thesis emerges that, as the
stories of Genesis unfold, economic modes increasingly replaced behavioural ones.

At the end of Genesis, a topical focus on social conflict culminates in one of the richest and longest stories of the Old Testament – the Joseph story. This chapter pays special attention to this story, which also directly connects Genesis to the book of Exodus. I interpret the Joseph story as the climax of economic, societal contracting in the Old Testament. Then, peaceful coexistence and productive cooperation emerged between Egypt and Israel and interaction problems were resolved in a mutually beneficial way. The Joseph story mastered interaction conditions, such as the desert problem and pluralism, through the skilful intervention of the Israelite Joseph at the top of Egypt's industrial hierarchy. I critically examine and discount conventional characterizations of Joseph as an anti-hero or even as a non-hero. I derive implications regarding the emergence of an economically based societal contract from Egypt's and Israel's successful interactions, namely in relation to economics' normative imperative to organize social interactions as a matter of creating mutual gains – the 'wealth of nations', as Adam Smith put it. This ideal postulates mutual benefits as interaction outcome. The chapter examines how far this normative imperative and implications derived hereof can be reconciled with biblical ideals on cooperative behaviour, for instance, on successful cooperation among nations.

In the subsequent, first, I examine evidence of behavioural contracting in some of the early stories of Genesis (section 3.1). Second, the chapter identifies a changing orientation in Genesis towards non-behavioural, economic governance and economic contracting (section 3.2). Third, the heuristic role of economic man in Genesis is stressed for organizing economic contracting (section 3.3). Fourth, I pay special attention to the Joseph story and its high relevance for an economic reconstruction of the Old Testament (section 3.4).

3.1 Evidence of behavioural economics in the early stories of Genesis: Social ordering in value homogeneous settings

The subsequent examines how far the Old Testament went down a behavioural route to societal contracting and solving institutional interaction problems. Here, I address the question whether and, if so, how far, already early behavioural ordering in Genesis was supplemented in certain respects by economic ordering, especially *behavioural economic* ordering.

The early societal contract: Value contracts with God as sovereign

There is some evidence that in the very early stories of Genesis, especially the ones which involved Noah, Abraham, Lot and Isaac, value-based contracting between God and humans was the goal. The achievement and maintenance of value homogeneity was then an important interaction condition for cooperation to succeed among humans. This hints at a non-economic approach or, from an economic perspective, at best at a behavioural economic approach to social ordering and institutional regulation. The question arises how far the Old Testament here promoted behavioural, societal contracts through theological or socio-psychological ordering, namely through behavioural, internalized institutional structures, for example, in the tradition of a communitarian, ethical approach. Evidence for such behavioural structures, which hint at a behavioural societal contract, is the presence of social values, moral precepts, virtues and religious beliefs that are (to be) shared by the group. Such value structures can be interpreted as institutions that are behaviourally enacted, for example, through virtuous character education in an Aristotelian tradition or through practices of religiosity. The human condition is then focused on. If well enacted, behavioural intervention nearly instinctively predisposes choice makers towards cooperation in social exchange. Figure 1.2 illustrated such a behavioural approach from the point of view of theology.

Following a contractarian approach, the related image of God is here the one of a value contractor who, as sovereign, facilitates the sharing of values among humans and thus cooperation among humans. More precisely, God could here be thought of as a 'central contracting host' who hosts value contracting. He is 'sovereign over all the hosts' whereby 'hosts' are understood as God's 'powers', 'armies' (see the *Preface*, p. 50, of Gideon's edition of the Holy Bible, New International Version, International Bible Society, 1984). It appears that at least in the early stories Genesis seemed to aim theoretically and practically at value contracting in order to handle the institutional problem: It invoked a 'covenant', even an 'everlasting covenant' (Genesis 9: 8, 12; 17: 4–7, 19; 17: 7, 19; 22: 18) between God and humans which was behaviourally grounded in human faith in God and the sharing of same values among humans (see Spriggs 1974: 4).

Based on a value-oriented covenant, Genesis approached the resolution of the institutional problem in a behavioural manner, being made dependent on the clear conscience of the individual and being connected to the religiosity of humans and their personal mastery of living in the image of God (e.g. Fromm 1967: 55–6). The Old Testament's behavioural approach compares in this respect to an institutional sociology or a social psychology, and similarly to a religious economics, or, of course, to the theological approach. It may be related to a behavioural, communitarian ethics, for example, a virtue ethics, which suggests that through the '[behavioural] regulation of the individual soul' (Plato 1999: 174), namely by leading a godly life, the institutional problem can be solved; in Plato's words, the 'good and true city and state ' can be achieved (Plato 1999: 174). This underlines the idea that God was a contracting host for *value* contracting. In this way, the original sin was to be behaviourally healed.

In this respect, Genesis followed a sociological, socio-psychological or theological approach in the aftermath of the collapse of order in the paradise scenario. Schein's (1980) suggestions on organizational, psychological contracting could here be linked to the Old Testament. Thus, a behavioural route to constitutional contracting remedied the 'precontract state of nature' (Buchanan 1975: 25), which could be observed as final outcome of the paradise interactions (see Chapter 2). A potentially anarchic situation regarding human behaviour, as reflected by Adam and Eve's defection behaviour in paradise, was overcome. The first covenants between God and humans (Noah, Abraham) were clearly of such a value-based, behavioural nature.

However, not only humans but also the sovereign was in this way bound by behavioural norms: 'God [too] is bound by the norms of justice and love', as Fromm (1967: 28) noted (see also Fromm 1967: 51, 53, 62, 182–4). Interesting in this connection from an institutional economic perspective is that the first covenants transformed the role of God from that of an absolute and arbitrary ruler to the one of a 'constitutional monarch' (Fromm 1967: 25). Binding both parties, sovereign and subjects, is a very significant issue for a democratic approach to constitutional contract, especially the involving of a sovereign in societal contracting, binding the sovereign by same or similar rules as the subjects. Of course, after the Paradise events, both parties had an economic incentive to engage in constitutional contracting, even a behavioural one, since this reduced the effort, time and energy they had to invest in predatory or defence activities regarding good x, the one good that was scarce in the precontract, natural distribution state of Hobbesian anarchy (Buchanan 1975: 28; see also Chapter 2).

Through stories which depicted role models of highly religious humans, nearly holy human beings, the Old Testament indicated how humans should aim to live in the image of God and thus make sure that a value-based covenant with God was not broken. Social values such as righteousness, justice or non-violence were upheld (Genesis 4: 7; 6: 9–11,

22; 9: 6; 20: 6; 22: 15). Key role models discussed for a behavioural approach to the institutional problem were Noah, 'a righteous, blameless man' (Genesis 6: 9; 7: 1; see also Kugel 1997: 116; Buber 1982: 31–2), and Abraham, a 'right and just man' (Genesis 18: 19; see also Shields 2003: 33, 47; Buber 1982: 32–3, 40) and to a lesser degree also Lot and Isaac (see also Kugel 1997: 152–3, 182–3). Religious faithfulness was then the key driver of behavioural, constitutional contracting between humans and God and post-constitutional contracting among humans. This role model of human nature, as exemplarily well depicted through Noah or Abraham, compares to that of a 'faithful priest' who leads his people in the name of God (Buber 1982: 34). For Abraham, even the term of a 'prophet' and 'seer' was reserved (Buber 1982: 37). On a related point, the idea of the paradise was behaviourally (re)interpreted as the 'garden of the righteous' (Kugel 1997: 79).

The early value-based contracts in Genesis were ambitiously posed: They were *intergenerational* and *universally* oriented. Genesis (9: 12) touched upon intergenerational contracting among nations – an idea also prominently discussed in Rawls' *Theory of Justice*. Genesis invoked in this connection the idea of a 'covenant for all generations to come'. The accounts of lengthy family trees in the Bible also reflect a focus on intergenerational contracting (e.g. Genesis 5: 3–32; 10: 1–31; 11: 10–30; 25: 1–19; 36: 1–40; 46: 8–25). Genesis interrelates generations, in particular the generations of Israel, but as Buber (1982: 25, 28) noted, this focus on Israel's generations is ultimately linked to the human race and mankind as such. Fromm (1967: 24–6) similarly stressed that the first, largely value-based covenant between God and the human being (Noah) was universally oriented. Rights of *all* living beings were to be protected (Genesis 9: 11). Equally, the second covenant between God and humans (Abraham) was to be projected to mankind in general. Although Genesis (12: 1–3; 17: 7–10) put forward the second covenant with specific reference to the Hebrews it subsequently extended it to mankind.

Clearly, it appears that in Genesis a universal, global philosophy can be made out for establishing social order:

> The nations, preserving their irrevocable division [after Cain's fratricide and the Tower-of-Babel event], ... [have to] bind themselves together in a single humanity. How shall this new situation come about? One people must set an example of harmony in obedience in God for the others. From a mere nation, ... it [Israel] must become a community ... whose members are connected not merely by origin

and common lot, but are also bound to one another by just and loving participation in a common life. But it can do this only as a ... people of God, in which all are bound to one another through their common tie to a divine center. A pseudo-community which lacks the center (Gen. 11: 6) must fall apart.

(Buber 1982: 86)

Buber here raises the question of a universal societal contract among societies – and answers it through the proposal of a religious, value-based, communitarian contract that centres on God. Israel is called upon to set a 'living *example* of a true people, a community' (Buber 1982: 87, emphasis added). All the other nations should follow this example. As Buber (1982: 88) makes clear, the idea of the 'people' or 'nation' is here not to be understood in a biological sense but in a sociological, communitarian one. Addressing the same question of a value-based maintenance of the societal contract, Fromm (1967: 52) specified:

Universal salvation [according to Old Testament theology] is not dependent on adherence to Judaism.... The human race will have achieved the condition of blessedness [solidarity and peace], providing only that it does not worship idols and does not blaspheme God.

(See also Fromm 1967: 53–4, 82–3)

Buber's and Fromm's interpretations of how a community of nations were to be created are similar but there are also important differences. Both agree that Israel and the covenants God made with Israel provide a role model of value-based, behavioural contracting among nations for achieving a universal community and the universal salvation of mankind. A key difference between their interpretations is Buber's largely theological, religious analysis of the value contract between God and humans, whereas Fromm, in a more enlightened, philosophical tradition, abstracts the concept of God to a high degree where the idea of God then finally stands for non-theistic, humanist values that behaviourally organize the universal community.

Behavioural economic ordering in the early stories of Genesis

Since the Paradise story the personal mastery to live in the image of God was under threat – and thus, one could speculate, were the new behavioural contracts that were closed in the aftermath of the original sin with God hosting value contracting. In the course of Genesis, the Abraham–Lot separation story already underlines this, with Lot choosing land that was closely located to the city. The city metaphor, as further discussed throughout this chapter, signalled in the Old Testament pluralism, ethnic diversity, moral disagreement and even value decay, such as 'sinfulness' and 'wickedness' and the breakdown of behavioural ordering. At least implicitly, the city metaphor also told of the coming of anonymous social exchange as it characterizes the modern market society. Hence, it will be interesting to see, as subsequently discussed in this chapter, how Genesis handled such threats to the behaviourally oriented value contracts between God and humans (e.g. Noah, Abraham) and among humans.

Even when the Old Testament favoured a behavioural route to institutional analysis in the early stories of Genesis it already seemed to back up conflict resolution with certain methods and concepts of economics. It appears that the Old Testament from the outset aimed at least at a religious, behavioural economics. There are various indications that support such a diagnosis.

From the very beginning, Genesis signalled an economic framework for behavioural contracting when living in the image of God was interlinked with 'ruling' over capital: 'God said: "Let us make man in our image, in our likeness, and let them rule over the fish of the sea and the birds of the air, over the livestock, over all the earth, and over all the creatures that move along the ground"' (Genesis 1: 26). As discussed above, Genesis initially answered the question of how to effectively 'rule' over capital with the recommendation of value contracting with God: faith in God and living a life in the image of God. Genesis seemed to propose here that, in line with humans approximating an image of God, a behavioural, institutional regulative could be enacted for organizing successful capital utilization. In this respect, Genesis' positive suggestions on humans *being* created in the image of God may have to be normatively interpreted in the first place, namely with regard to the successful maintenance of a value contract between God and humans.

Also, as discussed earlier in Chapter 2, from the very outset, the Old Testament hinted how, in the face of value pluralism and value decay, cooperation could still be assured – namely in economic terms through incentive structures. After Adam and Eve's defection 'he [God] placed on the east side of the Garden of Eden cherubim and a flaming sword flashing back and forth to guard the way to the tree of life' (Genesis 3: 24). Potential conflict was here no longer tried to be solved in a

pre-modern, tribal manner through intrinsic, behavioural value contracting and the handling of the human condition, for example, by trying to strengthen the religiosity of the human being. Rather, economic
institutions, including economic sanctions, were drawn upon. In this
context, God made costly armament investments to protect the one
remaining divine tree. Such investments characterize the unproductive
and uncooperative nature of the natural distribution state, as Buchanan
(1975) reminds us. These defence or predatory investments open up
room for cost savings by means of newly negotiated constitutional
order that involves the redistribution of wealth (specifically: the scarce
good x). By reducing armament investments, new constitutional order
becomes economically attractive. But initially, 'cherubim and a flaming sword' or, more pragmatically expressed, certain capital gains and
losses allocated to an agent in the wake of failing cooperation (or succeeding cooperation), actually changed calculated gains and losses of
decision makers in a way which made attack unattractive on grounds
of self-interested choice. A precontract, natural state equilibrium was
thus reached in the aftermath of Adam and Eve's first attack with God
making rearmament investments.

Furthermore, there are other economic elements which at least partly
defined the early behavioural contracts that were closed between God
and humans after the original sin. The type of interaction outcome that
was discussed in Genesis for value contracting reflects this: Not peace or
harmony in social relations as such was aimed at but the generation of
wealth for all choice makers. It was God who distributed earthly wealth:
Even the good, religious human being received ample capital distributions from social interactions. For living in the image of God, Noah and
Abraham *and* their families (their 'nations') were rewarded with fruitful
land, prosperity, longevity and surviving disasters (Genesis 13: 2, also
24: 34–5, 53). On the other hand, sinful humans were punished with
shorter life spans and even death (Kaiser 2001: 71, 74–5). Regarding the
good 'longevity', this can be interpreted with regard to the one remaining divine tree and the good x it reflected, specifically eternal life. It
appears that God rewarded the faithful human being by sharing out,
in degrees, this remaining, scarce good x, thus supporting behavioural
contracting by economic means. In this way, Genesis reached a new,
more stable and less costly equilibrium in constitutional ordering, overcoming the initial, natural distribution state equilibrium.

At times, Genesis further economically backed up behavioural
contracting through a hostage model – which could economically
test contract commitment: here, value commitment. Such a test was

prominently discussed through the story of God requesting Abraham to sacrifice his only son Isaac (Genesis 22: 1–3) or the story of Sodom and Gomorrah when Lot offered his daughters as hostages in exchange for travellers (for a review of this issue, see Morschauser 2003). In considerable degrees, these instances compare to a hostage model for analysing and ensuring effective, credible contract execution, as it is also elaborated on in institutional economics (Williamson 1985: 169–75; Williamson 1983). In this respect, Miller's (1993b) interpretation of Bible stories with regard to a sacrifice model can be linked to and deepened by the institutional economic analysis of hostage models. Miller argued that the purpose of the sacrifice scenario in Genesis was to establish certain behavioural rules, namely rules regarding cultic obligations. Similarly argued Davidson (1979: 94) who outlined that the purpose of God's request of Abraham to sacrifice Isaac was that 'men had to live in faith, stripped of many of the God-given things they most cherished', such as their next of kin or their land (see also Davidson 1979: 96). Although I cannot follow Miller or Davidson regarding their suggestions on rules for *cultic*, *religious* purposes, a rule-making purpose of a sacrifice-test model is convincing, especially to test out contract commitment in the absence of well established legal rules which came with unambiguous, effective economic sanctions. Miller's argument on cultic purposes and cultic regulation is tied to his assumption that a sacrifice model was useful for the tribal, archaic society. As much as Miller can explain some of the early stories of Genesis in this way, his analysis quickly runs into problems (1) when in Genesis written contracts are set out, (2) when complex interaction sequences are encountered, (3) when complex institutional ordering can be observed and (4) when pluralism as an interaction condition prevails (e.g. through discussing the city metaphor), or in short – when the archaic society was exited from and a modern, pluralistic society was entered into. In the Old Testament this happened in force at least from the stories of Jacob onwards but it was also already hinted at by some earlier stories, for example, the Tower of Babel story and the Sodom-and-Gomorrah story or the type of contracting Abraham and Abimelech were involved in, as discussed below in section 3.2.

   In sum, it seems quite clear that Genesis was not written as a pure behavioural ethics: Even from the outset, it seemed to aim at least at a behavioural economics, questions of value contracting between God and humans being tied to issues of effective capital utilization and economic rewards. The Old Testament apparently viewed religiosity and value contracting as means for effective capital utilization. The subsequent discussion details whether, and if so how far, Genesis qualified such a behavioural approach and moved towards a purer, economic approach. I suggest then that Genesis set out proposals on 'truly' economic institutional ordering, favouring economic ordering over value contracting in order to solve the institutional problem. The subsequent discussion proposes that such a switch in perspectives can be explained with respect to a superior capability and with respect to efficiency gains of economic institutions to handle cooperation problems for certain interaction contexts, namely *modern* ones where pluralism, cultural diversity, moral disagreement and even value decay are encountered as interaction conditions.

3.2   Towards institutional economic order in Genesis: Capital scarcities, dilemmatic capital exchange, incentive structures and mutual gains

At the heart of institutional economics lies a capital exchange model: Agents contributing capital to an interaction and, in return, they receive capital distributions. An interaction is only expected to materialize if interests of interacting agents can be 'equilibrated' in a pareto-superior way, that means as a result of capital contributions made and distributions received, *all* parties involved are left better off. In the following, first, the role of capital scarcities in Genesis is analysed. Second, I outline how scarcities induced dilemmatic, conflict-laden capital exchange in Genesis. Third, I discuss incentive structures of Genesis as means of conflict resolution. Fourth, the goal of mutual gains as interaction outcome is examined. Finally, I spell out pluralism as a rising interaction condition when the stories of Genesis unfold. The discussion in the following sections focuses on the Genesis stories prior to the Joseph story. (The Joseph story is discussed separately in section 3.4.)

Scarcities in capital as starting point of biblical storytelling

In nearly every story of the Old Testament, scarcities of capital of one kind or another set the scene for interactions. The limited availability of certain desired capital, constrains choice behaviour of agents. This was already a key feature of the Paradise story. Besides a heuristic purpose as discussed above, the Paradise story dealt with substantial issues of capital scarcities, too, such as scarce free time of Adam and Eve. Becker (1965) would speak of scarce 'time capital'. To recapitulate: Adam and Eve were expected to work six days a week, keeping paradise cultivated. Hence, their free time was severely curtailed. An economic problem existed here in paradise. This capital contribution model concerning time capital can be detailed: Adam and Eve spent most of their time working for God. Besides time capital, they were also expected to contribute capital in the form of skills or 'human capital'. For their work contributions, they received capital distributions in return, namely free access to harvest fruits in Paradise, except fruits from the tree of life and the tree of knowledge. As discussed in Chapter 2, the Paradise story implied through the ban not to eat from the tree of life scarcities in 'life time capital' and 'eternal life' (Genesis 2: 9; 3: 22; 6: 3). Regarding the ban not to eat from the tree of knowledge, Genesis implied scarcities in human capital, such as certain knowledge and skills (Genesis 2: 9, 17; 3: 6).

In general, the Old Testament's ideas on skills and human capital not only reflects agricultural skills but also managerial ones, as found in the Jacob story (and the Joseph story, too). Human capital of an altogether different kind was traded when it came to slave ownership. Even Abraham, one of the key role models of the highly religious, nearly holy human being in the Old Testament, was seemingly involved in slave trading and slave ownership (Genesis 12: 5; also Genesis 17: 13; 29: 19, 27; 37: 26–8). Employment relationships and human capital management issues here become a topic on a large scale. A further type of human capital plays a prominent role when it comes to marriage arrangements. The Old Testament outlines problems in finding suitable marriage partners, especially fertile ones. The Lot story, the Abraham story or the Jacob stories are illustrative (Genesis 19: 31–2; 20: 11; 21: 1–2; 24: 3–5; 25: 1–4; 28: 2–4; 29: 15–30). In a sense, scarce biological human capital is the topic. In the background loom issues concerning the economics of reproduction, population management and gene pool management. In nomadic, tribal societies, located in a desert area, it was anything than easy to make marriage arrangements that prevented the decline of biological human capital within the tribe, with infertility threatening to rise, for example, through inbreeding (Genesis 19: 36–8, also Genesis 20: 11, 28: 2–3, 29: 31).

Other scarcities in capital encountered in the Old Testament reflect site capital, physical capital and farming capital, such as fertile land, wells for drinking water, animals and plants. They are frequently discussed in stories that follow the Paradise story. The Abraham–Lot story is an early example. Genesis (13: 6–7) points out that there was not enough fertile land and drinking water that could support both Abraham and Lot and their families and herds. The commons dilemma looms here, instructing the analysis of social interactions and interaction conflict (discussed in more detail below). These scarcities encountered by Abraham and

Lot contradict Meeks' (1989: 12) view that scarcity was no issue in the Old Testament '*if* the righteousness of God is present' (emphasis as in original). As discussed above, Abraham and Lot were very much righteous and God-fearing human beings and hence, one could argue, should not have met scarcity, at least not in the way Meeks' seems to imply. Apparently, the Old Testament's analysis of scarcity even among righteous and highly religious human beings stresses that we are dealing here with an ever-present interaction condition. Indeed, the absence of this condition would render most treatises of social order, societal contracting and institutional governance irrelevant. The Paradise story, as discussed in Chapter 2, made a similar point, both in theoretical and in heuristic perspectives.

Following the Abraham–Lot story, Genesis (26: 12, 19–24) further discusses scarcity in the Isaac–Abimelech story. It then states that food and water were in short supply and famine was raging in the Israelites' homeland. Or, in the Jacob story, clever breeding tactics lead to imbalances in the distribution of farming capital between Jacob and his master Laban (Genesis 30: 37–43; discussed in detail below).

Genesis assessed capital scarcities of yet another type when it comes to problems in intergenerational capital transfer, for example, through the allocation of inheritance rights. The Esau–Jacob story (Genesis 25: 31), or the story of Rachel and Leah (Genesis 31: 14) are illustrative. Also, the 'Table of Nations' can be similarly read, implying intergenerational capital transfer problems (Genesis 10: 1–26, 11: 10–32). The ideal of a community of nations through time is touched upon by the genealogies of the Old Testament, as also hinted by Rogerson and Davies (1989: 55).

All these capital scarcities are sufficient to set the scene for potentially dilemmatic social conflict. A critical question for Genesis is here: How could interacting agents handle these encountered scarcities and what suggestions did Genesis make in this respect? The following addresses this question.

A dilemmatic conflict model of capital contributions and capital distributions

As much as Genesis examines capital scarcities, this is not done for its own sake. Rather, they are the integral elements of a conflict model, even a *dilemmatic* conflict model. Old Testament stories seem to typically approach questions of capital utilization as dilemmatic interaction conflicts over capital contributions to and capital distributions from an interaction. In Genesis, dilemmatic interaction conflicts are prominently encountered by Adam & Eve and God (as already discussed), Abraham and Lot, Abraham and Abimelech, Isaac and Gerar, Isaac and Abimelech, Esau and Jacob, Isaac and Jacob, Laban and Jacob, Joseph and the pharaoh of Egypt.

What these stories have in common is that cooperation problems and the societal contracts they stand for are discussed as dilemmatic interaction problems among a mere handful of persons, in most cases two-person models. Such a scenario, in which only a small number of persons interact, compares to the approach of the theories which form the conceptual backbone of institutional and constitutional economics, such as game theory, property rights theory, principal-agent theory and transaction cost economics. Besides enabling a detailed discussion of interaction problems, a small number's focus analytically reflects that only in an interaction context with a finite number of agents can dilemmatic social conflict arise that is caused by interdependent choice behaviours (Homann 1999a, 1999b; Axelrod 1997, 1984; Williamson 1985, 1975; Buchanan 1975; Luce and Raiffa 1957; von Neumann and Morgenstern 1947).

Noth's (1966: 9) suggestion that Genesis is interested in distinctive *individual* figures while Exodus examines Israel as collective can be clarified in this respect. Already Genesis examines *interactions*, mostly two-person interactions, which at times are intricately interconnected, on the one hand, and which need to be projected to larger group interactions, on the other. Also, the Joseph story predominantly does not tell of interactions between Joseph and the pharaoh but above all between Israel and Egypt. Hence, a *social* focus on *inter*action analysis can be made out for Genesis. To underline this important point: As much as biblical conflict models are focused on two-person interactions in conceptual and practical, normative perspectives, the Old Testament, like a constitutional and institutional economics, is not primarily interested in cooperation problems among a mere handful of people. Bible stories typically project the resolution of interaction problems between individuals to the groups, tribes and nations they represent. The patriarchs stand for their people (Westermann 1986: 417; similarly Davidson 1979: 137). Genesis targets the welfare of the 'city' (Genesis 11: 4, 22: 18, 44: 3), the 'nation' (Genesis 10: 1-32, 12: 2, 18: 18, 27: 29) and even a 'community of nations' (Genesis 35: 11, 48: 4, 19, also Genesis 18: 18, 22: 18). Davidson (1979: 27) very clearly spelled out in this connection that two-person quarrels over land usage in the Old Testament, such as the quarrel involving Abraham and Lot (Genesis 13: 1–13), reflect multitribal or multinational interaction problems in a certain region, which for the Abraham–Lot story seem to involve up to eleven nations. In abstract, conceptual terms, comparisons to game-theoretical analysis can be made (e.g. Axelrod 1984).

Also, from the outset, Old Testament stories begin to discuss cooperation problems in *modern* social arenas, namely the nation and the international community, and the capitalist market economy in general, where anonymity, value pluralism cultural diversity, moral disagreement and even value decay reign in social interactions. Then, traditional, behavioural, institutional mechanisms of social ordering, for example, family-type bonding and value contracting, can be expected to be largely ineffective (discussed in more detail below and in section 3.4 as the 'condition of pluralism' and the 'condition of modernity'; see also Wagner-Tsukamoto 2008a, 2008c, 2003). Such an intergroup focus which hints at institutional analysis for modern contexts becomes equally apparent when the 'Table of Nations' is set out in Chapter 10 of Genesis, or when the final stories of Genesis culminate in a large-scale migration story, with the Israelites relocating as expatriates to their affluent neighbour Egypt, and subsequently, in Exodus, large-scale conflict emerges between the two nations (see section 3.4; also Wagner-Tsukamoto 2008a, 2000b).

In finite scenarios of two-person or two-nation interactions, the negotiation of capital contingencies in an interaction is a critical issue. An excellent example here are so-called asset specific skills, as reflected by Jacob's knowledge of cross-breeding tactics for sheep (Genesis 30: 33, 37–43) or his salesman-like knowledge of how to close a contract despite conditions not being staked in his favour. This happened when he extorted Esau's birthright or when he extorted Isaac's blessing (Genesis 25: 31–4, 27: 24–5). Exploiting an emergency situation when his elder brother was close to starving, Jacob 'enticed' Esau to sell his birthright to him (Miller 1994: 759). The Old Testament literature notes in this respect that Jacob knew how to bend and interpret a contract to his advantage without breaking it: 'Jacob drives a hard bargain' (Davidson 1979: 124). Or, Pfeiffer (1948: 144) linked 'astute schemes for acquiring wealth' to Jacob's personality. Apparently, Genesis no longer models Jacob as a choice maker who is behaviourally disposed towards cooperation in social interactions, as earlier invoked by Genesis in relation to the righteous, quasi-holy, religious figures of Abraham and Noah. Jacob's behaviour closely reflects the model of economic man, even in the worst sense as Williamson (1967, 1975, 1985) interpreted economic man with regard to opportunism and guile and Buchanan (1975) or North and Thomas (1973) with regard to predation behaviour. Plaut (1981: 35, 187) explicitly invoked here the idea of guile for Jacob, too, which he also associated with the snake in Genesis 3. Opportunism in extreme degrees is here encountered. (Section 3.3 follows up with regard to economic man-behaviour.) Armstrong (1996: 96) even suggested that Jacob's wealth was achieved by 'the guile of the serpent'. In general, Genesis (Chapters 30–1) seemingly unfavourably depicts Jacob as being inclined towards deceitfulness and cheating.

Jacob's knowledge of haggling tactics, of 'perfunctory cooperation' or 'organizational misbehaviour', as Williamson (1985: 262–3, 1975: 68–70, 80–1) or Ackroyd and Thompson (1999: 1–3, 25) might call it, becomes more apparent in interactions with his employer Laban. Genesis here tells of a classic contribution–distribution conflict, reflecting the commons dilemma (Genesis 30: 31–43 and 31: 1–2, 3–24, 26, 38–42). Besides the payment of a fixed wage by Laban to Jacob, Jacob and Laban agreed to share capital gains from farm production: Their contract detailed that Jacob was allowed to keep all newly bred speckled and spotted sheep and goats of Laban's herd. However, since Jacob was the shepherd and thus the producer of livestock capital he could influence through clever breeding tactics the number of spotted and speckled animals. The agreement between Jacob and Laban did not explicitly forbid Jacob to apply such tactics. A problem of so-called incomplete, relational contracting existed, as Williamson (1985: 71–9) might put it. Such conceptual grey areas open up room for discretionary employee behaviour (see also Wagner-Tsukamoto 2007a, 2003, 2000a; Williamson 1967, Berle and Means 1932). I disagree here with Kugel's (1997: 222) interpretation that it was divine intervention which allowed Jacob to acquire substantial parts of Laban's flocks and rather stick to the biblical account itself (Genesis 31: 37–43) which suggests that Jacob's clever breeding tactics were the source of his success. Also, the institutional problem here begins to emerge in the Old Testament as the *organizational* problem, that is, how to handle and control delegation in a hierarchical, contractual relationship.

Once Laban discovered that Jacob had exploited a contractual grey area, he could not do much about it: In this specific instance, God – the sovereign, the central contracting host – explicitly forbade him to settle the dispute in a violent, physical manner (Genesis 31: 24, 42). In Buchanan's terminology (Buchanan 1975: 67–9; also Friedman 1962: 15, 25), seemingly existing order at the constitutional stage of the 'protective state', as reflected by God's *judicial*, umpire-like intervention, successfully channelled and constrained post-constitutional, private goods contracting between Laban and Jacob. The role of God can in this respect be compared to the one of an umpire or law enforcement agency which monitors the fulfilment of contractual claims but does not intervene in actual contractual bargaining or the establishment of the rules of the game itself. As a result, Laban was forced to negotiate a new contract with Jacob that settled the conflict by changing contractual incentive structures: by setting out new property rights to shepherding (Genesis 31: 44, 52). This yielded a new post-constitutional, private goods contract between them and it seemed to ensure mutually beneficial (pareto-superior) capital utilization over time since both parties could reduce investments in efforts to predatory or defence activity regarding contractual grey areas.

Such instances, in which one party gained and another party lost, however, are not presented in isolation in the Old Testament. Hence, it is difficult to speak of winners and losers. Most of these stories are part of an intricate web of bargaining processes for capital, tit-for-tat retaliation in the case cooperation broke down, and the institutional (re-)regulation of it. This reflects *interaction* economics when projected to post-constitutional contracting. For example, Jacob's thefts of Esau's birthright and blessing as first-born are later compensated for when Jacob makes payments to Esau in the form of livestock gifts, which were meant to 'pacify Esau' (Genesis 32: 20; see also Genesis 32: 13–21, 33: 10–11). New distributions from Jacob to Esau thus came into place. Apparently, there are some fine retribution arrangements in place in the Jacob–Esau interactions that ultimately resolved their conflict in economic terms. Brams (2002: 66) overlooked this when he suggested that the Jacob–Esau conflict remained unresolved economically, Esau just somehow forgetting about the wrongs that were initially done to him by Jacob: 'Esau bore no grudge [against Jacob] in the end, for reasons that are less than clear. The best guess that I can make is that he had a mercurial temperament … which would make him quick to forget the wrongs done to him.' My economic interpretation of the lengthy tit-for-tat interactions involving Jacob, Isaac, Laban and Esau shed here a very different light on why conflict could ultimately be resolved among the parties involved. Indeed, as Figure 3.1 shows (see below), the tit-for-tat interactions from Isaac (tit 2) up to Laban (tat 4) can be read as meta-tat payments that were meant to pacify Esau economically. I now spell out this interpretation of dilemmatic interpretation processes that involved Jacob in more detail.

Jacob is substantially punished for the theft of Esau's birthright and blessing when Isaac sends Jacob to Laban to take one of Laban's daughter's as wife (Genesis 28: 1–2). Isaac must have been well aware of Laban's cheeky character, who ultimately made Jacob work for 14 years

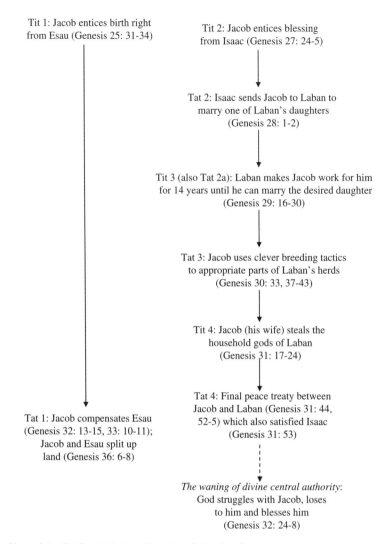

Tit 1: Jacob entices birth right from Esau (Genesis 25: 31-34)

Tit 2: Jacob entices blessing from Isaac (Genesis 27: 24-5)

Tat 2: Isaac sends Jacob to Laban to marry one of Laban's daughters (Genesis 28: 1-2)

Tit 3 (also Tat 2a): Laban makes Jacob work for him for 14 years until he can marry the desired daughter (Genesis 29: 16-30)

Tat 3: Jacob uses clever breeding tactics to appropriate parts of Laban's herds (Genesis 30: 33, 37-43)

Tit 4: Jacob (his wife) steals the household gods of Laban (Genesis 31: 17-24)

Tat 1: Jacob compensates Esau (Genesis 32: 13-15, 33: 10-11); Jacob and Esau split up land (Genesis 36: 6-8)

Tat 4: Final peace treaty between Jacob and Laban (Genesis 31: 44, 52-5) which also satisfied Isaac (Genesis 31: 53)

The waning of divine central authority: God struggles with Jacob, loses to him and blesses him (Genesis 32: 24-8)

Figure 3.1   Tit-for-tat interactions involving Jacob

in order to marry the one of the daughters he desired – Rachel (Genesis 29: 16–30). Jacob was in this connection deceived by Laban and Laban's other daughter, Leah:

All that night he kept calling her 'Rachel' and she kept answering him 'Yes?' 'But the next morning, behold, it was Leah' [Genesis 29: 25].

He said to her, 'Liar and daughter-of-a-liar!' She answered: 'Can there be a schoolmaster without any pupils? Was it not just this way that your father called out to you "Esau" and you answered him [see Genesis 27: 24]? So when you called me I likewise answered you.'

(*Genesis Rabba* 70: 19 quoted from Kugel 1997: 219)

Kugel (1997: 222, 229) spoke in this connection of the 'slippery' character of Laban. Graves and Patai (1964: 211–12, 224) characterized Laban as a scheming deceiver. Von Rad (1963: 286) even talked of 'shameless treachery'. A further 'revenge' element of Isaac's request of Jacob to take one of Laban's daughters as wife was the close kinship relation Laban shared with Isaac and Jacob (Genesis 28: 1–2). Infertility or other inbreeding problems loomed here. An appeasement element regarding Isaac is clearly referred to in the Jacob–Laban story when Jacob and Laban finally come to a 'peace' settlement (Genesis 31: 53), which was also meant to satisfy Isaac (Genesis 31: 53–4; see Figure 3.1, Tat 4). A complex web of tit-for-tat interactions, mirroring an evolutionary, interaction economics, emerges (see Figure 3.1). In this connection, a tit-for-tat strategy can be simply defined as a strategy that 'rewards cooperation with cooperation and punishes defection with defection.' (North and Taylor 2004: 8). In the case a central authority is unwilling to intervene in private goods exchange, or a central authority is absent altogether, tit-for-tat can be a valid and rather successful strategy to induce cooperation over time in dilemmatic conflict situations, as the economic literature has well documented (e.g. Axelrod 1984). In order for cooperation to emerge, 'it pays to be nice, [but] it also pays to be retaliatory' (Axelrod 1984: 46). In interactions that involved Jacob, such tit-for-tat interactions seemingly contributed to the emergence of cooperation even among rather egoistic actors.

Those who came with guile were visited on with guile, as Plaut (1981: 187, 190) put it for the cheeky character of Jacob, who met his counterpart in Laban (similarly Westermann 1986: 480). Or, in the terminology of Graves and Patai (1964: 224), 'deceit is matched against deceit.' Guile and predation, or in a figurative sense 'the snake', show up here reciprocally in social interactions. Genesis spins in this respect a web of interrelated conflicts regarding capital contributions and capital distributions through the characters depicted and their interaction sequences of wins and losses. Different types of capital are involved. As noted, Jacob's interactions are here an excellent example (see Figure 3.1): He steals Esau's birth right and blessing, the latter by deceiving their father Isaac; he contributes in return human capital, namely work capital and agricultural skills, to Laban; he receives, finally, the desired daughter of Laban as his wife, after Laban had made him marry first another of his daughters and work for him for a long time; and Jacob then gets his counter-revenge on Laban through his clever breeding tactics concerning Laban's sheep and goat herds; this, in turn, leads to a further compensation agreement between the two parties; subsequently, Jacob (more precisely, his wife) steals the household gods from Laban (Genesis 31: 17–24), before he finally makes a peace treaty with Laban (Genesis 31: 53–4) and reaches a peace settlement with Esau (Genesis 32: 13–21, 33: 10–11).

These considerations put into perspective some of Miller's (1993a) or Brams' (2002) suggestions which implied that the Jacob–Esau conflict was settled once Jacob had acquired Esau's birthright and Isaac's blessing and that Jacob basically got away unpunished with his extortions. Although Jacob's extortions were not overturned by subsequent interactions, there were certain intricate compensation and 'revenge' strategies in place.

Miller's (1994; 1993a) legal–economic approach to analysing Bible stories falls short of identifying both *inter*action problems, (i.e. tit-for-tat problems of contractual ordering) and issues of constitutional, economic ordering, which reflect the larger purpose of tit-for-tat when it comes to the establishing of a new societal contract. Miller focused on the single transaction or simple contract. Although his legal–economic analysis generally moves in the right direction, it cuts short an institutional and constitutional economic analysis of dilemmatic interaction conflict. And as indicated, he ignored constitutional, legal aspects of establishing social order. The interaction webs identified in the present book go beyond the diagnosis of a 'linear succession' of events in Genesis (e.g. Kaiser 2001: 83). In general, theology struggles to identify such interaction relationships among stories because of its research focus on the verse rather than the collection of verses that make a story or chapter and even more so interrelationships among chapters. Good examples are here Kugel's (1997: 199–210) or Eissfeldt's (1974: 196–7) theological interpretations, which fail to detail conceptual relationships among the stories that involved Jacob. Similarly, a lacking understanding of interaction economics led Valiquette (1999: 60) to suggest that 'rejection/acceptance' themes, as seemingly present in the stories of Esau and Jacob or in the Joseph story, were of an ironic and provocative nature. As outlined earlier and as section 3.4 for the Joseph story details, from an economic point of view, irony and provocation can be rationally, heuristically reconstructed in relation to ideas of 'rational fools' and 'opportunism' and how these ideas were constructively applied in the Old Testament to analyse the institutional problem.

In certain respects, Axelrod's evolutionary economics is here more helpful, especially for the Jacob stories, although such analysis runs into economic reconstruction problems as soon as questions of central authority, in particular God's involvement, arise. This also generally curtails the usefulness and relevance of evolutionary economics for reconstructing the Old Testament since questions of central authority that either involves God, in one way or another, or involve human attempts at governance are frequently an issue in the Old Testament. The subsequent analysis in this book will further demonstrate this. A constitutional and institutional economics, in the tradition of Buchanan and Williamson, is here of higher relevance for interpreting the Old Testament because their analyses explicitly cover questions of 'central authority' or, differently put, 'governance'. To follow up this point: The issues depicted in the Jacob stories can be closely linked to evolving economic, constitutional contract as set out by Buchanan, when a precontract, anarchic state of social life is overcome and constitutional contracting develops step-by-step. In the wake of the interactions involving Jacob, various compensation payments ('disarmament payments') were made to parties which had been disadvantaged by previous predatory, opportunistic behaviour of other agents. Ultimately a 'peace treaty', a social contract emerged. Such disarmament payments characterize the emergence of constitutional contracting out of the anarchic, natural distribution state, as Buchanan called it. This also qualifies the suggestion that the Jacob–Laban interactions merely reflected tit-for-tat interactions. Tit-for-tat came *with a purpose*: To a considerable degree, wider issues of developing constitutional order, through changing and constraining rules for choice behaviour, loom already at this stage of storytelling in Genesis. Specifically, Jacob's interactions reflect what Buchanan (1975: 70–1, 94, 109–10) called 'primal disarmament contracts'. They are payments through which the parties involved in social exchange can escape from an initial, anarchic, precontract, natural distribution state, bettering their respective economic positions as a result of saved armament costs regarding predatory and defence efforts in relation to scarce goods (good x, in particular).

As Buchanan (1975: 71) noted in this connection: 'Persons lay down their arms – in order to save defense and predation costs and reap gains from cooperation.' Buchanan's reference to 'arms' has to be figuratively interpreted, as Buchanan made amply clear, namely regarding costly 'armament' investments into predatory and defence activities as they characterized the natural distribution state. On this basis, precontract, anarchic states are overcome and existing, dysfunctional constitutional order is restructured. The key guiding principle for both is: '*Free relations among free men* – this precept of ordered anarchy can emerge as principle when successfully renegotiated social contract puts "mine and thine" in a newly defined structural arrangement' (Buchanan 1975: 180, emphasis as in original). I thus read the Jacob–Laban interactions and the other interactions that involved Jacob with reference to such an initial state of constitutional economic contracting in which limits to choice behaviour were set out, reversing the state of natural anarchy. Genesis here begins to hold up the principle of 'Free relations among free men' for social ordering and contracting. This was, for example, explicitly made clear in the story when God forbade Laban to physically punish Jacob for his questionable tactics and when God refrained from actually solving this conflict (apart from his umpire-like intervention).

For the early, nomadic and archaic society characterized at this point of storytelling in Genesis, the seemingly simple tit-for-tat strategies and bargaining processes and the seemingly simple institutional structures and basic evolutionary economics they reflected may have been sufficiently effective and efficient. Traditions of oral contracting coupled with simple compensation mechanisms and evolving governance structures seemingly sufficed to resolve capital exchange conflicts. When read from an institutional economic perspective, Miller (1993a) basically implied this, too, by providing snapshots of tit-for-tat interaction analysis. Over time, as Axelrod's (1997, 1986, 1984) evolutionary, game-theoretical economics spelled out, tit-for-tat is a valid strategy for interactions to stabilize and for interaction partners to avoid loss–loss situations, especially when a central authority is not present. However, as noted, tit-for-tat is a time consuming strategy and it is a passive, non-interventionist one from the point of view of a *normative* institutional and constitutional economics. It assumes the absence of a central authority, which for the Old Testament can be very frequently reconstructed in relation to God's involvement in human interactions or through human attempts at institutional governance. Axelrod and Miller underestimated these issues and wider issues of constitutional economic contracting. Axelrod does so in abstract terms and Miller specifically so in his analysis of cooperation problems in Genesis. In contrast, 'active', normative institutional economic intervention aims to resolve interaction conflict through direct intervention with rules that govern capital exchange. And questions of *purpose* of tit-for-tat regarding central authority are here strongly focused on. Normative institutional and constitutional economics can in this respect more directly analyse and more speedily and more effectively resolve interaction problems. Subsequent sections of this chapter, especially section 3.4, examine how far the Old Testament went down this route, of active rule-making that could prevent lengthy tit-for-tat exchanges and lead to win–win outcomes more efficiently and more effectively.

Incentive structures and institutional ordering in the early biblical society

As Libecap (1989) spelled out, following the approach of Williamson (1975, 1985) and North (1993a, 1993b), economic performance of a society is shaped by the governance structures and property rights institutions it has installed for regulating capital exchange. Buchanan (1975) argues along similar lines for constitutional contract issues.

Miller (1993a) noted in the early biblical society in Genesis that it was mainly oral contracting which governed capital exchange. And once an oral contract was entered, it was valid. Written contracting that was governed by complex laws was not yet in place. An oral contracting model implies various things. First, the contracting partners had to negotiate, for the interaction, everything they wanted to exchange and how the exchange would occur. No contract laws could help them. Second, one party could easily exploit the other party if power imbalances existed; for instance, Jacob exploited Esau who was starving or he exploited Isaac who was blind. Under the oral contracting practices in place, the contract would still be valid because this ensured at least stable although unfair interactions (Miller 1993a). In a figurative sense, which can be methodically interpreted regarding the way storytelling proceeds in the Old Testament, the theft scenario of the original sin is here re-encountered. However, this is not the end of the story, as Miller seems to imply. Already for the simple tribal society depicted prior to the Joseph story, punishment strategies were in place for unfair oral contracts. As noted above, tit-for-tat strategies were in place which compare to 'eviction' policies for Adam and Eve that followed the original sin. The Jacob story and the interactions that result are a good example too. After Jacob's deceits, he suffers retributions for his deceitful behaviour and he has to compensate Esau, Laban and Isaac (see Figure 3.1). As much as Jacob shows anarchic tendencies in disadvantaging his contracting partners, he is later tamed by new contractual arrangements that more fairly balance exchange contributions and distributions between the agents.

Similarly, Genesis early on hinted at economic proposals on restructuring incentive structures for conflict resolution when Abraham and Lot split up land (Genesis 13: 6–9). These issues of economic tit-for-tat strategies are not clearly spelled out by Miller. As already hinted above, Buchanan's concepts of anarchic, precontract natural distribution states, constitutional contract, disarmament payments and the move from anarchy to constitutional order are here more helpful to understand evolving social order in Genesis. In general, if an agreement had been entered in an unfair, forced manner, which failed to reflect an incentive-compatible, mutually advantageous, 'fair' arrangement, some kind of retribution process started in the Old Testament. Repayment schemes of one kind or another were put into place, for example, straightforward payments of animals or money or the contribution of human capital. And additional, new treaties were made in this respect, too, healing previous contractual loopholes. These instances all very closely reflect on Buchanan's idea of 'disarmament payments', which are necessary in order to move from conflict-laden anarchy to stable, constitutional contract. One of the well-known stories here is the treaty finally reached between Jacob and Laban (Genesis 31: 51–4; see above). Over time, such instantaneous practices of conflict resolution which had to be newly negotiated from event to event were laid down as laws. This reflects an important step in constitutional, societal contracting and in a nation-building and state formation process of a society.

The simple capital exchange models and tit-for-tat strategies of the early stories of Genesis reflect on the type of incentive structures at this stage of storytelling in the Old Testament. In a very simple manner, most of them set payments for an agreed action, whereby agreement could be entered by force, through extortion or by free will. Regarding the latter, the bargaining process came to an end when the exchange of goods was agreed. For instance, the treaty of Beersheba between Abraham and Abimelech, later renewed between Isaac and Abimelech (Genesis 21: 22–31; 26: 19–23), settled a dispute on the use of water through the design of incentive structures: a rule – here a sworn oath, a 'promise' – on how the dispute was to be settled, and a sanction – here: a payment of seven lambs by Abraham to Abimelech – to sanction the rule. Again, 'disarmament payments' are here visible. A stable, 'incentive-compatible' solution was thus reached between Abraham and Abimelech. Interest conflicts between the two parties were equilibrated. Hence, regarding the treaty of Beersheba between Abraham and Abimelech, I find nothing grotesque, as suggested by Westermann (1986: 348), that concerns the contracting status between the nomad

Abraham and King Abimelech, especially since Abraham had acquired great wealth during his stay in Egypt and thus was in a sense equal to Abimelech. Also, as Buchanan's constitutional economics made amply clear, effective constitutional contract can emerge for the parties involved even if they enter bargaining over rules and disarmament payments in unequal terms (Buchanan 1975: 11–12, 54–5). An equal standing of parties is not a necessary principle or condition for social order to emerge, but the generation of mutual gains as a result of constitutional contract is. Once the parties can better their economic position as a result of constitutional contracting, an initial, anarchic state of social order, in which a good x may have been highly one-sidedly, unequally distributed among parties (see Chapter 2), is overcome.

In the interactions, Abraham–Abimelech, Jacob–Esau or Jacob–Laban, cooperation problems were solved not through a behavioural value contract via God as contracting host but through incentive structures, (re)designed by humans through 'private ordering' and 'governance' to use Williamson's (1985: 9–10, 28–9, 33–4, 72–9) terms. The bartering of an economically inspired societal contract emerges here. Incentive structures reflect the 'economic institutions of capitalism', as Williamson (1985) referred to. The constitutional contract, and the kind of incentive structures it draws upon, looms large here too. If well enacted, incentive structures systemically realign, 'equilibrate' self-interests among choice makers by means of allocating capital contributions and capital distributions to them so that cooperation emerges on grounds of self-interested choice. The thesis emerges that the Old Testament increasingly favoured social ordering through economic institutions as the stories of Genesis unfold (with pluralism, moral disagreement, etc. also rising as interaction conditions; see below). The 'situation' and thus a systemic condition were interfered with but not human nature or the human condition (via religiosity and living a godly life, as religious economics or theology promote). Constitutional economic ordering began to take the centre place, at least since the stories that involved Jacob. In this respect, the original sin was overcome as a matter of organizing incentive structures and the related intervention with capital contributions and capital distribution. Theological interpreters, for example, Davidson (1979: 90), tend to overlook such economic issues when the giving of cattle by Abraham to Abimelech is interpreted as 'solemnizing the agreement by a rite'. As indicated, an economic interpretation relates the sworn oath not to a mere rite but to economic contracting and compensation as is the giving of lambs related to economic capital exchange that sanctioned the 'rite'. Constitutional economic order, which ensures cooperation and prevents anarchy, emerges here.

In the early stories of Genesis, clearly some bargaining goes on regarding what constitutes a fair contract. Libecap (1989: 7) would speak of bargaining processes that concern governance structures such as property rights institutions: institutional structures that define decision-making rights of agents, set contributions standards and distribution standards. Once such governance structures are in place, law courts can support the task of deciding fair contractual practices (Buchanan 1975). Although, as Williamson (1985) reminds us, for complex, incomplete contracts, which involve asset-specific skills, law courts may not be the best solution to solve contractual disputes. In the tribal society, which was at an early stage of nation-building, 'temples' are likely to have well performed such a court function for contractual disputes. Miller's (1993b) discussion of ritual and regulation can be projected in this direction. Later, such a function was taken over in the Old Testament by 'judges' and 'kings' (see Chapter 5). Buchanan's (1975) ideas on neutral state activity regarding law enforcement can here be related to Genesis, too.

Wealth of nations (mutual gains) as goal of conflict resolution

The previous already hinted that interactions between two parties only came to an end in the Old Testament when a solution was reached which was satisfactory and acceptable to both parties. If an outright deceit or extortion had happened in the first place, bargaining over compensations continued until a satisfactory arrangement was achieved. Economics invokes here the idea of mutual gains ('pareto-superiority') as interaction outcome. It plays a prominent role in institutional economics, for example, Buchanan and Tullock (1962), Buchanan (1975) or Williamson (1985). The same idea is in principle invoked when concepts like the economic performance of a nation or the idea of the wealth of nations is referred to. These latter ideas reflect important normative, moral principles of economics which date back at least to Adam Smith (see also Wagner-Tsukamoto 2007b, 2005) and even much further, following the economic reconstruction of the Old Testament in the present study.

Even Abraham, one of the few role models in Genesis who reflected a righteous, value adhering figure who had succeeded to live a godly life was rewarded with increases in wealth: Through his interactions with the Egyptians, he 'had [in the wake of his emigration to Egypt] become very wealthy in livestock and in silver and in gold' (Genesis 13: 2, also Genesis 24: 34–5, 53). Such biblical themes compare in considerable degrees to Adam Smith's suggestions on the *Wealth of Nations*: Gains from social interactions over capital utilization were to be shared among all agents. Otherwise, as Smith pointed out, social exchanges could not be expected to materialize (see also Tullock 1985). Smith discussed as ordering mechanism primarily the 'invisible hand', that is, the incentive structure 'price mechanism', although he proceeded in a more governance-oriented, contractarian, institutional economic tradition in Chapter 6 on the *Treaties of Commerce* among nations (Smith 1976).

The Old Testament's favoured strategy for conflict resolution can be characterized as an economic, 'capitalistic' one: Not peace or harmony in social relations as such is the goal of conflict resolution, as theology possibly might expect (e.g. Tullock 1981: 45, Lace 1972: 106; see also Figure 1.2), but the creation of wealth for all choice makers (Genesis 14: 11, 17–24). In a sense 'economic peace' or 'industrial peace', even industrial democracy was aimed at. Normative ideals like the wealth of a city (Genesis 11: 4, 22: 18), the wealth of a nation (Genesis 10: 1–32; 12: 2; 18: 18; 27: 29) and even the wealth of a community of nations (Genesis 35: 11, also Genesis 18: 18; 22: 18) strongly hint at such an economic rationale for handling the institutional problem.

> May God give you of heaven's dew and of earth's richness – an abundance of grain and new wine. May nations serve you and peoples bow down to you. Be lord over your brothers, and may the sons of your mother bow down to you. May those who curse you be cursed and those who bless you be blessed.
>
> (Genesis 27: 28–9)

Ideas like 'heaven's dew', the 'earth's richness' or an 'abundance of grain and new wine' imply a very concrete, non-spiritual understanding of wealth. In the Joseph story, this became pre-eminent too (discussed in detail below). Then, Joseph ensured that both Israel and Egypt benefited from their interactions. In strong degrees, an industrial democracy emerged. As Pfeiffer (1948: 144) put it: 'The seeds of Abraham [Joseph] became a blessing to "all families of the earth."' In the more technical economic speak of Buchanan and Williamson, Genesis seemingly advocated mutuality of gains and pareto-superiority as goal for resolving conflict. Taken together with the idea that conflict was to be resolved by intervening with incentive structures, the idea of mutual gains implies an economic resolution of the original sin.

Pluralism as a rising interaction condition in Genesis: Towards an economic societal contract

Effectiveness and efficiency limits of behavioural ordering and contracting in a religious economic, theological, sociological or socio-psychological tradition are quickly reached in certain interaction contexts, namely when pluralism, moral disagreement and value decay are encountered and taken seriously. In social arenas, such as the city, the nation state and the more so a community of nations, behavioural value contracting and the maintenance of a value consensus may become too difficult and too expensive (Wagner-Tsukamoto 2008a, 2008c, 2003: Chapter 1 and 8, 2001b; also MacIntyre 1985: 1–5; Hardin 1968: 1246). The 'condition of modernity' arises here. Mill might speak of 'liberty'. Or, negatively formulated, a lacking value consensus and even value decay characterize social interactions. Questions regarding the quality of morality of a behavioural ethics as compared with an economic approach to ethics can in this respect be raised too (see Wagner-Tsukamoto 2008c, 2005, 2003, 2001b).

Although this book does not follow a historiographical approach to Old Testament analysis, it seems clear that the historic–economic and socio-geographic environment in which the Old Testament emerged and the social conflicts it reflected closely mirrored problems of value pluralism. And it can be argued that this is thematically reflected by the intertribal and international conflicts discussed throughout the Old Testament. One of the best examples is the multicultural interaction scenario depicted in the Joseph story and the Exodus story, once Israel had emigrated to Egypt. Section 3.4 analyses the Joseph story in this respect (see also Wagner-Tsukamoto 2001a) and Chapter 4 does so with regard to the Exodus story (see also Wagner-Tsukamoto 2008a, 2000b).

But already prior to the Joseph story, pluralism began to characterize social exchange in the Old Testament. Initially the Old Testament entered a behavioural ethics – which was then already supported by an economics, namely a *behavioural* economics – through discussing the religious figures of Noah and Abraham. It can be speculated that the Old Testament initially sought out a behavioural value contract between God and humans in order to later qualify such an approach in relation to the condition of modernity. Of course, the fragility of value contracting was also early on implied by the paradise story, but the more so through various stories that involved – failing – family-type, behavioural contracting that followed Adam and Eve's eviction from Paradise, such as the interactions of Cain–Abel, Jacob–Esau, Jacob–Isaac or Joseph and his brothers. Especially for these family-type interaction

scenarios one would normally expect that behavioural value contracting succeeded, being more (cost-)effective than economic ordering.
However, the message emerging from these family-type interaction scenarios is a discomforting one. The Old Testament seems to be rather wary
regarding family bonds being an effective institutional (behavioural)
regulative. Westermann (1986: 444) speaks in this connection even of
the 'collapse of the old [family-based] community order'. Figure 3.2
interprets this collapse economically and locates the collapse at the
point of Old Testament storytelling when Jacob is reborn as 'Israel'
(discussed in more detail below). At least from then onwards, mutually
advantageous, societal contracting in an economic tradition seemed to
be more cost-effective (pareto-superior) than a behavioural approach
(even when supported by a behavioural economics). Pluralism is the
important underlying interaction condition that changed the efficiency
and effectiveness of behavioural ordering and economic ordering.

Through stories that involved the 'city metaphor', Genesis very explicitly began to spell out limits of a behavioural approach to societal contracting and the resolution of interaction conflict under the condition
of modernity when pluralism is encountered. Genesis did this especially
through the Tower of Babel story (Genesis: Chapter 11) and through the

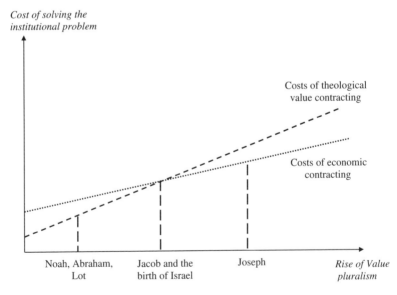

Figure 3.2   The rise of pluralism and cost implications

Sodom-and-Gomorrah story (Genesis: Chapter 19). Most dramatic here is the story of the destruction of Sodom and Gomorrah. In this story, a value consensus and apparent value contracting had broken down. Value diversity and moral disagreement were widespread and possibly even value decay was emerging. For example, we are reminded in the Sodom-and-Gomorrah story that Lot, a highly religious, noble and God-fearing character in the mould of Abraham, remained an alien in Sodom. The citizens of Sodom 'were not prepared to allow the scruples of this alien to dictate what they may or may not do' (Davidson 1979: 73). This city and the idea of the 'city' in general is a key metaphor of the Old Testament to refer to 'wickedness' and 'sinfulness' (Genesis 13: 13), or, more positively formulated, to pluralism, and the tolerance of moral disagreement among interacting agents. It appears that the city, with its large-scale and potentially anonymous arenas for social inter-action, directly undermines behavioural, institutional contracting that aims at a value consensus and the kind of value-based covenants Noah and Abraham had made with God. Hence, the city poses a threat to value contracting. What should be done? Should and could the threats of the city to behavioural contracting be eliminated?

In the sequence of events depicted in the course of Genesis, the city metaphor and the condition of modernity and pluralism it stands for is encountered and handled time and again, first in a rather destructive manner but later in a more constructive approach. Problems of behav-ioural, societal contracting in the city are comparatively destructively handled in the Tower of Babel story and more so in the Sodom-and-Gomorrah story (Genesis 11: 8–9; 13: 13; 19: 24–5). In the Tower of Babel story, Babel's inhabitants are punished for aspiring to reach the heaven and be like God. God broke down communication through the imposi-tion of a multicultural context, which explicitly also imposes pluralism as an interaction condition. In the Sodom-and-Gomorrah incident, the Old Testament resorted to an apocalyptic, religious fundamental-ist approach to 'solving' the institutional problem – by raining 'down burning sulphur' (Genesis 19: 23) on Sodom and Gomorrah. This wiped out these cities. Or, the city of Shechem was punished with eradication for the claimed defiling of one of Jacob's daughters, Dinah. In this case, punishment came about through the swords of Jacob's sons, Levi and Simeon (Genesis 34: 25–6). Ultimately even Jerusalem suffered a similar fate of destruction because of the unfaithfulness of Israel. Such value fundamentalist conflict 'resolution' reflects the theoretical and practical exhaustion of behavioural, institutional contracting when the condition of modernity is encountered (see also Wagner-Tsukamoto 2008c, 2001b).

Such anti-pluralistic implications are frequently not seen by theology, for example, Westermann (1986: 297) with regard to the destruction of Sodom and Gomorrah. For a behavioural ethics, such as a virtue ethics and a religious ethics, some rather grim moral implications emerge from these suggestions (see Wagner-Tsukamoto 2008a, 2008c, 2003: Chapter 8, 2001b). Even Plato (1999: 1317–18) rather similarly proceeded in a value-fundamentalist tradition, suggesting protectionism, the banning of international travelling, and a 'war for values' as means to ensure the effectiveness of behavioural, institutional ordering.

In contrast to behavioural ordering via an intrinsically enacted value consensus, a conventional ('non-behavioural', 'situational') institutional economics analyses interaction problems as problems of pareto-effective capital utilization in relation to economic institutions, namely incentive structures of one form or another. The approach is highly 'individualistic', especially in methodological perspective (Brennan and Buchanan 1985; Buchanan 1975). The advantage of such an approach is that it can solve the institutional problem *while tolerating the condition of modernity at the same time*. This happens as a mere by-product of economic analysis and intervention. Pluralism, moral disagreement or value inhomogeneity among agents are uncritical 'capital contingencies' or (behavioural) 'institutional rules'. This is generally overlooked by theological interpreters of 'pluralistic' Old Testament stories, such as the story of the destruction of Sodom and Gomorrah (e.g. Kugel 1997: 185–9; Westermann 1986: 297). As it emerged in force from Buchanan's studies and more implicitly also from Williamson's studies, interaction problems over capital contributions and distributions – the potential 'war about goods' in the Old Testament's terminology – can be more successfully handled in this way, both theoretically and practically.

The Old Testament seemed to be very much aware of shortcomings of a behavioural ethics to solve problems of societal contracts constructively. This is reflected by how Genesis developed a discussion of the institutional problem after the Sodom-and-Gomorrah incident – when a more constructive, economic reorientation was sought. The city metaphor was then more constructively handled too. Especially in the stories of Jacob's struggle with Esau, Laban and God, and in the in-depth 'case study' of the epic struggle over 'industrial justice' between Egypt and its expatriate Israelite work force. Then, the Old Testament seemingly advocated a conceptual, economic reorientation which enabled a constructive resolution of social conflict under *tolerance* of value pluralism or even value decay.

After the destruction of Sodom and Gomorrah, a conceptual reorientation of institutional analysis in Genesis is most obvious in the story of God's failing chastisement of the opportunistic Jacob. Jacob was one of the key role models of the Old Testament of an opportunist and failing value contractor (see above and also section 3.3). His behaviour hints at the limits of value contracting under the condition of modernity. In this respect, Genesis tolerated value decline in social interactions. In dramatic figurative fashion, Genesis illustrated this failure of value contracting in the story of God turning into a man, fighting with Jacob, and losing to Jacob:

> So Jacob was left alone [by his servants], and a man wrestled with him till daybreak.... Then the man said, 'Let me go, for it is daybreak.' But Jacob replied, 'I will not let you go unless you bless me.' The man asked him, 'What is your name?' 'Jacob', he answered. Then the man said, 'Your name will no longer be Jacob, but Israel, because you have struggled with God and with men [Esau, Isaac, Laban] and have overcome.'
>
> (Genesis 32: 24–8)

Can there be a more poignant example of anarchy under conditions of economic conflict? Adam and Eve, of course, spring to mind but God's fight with Jacob is very telling too. Economic conflict shows up here by Jacob's 'request' for the blessing, which the Old Testament even since the covenants involving Noah and Abraham had economically interpreted (e.g. regarding prosperity, fertility, longevity, etc.). And economic conflict is also referred by God's explicit mentioning of Jacob's previous struggles (with Esau or Laban, for instance, which were struggles over capital). Thus, this story of God's fight with Jacob seems to spell out the limits of solving – through value contracting – social conflict, namely 'struggles' and interaction problems arising from anarchy in general. Like MacIntyre (1985), Genesis apparently asks here what comes *After Virtue*, more precisely: after the limits of a behavioural ethics in a theological, philosophical or socio-psychological tradition (even if supported by a behavioural economics) have been reached, and where as a result a value contract collapsed in which God had been initially involved as a quasi-Hobbesian sovereign master that hosted value contracting in the aftermath of Adam and Eve's defection (e.g. with Noah, Abraham or Isaac). In Genesis, such a turn away from behavioural contracting is reflected by God making no further appearance in Genesis after he lost to Jacob, as noted by Armstrong

(1996: 92) and similarly by Davidson (1979: 212) – Davidson with explicit reference to the Joseph story.

However, it is difficult to see, as suggested by Armstrong (1996: 90), that Jacob's fight with God would 'heal the conflict in his soul and [make him] experience the healing power of the divine' (similarly, Armstrong 1996: 97). Such a positive, behavioural interpretation of God losing to Jacob may be difficult to uphold for various reasons. Firstly, Armstrong (1996: 92) later finds that God left Jacob alone through the remainder of Genesis after the fight. This hints at a break rather than a healing, reconciliatory encounter between God and Jacob. Secondly, Jacob basically extorted a blessing from God as a result of their fight. The story is quite clear in this respect. This again does not hint at a friendly, reconciliatory encounter that helped to mend claimed psychological troubles of Jacob's soul. Thirdly, Armstrong (1996: 78; see also above) stated in an earlier passage that the idea of the blessing may have to be interpreted in an economic way in the first place, blessing implying wealth, success, power, etc. for Jacob's nation. Such an interpretation, again, is far away from religious healing effects that come with a blessing. Finally, there is the issue of pluralism as an explicit inter-action condition of the story when Jacob and God are fighting, which Armstrong and so many others do not see. I suggest that pluralism as an interaction condition underlines the very special meaning of this story. In the story of God fighting with Jacob, Genesis stressed the presence of value pluralism and the condition of modernity by explicitly locating the fight 'within sight of the city' (Genesis 33: 18). Of course, the 'city' has been a key reference of the Old Testament to value pluralism, moral disagreement and even value decay since Genesis discussed the Tower of Babel story and the Sodom-and-Gomorrah incident. Similarly, when the 'city' is later referred to, for example in Genesis (44: 4) or Exodus (9: 33), this implies a metaphorical reference to value pluralism, too.

Seemingly, the outcome of Jacob's fight with God signalled the end of an era:

> '*For the first time*, man seemed to be offered a prospect for jumping out of his evolutionary history [of being bound by a Hobbesian slave contract; in the Old Testament: a tight, authoritarian value contract with God]. Man, in concert with his fellows, might change the very structure of social order'
>
> (Buchanan 1975: 148, emphasis added)

Buchanan made this comment with regard to the specific, historic evolution of moral philosophy from Hobbes, Spinoza and Locke onwards, when the ideas of the Enlightenment emerged, and Buchanan apparently was sceptical in this respect that moral philosophy prior to the era of the Enlightenment had made significant attempts to conceptualize a social, constitutional contract in which rulers where held accountable by subjects, and more generally, where subjects could act independently of other humans and especially of God. If one looks carefully at the stories of the Old Testament, in particular those involving Jacob (but also Adam and Eve), such scepticism of Buchanan can be reversed. In considerable degrees, we find already in the Old Testament moral philosophical thought in which humans began to seriously question the nature of an authority relationship (with humans and, above all, with God). The anarchic figure of Jacob and the kind of conflicts he instigates is here a prime example. It signals a conceptual reorientation in societal contracting, with the influence of divine central authority waning (section 3.3 follows up).

In general, theology agrees that 'there is no more strange or perplexing narrative than this [Jacob's fight with and win over God] in the whole of the Old Testament' (Davidson 1979: 184). What startles theology in particular is that God did not win over Jacob and that the economic man-like, opportunistic and, at times, even predatory figure of Jacob was chosen and 'blessed' by God to become 'Israel'. I suggest that this implies a fundamentally new type of covenant being brokered between God and humans in order to solve the institutional problem and to create the good 'city' and good society – a covenant which resembles an economic, constitutional contract in the tradition of Buchanan, with God taking a very backseat role. As indicated, an economic interpretation can begin to unravel such perplexities by invoking the condition of modernity and pluralism as an interaction condition, especially in Bible stories from the Jacob stories onwards, and by methodically interpreting the opportunistic aspects of the figure of Jacob as a tool to test out economic institutions for ordering social interactions (see section 3.3). The latter implies that with the appearance of anarchic Jacob, economic man fully enters the stage of biblical storytelling and that behavioural man and related behavioural economics, as previously encountered in considerable degrees in the stories involving Noah, Abraham or Lot, retreats from the stage (see also below, section 3.3, when the figure of Jacob is more explicitly linked to economic man-behaviour).

As discussed, the early patriarchs, like Noah, Abraham, Lot and Isaac, were involved in – largely value-based – contracting with God. One should not underestimate that this already transformed the governance relationship between human beings and God. An absolute ruler no longer ruled the people. It goes undisputed that this was already a considerable achievement in reforming constitutional contract. God's role then began to resemble one more of a constitutional monarch – albeit still 'only' a behaviourally bound one:

> With the conclusion of the covenant, God ceases to be the absolute ruler. He and man have become partners in a treaty. God is transformed from an 'absolute' into a 'constitutional' monarch. He is bound, as man is bound, to the conditions of the constitution. God has lost his freedom to be arbitrary, and man has gained the freedom of being able to challenge God in the name of God's own promises, of the principles laid down in the covenant.
>
> (Fromm 1967: 25)

Fromm here clearly outlined that the idea of the 'covenant' implied that the concept of God

> progressed into a much more developed and mature vision. *The idea of the covenant constitutes ... one of the most decisive steps in the religious development of Judaism,* a step which prepares the way to the concept of the complete freedom of man, even freedom from God.
>
> (Emphasis as in original)

Fromm followed up through a philosophical humanist critique to outline a progressive liberation of humans – from God – in the Old Testament. The present study suggests here a different 'humanism': a radical, economic humanism – one that draws on the institutional and constitutional economic approach to map out a changing contractual relationship between God and the people in the Old Testament, which, so I subsequently argue, found its climax in the Joseph story. Gilboa (1998: 215–17, 228), in degrees, touched upon such emerging differences in covenant relationships between God and Abraham, on the one hand, and between God and Jacob, on the other. She stated, that Jacob, in difference to Abraham, initiated interactions with God and that Jacob stated his own terms of rewards for following God. I further detailed these insights in relation to the city metaphor and pluralism as an interaction condition and the emergence of enlightened constitutional order in the tradition of Buchanan (as discussed above, and with regard to economic man-behaviour of Jacob; the latter is discussed in section 3.3). Seemingly the Old Testament pointed out when discussing Jacob's interaction with God that under certain circumstances behavioural institutional ordering via religiosity was unsuccessful and too costly (or at least less successful and more costly than economic ordering). Similarly, Gilboa (1998: 228) argued that Jacob set the terms for a 'pact' between God and the nation of Israel, thus coming to a very different understanding of nation-building and contracting with God than the one inherent in the interactions between God and Abraham or between God and Isaac. This change in the covenant relationship between God and humans is underestimated and not seen by Fromm (1967: 47). As a key result of the Jacob story, as outlined above, the constitutional monarch 'God' was losing further powers to humans regarding societal contracting among humans, and a rather enlightened, modern approach to societal contracting is emerging.

Not surprisingly, the story of God's fight with Jacob ultimately finds an economic resolution in Genesis: Unlike his religious forefathers Noah or Abraham, who were still given land by God for showing faith in God and living a godly life, Jacob bought land and paid for it with money earned from his rather dubious interactions with Esau and Laban, so setting up his nation: 'For a hundred pieces of silver, he bought ... the plot of ground where he pitched his tent. There he set up an altar and called it El Elohe Israel' (Genesis 33: 19–20). In this respect, I do not see Jacob emerging from the story in which he fought with God as a 'new Jacob' with a 'new name' and a 'new character', as Davidson (1979: 186) argued. The way he acquires land for his nation is rather true to his previous, economic approach to handling social problems. Jacob's renaming as Israel, so I suggest, rather reflects a fundamental reorientation in societal contracting regarding the nature of the covenant between God and humans. Value-based contracting was increasingly replaced by more enlightened, economic contracting. By doing so, the initial ideal of a universally beneficial covenant between God and mankind that went beyond the interests of the Hebrews (Genesis 9: 11; 12: 3) could be realized in a different and more successful way than through mere value-based contracting – which increasingly had reached its economic limits in the face of value pluralism (see Figure 3.2 above).

Interestingly, Genesis (33: 18) and the 'within sight of the city'-reference of the struggle of Jacob with God, which implies pluralism as an interaction condition, also directly connects to the city of Shechem, which in Chapter 34 of Genesis becomes the stage of the Dinah–Shechem story (for a review of the story, see van Wolde 2003). In this story (claimed) value decay was a big topic, namely in relation to the theft and (claimed) defilement of Jacob's daughter Dinah by Shechem. Ultimately, the Jacobites, namely Levi's and Simeon's armies, took in a rather anti-pluralistic manner revenge by killing all male inhabitants of the city of Shechem. Van Wolde (2003: 447) spoke in this connection of the failure of a love story in a multiracial society, specifically the 'danger of monotheism when it is closely related to monoethnicity'. Armstrong (1996: 95) talked of one 'of many Israelite massacres of the indigenous population of the Promised Land'. Davidson (1979: 196) found that the Dinah story 'is one of the few places in the patriarchal stories where the writer makes a specific moral comment on what is happening.... Jacob's sons are worthy of their father at his worst'. Or, Pirson (2002: 25) hinted at an economic threat that was unleashed by Simeon's and Levi's action: 'They [Simeon and Levi] are men who do not keep their word, and who act against their father's wishes and risk the welfare of the family by their rash actions.' Tit-for-tat could be expected at a later stage and pluralism as an interaction condition was here not mastered. In this respect, the behavioural goals and ideals envisioned by the early, value-based covenants between God and humans, which involved Noah and Abraham, could not be realized. Seemingly, in pluralistic settings, the question regarding a new type of covenant arose.

Apparently, Genesis develops the conclusion in relation to the final outcome of the Jacob story and similarly the Dinah story that for solving the institutional problem in the face of value pluralism, theological–psychological contracting and related value ordering should no longer be favoured. A new and different type of societal contract or 'covenant' between God and the people became necessary. Figure 3.2 captures related hypotheses. For maintaining the integrity of a behavioural ethics it could even be argued that to let God lose to Jacob was a necessity: Only in this way could 'God', understood as a principle of unconditional good, of 'humanity' in a very noble sense, theoretically and practically be left intact. Otherwise, God had to take on the role of a value-driven 'terrorist' who could only 'solve' the institutional problem in a radically destructive way, as most dramatically depicted in the story of Sodom and Gomorrah. This reflects a desperate but also an enlightened, highly emancipatory and coming-of-age message of Genesis: Society seems to be called upon to solve conflicts and cooperation problems without (primarily or solely) relying on value contracting and the maintenance of a value consensus as it was promoted in the stories involving the early, religious patriarchs, such as Noah, Abraham and Isaac.

3.3 The prevalence of economic man in Genesis after the Paradise story

The subsequent traces economic man in stories of Genesis that follow the Paradise story. Ideas of self-interested behaviour are looked for, for individuals and for groups. I examine a methodical purpose of invoking outright predatory and opportunistic behaviour in Genesis. It becomes apparent that economic man in its different shades and appearances is widely present throughout Genesis. This underlines a strong, economic message of the Old Testament. In turn, this should encourage theology (and other social research too) to reassess its negative perception of the model of economic man. I argue that the model of economic man is mainly a useful, methodical instrument of economic theory-building but not an empirical or even prescriptive image of human nature.

Self-interest, wealth accumulation and wealth creation

Self-interest can be indirectly diagnosed when looking at interaction types, interaction outcomes and intervention techniques (see Figure 1.1). They were already discussed in previous sections in some detail. The idea of wealth creation and wealth accumulation is here especially interesting since it is an economic idea that is shared by both behavioural economics and conventional (non-behavioural) economics. Wealth accumulation is closely linked in the Old Testament to the idea of the 'blessing', which is given to key patriarchal figures, such as Abraham, Isaac or Jacob. For these figures, 'the imagery of blessing evokes fertility, wealth, success, and might' (Armstrong 1996: 78). Regarding wealth accumulation, nearly all key figures of Genesis (and of the Torah and the books of the Deuteronomic history too) show economic man-behaviour to a high degree. The riches they accumulated for themselves and for their tribes or nations reflect this. Fertile land, livestock, longevity or 'time capital', rights over water usage, gold, silver, serfs and slaves are among the riches discussed. Even behavioural role models accumulate riches in this rather 'economic' manner: Noah is given survival and 'everything that lives and moves will be food for you. Just as I gave you the green plants, I now give you everything' (Genesis 9: 3). Abraham, who is another behavioural role model of the early storytelling of Genesis, also got very wealthy for being faithful, religious and God-fearing: In his self-chosen work emigration to Egypt, '[he] had become very wealthy in livestock and in silver and gold' (Genesis 13: 2). And, in difference to sinful humans, he grew into old age (Kaiser 2001: 71, 74–5), which reflects the accumulation of time capital and an attractive share into the one scarce good x 'eternal life' that was left in the aftermath of the Paradise interactions.

Jacob is a key character who initially acquires wealth through skilful, opportunistic interventions. For basically nothing, he takes away the birth right from Esau and deceives their father Isaac regarding 'inheritance rights'. Also, he appropriates a considerable number of Laban's animals through clever breeding tactics. Although he later compensates Esau, Isaac and Laban in one way or another, his opportunistic strategies enabled Jacob to accumulate considerable wealth, at least enough wealth to acquire land for his family and tribe (Genesis 33: 19–20).

Joseph made his way to the top of the Egyptian hierarchy, overseeing Egypt's economic policies (see section 3.4 below). In this process, he acquired wealth to a very high degree. He received rewards such as the 'best land', a mansion, jewellery, fine cloth, a wife of high social standing ('the daughter of Potiphera, priest of On'), a chariot and other riches (Genesis 41: 41–51; 47: 6). Joseph also ensured that his people, once they had emigrated to Egypt, were given the 'best land' by the pharaoh (Genesis 47: 6). This was due to the type of human capital they could offer to the pharaoh, namely special farming and supervisory skills (Plaut 1981: 298). At this point in time, a potential dilemma regarding capital interactions between Israel and Egypt was resolved, with both sides benefiting and mutual gains resulting as interaction outcome (see section 3.4). On the other hand, as discussed in Chapter 4, in the Exodus story both sides considerably lost wealth as a result of their interactions.

The plundering and raiding of cities, depicted in the Old Testament, is a common way to acquire wealth. A war about goods and capital is then actually played out. This generally hints at institutional ordering and societal contracting at an early stage, with concepts like the nation or international community still in its infant phase. Buchanan (1975) might diagnose war-like, predatory interactions in a precontract, natural distribution state. In one of these battles among cities, Abraham's nephew Lot is taken slave (Genesis 14: 11): Abraham then came to the rescue of Lot, recovering him and his possessions (Genesis 14: 16). The Dinah story, especially the killing and plundering intervention of Simeon's and Levi's men, is another good example (Genesis 34: 25–9). Plunder is here an economic asset.

In general, a focus on wealth and mutual gains/mutual loss is typical for an economic approach to institutional ordering and societal contracting. In a pure, theological approach, one would expect a focus on different interaction outcomes, namely peace and harmony in social relations, belief in a godly way of life, etc. From the very first story of Genesis such a focus is not apparent. The opposite is the case, ideas of wealth disputes, wealth creation and wealth accumulation and interaction outcomes like mutual gains and mutual losses are discussed – and economic man is here very much visible.

Darker shades of self-interest: The behavioural punishment of 'bad', opportunistic behaviour

Genesis discusses self-interest more directly, too. The Paradise interactions already imply darker shades of self-interest, with Adam and Eve stealing God's knowledge. In the Cain-and-Abel story this dark theme is directly picked up, too, with Cain killing his brother Abel in a nearly motiveless manner. God then complains about the wickedness of humans: 'The Lord saw how great man's wickedness on the earth had become, and that every inclination of the thoughts of his heart was only evil all the time' (Genesis 6: 5). What Buchanan described as the anarchic, war-like, natural distribution state, which so closely resembles Hobbes' war of all, here shows up in Genesis. Although Genesis puts forward the reference to wickedness among humans in an empirical, behavioural manner, it may have to be read in a heuristic, instrumental perspective in the first place, namely how to handle self-interest in social interactions – by means of establishing new, better societal contracts ('covenants') that could control opportunistic, predatory, 'wicked' behaviour.

At this early point of biblical storytelling, God still ponders a radical solution: to clean earth from such wickedness by nearly destroying all mankind. Only those who lived their lives in the image of God were meant to survive. This reflects a value-fundamentalist, behavioural solution to the problem that self-interest can show up in a nasty manner in social interactions. Genesis then favoured a non-economic while non-individualistic and non-self-interested approach to social order and societal contracting. The story of Noah's ark or the Sodom-and-Gomorrah incident are here the key examples. 'Economic men', especially those of an 'evil' disposition, were eliminated. The great flood or the destruction of Sodom and Gomorrah were meant to re-establish moral behaviour. This approach moves analytically, both theoretically and methodologically, in the opposite direction than Williamson's or Buchanan's institutional and constitutional economics. In addition to such a behavioural approach of early Genesis, the previous discussion diagnosed a behavioural economics for Bible stories, namely the backing up of behavioural strategies to live in the image of God with economic sanctions and rewards. As discussed, a behavioural economics can be attested for certain Bible stories, especially the early stories that involved good and quasi-holy figures like Noah and Abraham.

It can be speculated that the Noah story already hints at the failure of a normative, *behavioural* economics to reform economic man. The success of the 'flood project' is in doubt because immediately after the Noah story God agrees: 'Never again will I curse the ground because of man, even though every inclination of his heart is evil from childhood' (Genesis 8: 21). Seemingly, God realized that the moral costs of cleaning up the earth in a value fundamentalist way were just too high. This implies that darker sides of self-interest are not really to be confronted and remedied by behavioural intervention. Besides, interpretations of 'man's character being evil from childhood' are untenable, even on empirical, behavioural grounds. Indirectly, a behavioural misinterpretation of the idea 'economic man' is here met. The Old Testament and Old Testament theology in this regard seem to be unaware of how to handle the tool 'economic man' instrumentally, methodically as a research heuristic of (institutional) economic analysis.

On a smaller scale, namely with regard to cities rather than the entire world, the stories that follow the Noah story still continue to look at a radical, behavioural solution to solving social problems. The Tower of Babel story hinted at this but the Sodom-and-Gomorrah story spelled this out in detail. As in the Noah story, God sought a radical, fundamentalist solution, harming or even destroying places were its inhabitants did not live in the image of God. Sodom and Gomorrah were wealthy places. They were located in the fertile Jordan valley and their inhabitants enjoyed a prosperous lifestyle. As Kugel suggested, it may not have been sexually deviant behaviour that ultimately led to the destruction of these cities. The key reason for the destruction of these cities may have been that their inhabitants showed in high degrees an inclination to economic man-type behaviour. Kugel (1997: 187) pointed out that the Sodomites' 'fault was pride or stinginess, an unwillingness to help the unfortunate of this world.... [I]t was primarily the Sodomites' pride and their failure to aid the poor amidst their own prosperity that caused God to smite them.' Plaut (1981: 133–4, 1391) similarly points out in this connection that affluence of the inhabitants of Sodom and Gomorrah without social concern was self-destructive. The project of Old Testament theology is clear: Because of their greed, the Sodomites were to be punished. From here it is only a small step to accuse the inhabitants of Sodom and Gomorrah of economic man-type behaviour and call for the behavioural correction of such behaviour, which in this instance came through the eradication of Sodom and Gomorrah. Less severe corrective measure would have been behavioural, moralizing programmes that tried to make the Sodomites more benevolent, hospitable and generous when it came to aiding the poor.

A diagnosis of the greedy, erroneous behaviour of the inhabitants of Sodom and Gomorrah basically finds fault with the model of economic man and calls for the elimination of such behaviour in one way or another. Behaviour was judged as sinful because of its economic, self-interested qualities. And image of human nature criticism is more or less directly targeted at biblical economic man. This was repeated throughout the Old Testament when the sinful behaviour of Sodom and Gomorrah's inhabitants and the destruction of these cities were raised again as an issue (Westermann 1986: 298–9). Such criticism was developed not explicitly in the Sodom-and-Gomorrah story itself but by interpretations of this story. Kugel (1997: 187–9) reviewed here both interpretations in the Old Testament, specifically in the book of Ezekiel, and interpretations of the Old Testament by third parties.

Instead of punishing apparent 'economic men' who lived in Sodom and Gomorrah, a different way of intervening and aiding the poor in these cities was not pursued in this story, neither with regard to counteracting problems of 'too' self-interested behaviour nor with regard to preventing a destructive, value fundamentalist solution of the Sodom-and-Gomorrah problem. Institutional economics would advise that problems of aiding the poor were in the first place a systemic problem that should be remedied through the intervention with governance structures. For example, intervention could come through a tax system that raised revenues for social purposes. The advantage of this proposal is that it leaves intact a market system that has created prosperity. It also does not temper with values held by the individual. Regarding the latter, economic intervention would tolerate pluralistic, deviant or even stingy predispositions but also benevolent, compassionate ones. It is really up to the individual to decide what life to live and what role philanthropy and morals should play in this life.

Biblical characters getting away with opportunistic behaviour?

The story of the destruction of Sodom and Gomorrah was the final incident in Genesis to solve social problems in a radical, destructive manner. In most of the subsequent stories of Genesis, a constructive solution was sought. Economic man was then no longer confronted and destroyed, even if he showed up in a despicable manner, such as a fraudster, thief or killer.

One of the first examples of opportunism that seemingly went unpunished in biblical storytelling is the land separation problem of Abraham and Lot (Genesis 13: 8–13). Seemingly, Abraham and Lot encountered the commons dilemma. Their herds had grown too large to be supported by the same farm land (a 'commons'). Von Rad (1963: 166) touched upon this, as did Davidson who stated:

> The kind of quarrel which breaks out between Abraham's herds-men and Lot's is the kind of quarrel which must often have arisen between semi-nomadic pastoral groups, a quarrel over grazing rights. One area can only support a limited number of sheep and cattle.... The problem is intensified by the fact that Abraham and Lot are not the only people living off the land.
> (Davidson 1979: 27; see also Davidson 1979: 151)

Demsetz (1964) reviews a comparable historic example of the commons dilemma for Canadian Indians (see also Buchanan 1975: 22–23). Of course, the commons dilemma is not only prevalent in nomadic or tribal societies. In different shades and variations it is widespread and ever-present in all societies. Hardin (1968) and similarly Buchanan (1975: 179–80) unearthed a contemporary relevance of the commons dilemma with regard to global problems, such as overpopulation and environ-mental pollution. By invoking a scenario like the commons dilemma, the Old Testament based economic analysis on a dilemmatic conflict model, and on a related point, it modelled agents as economic men.

In the commons dilemma encountered by Abraham and Lot, Abraham resolved the conflict by behaving in a non-economic, unselfish, noble, friendly manner, as one would expect from a religious, nearly holy human being: Abraham gave Lot first choice in picking land for his herds, and Lot chose the fruitful land of the Jordan valley. Abraham got less fruitful land but God seemingly compensated Abraham for this dis-advantage when intervening in the transaction between Abraham and Lot. God made Abraham move his tents to a place which had certain advantages too. Also, only for the time being Lot's opportunistic choice went unpunished. As it turned out later, Lot's choice to enter the Jordan valley was not such a good choice after all since this place was close to the city of Sodom and Gomorrah, which later, in Genesis 19, attracted the anger of God. So there are some fine retribution mechanisms in place that concern the interactions between Abraham and Lot and in their final outcome the position of winners and losers may even have been reversed.

One of the cheekiest, most opportunistic characters of biblical story-telling, of course, is Jacob. As already noted above, he showed predation and opportunism in high degrees and seemingly got away with most of his fraudulent transactions, to the dismay of much theological research, as Miller (1993a: 24) or Westermann (1986: 479) diagnosed. There is probably no other character in biblical storytelling whose behaviour better fits what Williamson (1998: 1, 1985: 64–7, 1975: 26–30) termed 'self-seeking with guile' and 'subtle self-interest seeking' or Buchanan (1975) called 'predatory' behaviour. Jacob exploits and creates dilemma situations for others, he schemes and steals. He 'deceives', 'defrauds' and is involved in 'monstrous crimes' (von Rad 1963: 273, 276, 304; similarly Westermann 1986: 431–44). Graves and Patai (1964: 198, 200) speak of Jacob as the 'master-thief'. Jacob is characterized as practising 'outrageous deceit and being rewarded for his deed' (Plaut 1981: 190). As Davidson (1979: 140) noted: 'Jacob's name became synonymous in Israel with supplanter and cheat.' Or, Bloom (1982: xviii) found that Jacob was the 'most agonistic of characters'. Von Rad (1963: 261–2) less critically described Jacob as the culturally and economically advanced shepherd who outwits the hunter Esau (similarly Westermann 1986: 478–84, Davidson 1979: 137–8).

To detail this: In his interactions with starving Esau, Jacob extorts Esau's birthright for a little bit of food. As Armstrong (1996: 76, 88, 94) or Plaut (1981: 187) noted, Jacob came with 'guile' to Esau; Jacob then deceives their father Isaac to gain something like inheritance rights; and in his interactions with Laban he (ab)uses clever breeding tactics to appropriate animals from Laban's herds and he finally runs of with some of his possessions (see Figure 3.1 above). Through his 'astute schemes', Jacob acquires wealth (Pfeiffer 1948: 144).

As Kugel (1997: 199–200) found, a good deal of Old Testament theology tried to find good character traits of Jacob and bad ones of Esau in order to justify Jacob's selfish actions. For instance: 'Jacob was made out to be altogether virtuous and studious, [while] Esau's image was likewise modified by early interpreters .... He became utterly wicked, a crafty, bloodthirsty embodiment of evil' (Kugel 1997: 202). I argue that such behavioural (re)interpretations of Jacob's and Esau's characters and actions do not do justice to the ones depicted in Genesis. A methodical interpretation of Jacob's self-interested, economic man-type behaviour, reconnecting it in a figurative sense to the role the snake played in the Paradise story, may yield a more careful and balanced interpretation. Armstrong (1996: 88) here correctly summed up that Jacob's wealth was achieved by 'the guile of the *serpent*', although she – wrongly – disputed, as discussed above in Chapter 2, that the snake had no place in biblical stories after the Paradise story.

Jacob rather purposefully tested out social exchange for contractual loopholes, for incomplete contracting in a wider sense: By acting as an economic man in the extreme, showing high degrees of opportunism, predation and guile, he uncovered ways to disadvantage contracting partners. In a figurative sense, he reflected a good reincarnation of the cunning, crafty snake of the Paradise scenario. One might expect that God would have punished such behaviour through behavioural intervention, trying to turn Jacob into a good, religious person in the mould of Noah or Abraham. But this was not the case – although retribution came: As discussed previously, Jacob was forced into compensation agreements – 'disarmament contracts', as Buchanan (1975) might call it – with Laban and Esau and, indirectly, Isaac, too (see Figure 3.1 above). Over time, Jacob's deceit and scheming was matched by the deceit and scheming of his interaction partners. He was then outmanoeuvred. Tit-for-tat occurred. Jacob painfully found out that 'Laban was as smooth a double-dealer as Jacob' (Davidson 1979: 154). Graves and Patai (1964: 224) or von Rad (1963: 286) pointed this out for the Jacob–Laban interactions too. In this respect, new contractual arrangements that realigned previously incentive-incompatible governance structures tamed economic man.

In the Jacob stories, destructive anarchy rules biblical storytelling, the human being revealing an independent character, acting individualistically and with little consideration of other humans, God and the social order imposed by an existing city or state. Buchanan seems, in this respect, too sceptical that independent, 'pre-Hobessian anarchists' did not exist in social and moral philosophy prior to the Middle Ages:

> Only in the full emergence from the Middle Ages, only with Hobbes, Spinoza, and their contemporaries does man become possibly independent of other men, of God, of state and city.... In Hobbes's ability to visualize, to conceptualize, such an existence at all lies the critical difference with earlier philosophers. Can we conceive of pre-Hobbesian anarchists?
>
> (Buchanan 1975: 147)

As discussed here and already touched upon in section 3.2 above, in considerable degrees, a prime example of a pre-Hobbesian anarchist shows up through the figure of Jacob. Adam and Eve too should not be forgotten in this connection. Apparently, anarchy, the kind of economic conflicts it causes and the question of how to handle it, are the key issues of storytelling of the Old Testament. And as outlined, the answers developed by the authors of the Old Testament in relation to the figure of Jacob hint at a comparatively modern approach to this question which ventures in the footsteps of a constitutional and institutional economics.

In Jacob's interactions with other persons, God did not (yet) intervene to punish and remedy these misbehaviours, and when he later actually intervened and fought with Jacob, he lost to Jacob (see above). Does this mean opportunism and economic man-behaviour begins to win the day in biblical storytelling and that opportunism should be tolerated in social interactions? I think the key message is a different one, namely that opportunism and related 'Hobbesian anarchy' should be expected in social interactions and that it should be controlled by interacting agents – but control would (no longer) happen by waiting for godly, behavioural intervention to prevent 'bad', 'dark' behaviour. The modelling of agents as predators and opportunists functions as a methodical means to prevent the very occurrence of predation, opportunism and Hobbesian anarchy. As discussed, the larger purpose of economic man in these Bible stories can be said to be a functional, methodical one. Indeed, the stories involving Jacob showed ways of how predation and opportunism could be prevented through compensation payments and compensation arrangements of different kinds. The figure 'economic man', as so poignantly captured by the opportunistic side of Jacob's character, thus functions as a mere tool, complementary to the idea 'dilemma structure', for pioneering the organization of capital exchange transactions through better incentive structures. To put it very simply, through the model of the opportunistic figure 'Jacob', incentive structures, governance mechanisms and societal contracting in general can be examined for opportunism and thus be made incentive-compatible. Self-interests of competing agents are thus realigned in a manner so that mutual gains result. In the Jacob stories, pareto-superior, incentive-compatible governance emerged in this way step-by-step and the question of how to establish sound societal contracts received increasingly an economic interpretation in the Old Testament.

If one takes this into account, positive image of human nature implications result regarding Jacob's behaviour and the stories involving Jacob–Esau, Jacob–Isaac and Jacob–Laban. From here one can constructively address questions that have puzzled many theologians regarding the figure of Jacob:

How does all this guile accord with the description of Jacob as 'quiet' (*tam*), a word which usually denotes innocence and simplicity in the

Bible? From the outset, Jacob is a puzzle to us, and we never quite feel that we know him.

(Armstrong 1996: 76)

Or similarly, Davidson (1979: 138) noted an unresolved contradiction regarding Jacob's behaviour:

He [Jacob] schemes and cheats; he suffers the consequences of his own misdeeds. Yet this is the man to whom the blessing is given. In the midst of all the devious twists of his life God's purposes are being worked out, even when Jacob is least aware of it.

Theology here seems to struggle with the apparent conflict between Jacob's misdeeds and his elevation by God, which Jacob quite forcefully extracts from God (Genesis 32: 22–32; see also above). Through a methodical, functional interpretation of the figure of Jacob with regard to economic man-type behaviour, such contradictions can be addressed and resolved in economic terms. This also puts the occurring social interactions that involve Jacob in a modern, pluralistic context (see above, when Jacob's fight with God was linked to the city metaphor and pluralism as an interaction condition). As Westermann (1986: 500, 574) and similarly von Rad (1963: 307) noted, the Jacob–Laban encounters are full of legal and contractual principles that prevent war and help the emergence of peaceful coexistence. As I detailed, apparently, a state of Hobbesian anarchy was ultimately overcome. Institutional economic reconstruction spells this out. The Jacob stories hint at the development of a code for contracting, especially under conditions of incomplete contracting and pluralism. The ideal of mutual gains within a contractual relationship normatively prevails. And the idea of economic man and similar ones on guile and cunning behaviour need to be put into perspective regarding their heuristic nature in developing such economic schemes. This reflects a rather different theoretical strategy for assessing Jacob's self-interested behaviour than the one favoured by theology (or by behavioural economics) regarding its empirical and moral critique of economic man.

3.4 Economic ordering in complex, multicultural settings: Joseph and the Israelites in Egypt

In terms of richness and detail, the Joseph story is unrivalled in biblical storytelling, reflecting an 'organically constructed narrative of a special kind' (Schmidt 1984: 71; see also Soggin 1993: 336, 344; Davidson 1979: 211). Pfeiffer (1948: 29) suggested that the Joseph story, in contrast to many other, supposedly more rustic stories in the Old Testament, aimed at a cultivated audience. This immediately raises the question of why and how, which Pfeiffer did not address. The following here argues that the richness and 'cultivated', intellectual purpose of the Joseph story can be deduced from its institutional economic content and nature and from a further fundamental economic reorientation of addressing the institutional problem and issues of societal contracting in Genesis. In particular, in the Joseph story we encounter the institutional problem in its special version as the organizational problem.

The Joseph story places the discussion of social conflict in a very modern, pluralistic context. The city, the multicultural nation and international relations are ever-present interaction scenarios: 'Joseph freely mingles with Egyptians, becomes Pharaoh's right-hand man, and marries an Egyptian girl … all this without any word of disapproval or even comment [by Genesis]' (Davidson 1979: 212). This is in stark contrast to the chapters preceding the Joseph story where 'the attitude to the world outside the close-knit tribal group tends to be hostile [and] intermarriage with the local inhabitants tends to be discouraged' (Davidson 1979: 212).

As far as the Joseph story contains anti-behavioural elements, they largely relate to the behaviour of Joseph's own relatives. One of the story's key elements, namely Joseph being sold by his brothers to Egyptian merchants, here provides another warning against the effectiveness of socio-psychological and behavioural regulatives and, here especially, family bonds. The brothers were jealous of Joseph because of their father's apparent favouring of Joseph (Genesis 37: 3–10). They considered killing Joseph but once Egyptian merchants showed up, they decided to sell him off as a slave: 'So when the Midianite merchants came by, his brothers pulled Joseph up out of the cistern and sold him for twenty shekels of silver to the Ishmaelites, who took him to Egypt' (Genesis 37: 28). Like the Cain-and-Abel story and the Esau-and-Jacob story, this story implies the ineffectiveness of family bonds to serve as effective institutional regulative. The following firstly looks at the specific interaction conditions of the Egyptian society and its expatriate workforces. Subsequently, I review institutional economic ideas of capital exchange, incentive structures and mutual gains and I unearth a reorientation towards economic societal contracting in a rather radical sense in Genesis.

Dilemmatic scarcities as interaction conditions in the Joseph story

The stories discussed in the Old Testament reflect a specific *socio-geographic* and *economic context*, which can be linked to the one in which the stories of the Old Testament emerged. However, in the following, I want to stick to a historical–textual interpretation of the Old Testament and do not want to enter a 'real' historical context debate, as for example done by Muth (1997) or Hopkins (1996). In a historical–textual analysis of the Joseph story, the precise socio-geographical and political historicity of events is not the crucial issue (Paris 1998: 74–5) but only the environmental, socio-economic contexts described and implied in the Old Testament. This means, issues of sociographic, economic context are subsequently only elaborated on with regard to the information available in the Old Testament. (Although, of course, projections can be made between historical–textual analysis and 'real' historical one. But this is not the purpose of the present book.)

The Old Testament depicts a scenario in which little fertile land is available between oases and rivers, and famine and poverty are constant threats. Scarcities in capital were severely encountered, the commons dilemma loomed and as a result the institutional problem arose in dramatic fashion. Israel's homeland is depicted as infertile, being plagued by drought, natural disasters and problems arising from overpopulation and famine (Genesis 12: 10; 41: 27, 30; 45: 6). Different societies struggled with these scarcities in fertile land, all trying to access limited fertile land. Up till today, such dilemmatic questions over the utilization of scarce resources, like land and water, have remained a burning issue in the hot climate and desert-stricken areas of the Near or Middle East. This environmental context sets the scene for interactions described in the Joseph story.

Even in periods when natural and economic conditions were unfavourable, Egypt remained a place of abundance. It seemingly reflected the kind of paradise Adam and Eve had lost in the Eden story. Egypt was a 'good and spacious land, a land flowing with milk and honey', as the vision of the Paradise was renewed in Exodus (3: 8; 13: 5; see also Genesis 13: 10, Keller 1989: 73). As Davidson (1979: 28) noted: Egypt was 'synonymous with fertility.' A highly developed society lived along the shores of the Nile and in the Nile delta region. As the Old Testament states: 'All the other lands', 'all the world' aspired to emigrate to Egypt (Genesis 41: 54, 57). Indeed, the high economic development depicted by the Old Testament for certain areas in the Near or Middle East, specifically Egypt (see also Tullock 1981: 22–8, Ap-Thomas 1972: 11,

24, also Cohn 1981: 2), opened up affluence differentials with neighbouring regions. This is also underlined by international trade moving
towards Egypt (Genesis 37: 25, 43: 11–12; see also Keller 1989: 11, 89).
Affluence differentials provided incentives for Israel and other nations
in the region to migrate to Egypt (Genesis 41: 27, 30, 54, 57; 45: 6, also
Genesis 12: 10; 37: 25; 43: 11–12). And because of shortages in farming
skills, industrial skills, administrative skills and managerial skills, the
Egypt of Genesis welcomed immigration (Genesis 37: 28, 36; 39: 4–6,
22–3; 40: 2; 41: 2–7, 15, 40–7; 45: 5, 10–11, 18; 46: 3–5; 47: 6, 22–3).

Clearly, economic reasons existed why Egypt welcomed foreign
labour. Egypt and Israel shared an interest in the Israelites relocating to
the Nile. At least for the time depicted in Genesis when Israel moved
to Egypt, it is safe to conclude that their relationship did not resemble
the one of slaves and slave master: Relocation occurred voluntarily;
the Israelites were remunerated amply for working for the pharaoh
(see below), and the Israelites enjoyed freedom of movement inside
and outside Egypt (Genesis 41: 43; 42: 1–2; 47: 27, 50; 50: 7–11, also
Genesis 12: 10, Exodus 2:15; 5: 6–8). Of course, the archetypical case of
the Israelite 'non-slave' was Joseph: His brothers sold him as a slave to
Egypt (Genesis 37: 27–8, 36) but, once in Egypt, Joseph ascended to the
top of its industrial hierarchy (see below).

As much as the theological literature, for example, Sarna (1986: 46),
recognizes that Israel's relocation to Egypt gave them access to a 'land
flowing with milk and honey', it does not see or at least does not make
explicit a deeper economic rationale of establishing cooperative interactions, of maintaining shared interests and realizing mutual gains.

Pluralism as an interaction condition in the Joseph story

In the Joseph story, Egypt, the city and the nation in general no longer
reflected a 'family-oriented, archaic' economy and society, which Paris
(1998: 43) or similarly Miller (1993a, 1993b) diagnosed for the early
stories of the Old Testament. Besides the Old Testament's rather critical
approach to family bonds as effective means for value contracting and
social problem solving, the Old Testament strongly developed the idea
of the city and of multicultural interaction contexts, most dramatically
so through the final story of Genesis. As Paris (1998: 82) noted, it was
indeed Joseph who moved his people to the cities of Egypt. The condition of modernity (i.e. value pluralism) was then encountered in full
force once neighbouring tribes entered Egypt's workforce. A further hint
at the multicultural nature of contexts in the regions of the Near or

Middle East are the linguistic roots of the very word 'paradise', which is of Persian origin. Fascinating in this respect is Otzen et al.'s (1980: 42–3) comparison of the Paradise story to Babylonian narratives, such as the Gilgamosh epic (see also Rogerson and Davies 1989: 197; Westermann 1984: 226, 240; Tullock 1981: 43–4).

The Joseph story depicts an emerging multicultural interaction context, in which moral disagreement, social conflict and cooperation problems among migrating tribes and societies were a constant problem. Speculating on the purpose of the Old Testament, I want to advance the thesis that possibly for the first time in mankind's long history (1) a documented attempt was made to advise through the stories of the Old Testament on cooperation problems and societal contracting (i.e. the 'institutional problem'), *and* at the same time (2) the authors of the Old Testament conceptualized the institutional problem under the condition of modernity, with value pluralism, moral disagreement and even value decay prevailing. A related thesis here is that Genesis increasingly approached the resolution of cooperation problems in economic, non-behavioural terms, as the stories of Genesis unfold with the condition of modernity arising ever more. And, the condition of modernity, as a reflection of the city metaphor and interaction conditions of pluralism, moral disagreement, etc., heralds the coming of the free market society with its anonymous exchange transactions. As the subsequent further details, in the face of rising value pluralism, the Old Testament seemed to favour economic ordering via incentive structures ('economic institutions') over behavioural ordering via value structures ('behavioural institutions'), such as religious belief systems. This reflects a constructive reorientation of the Old Testament, which was already hinted at by the outcome of the stories involving Jacob, in particular Jacob's fight with God (see also Figures 3.1 and 3.2 above).

Also, keeping in mind an institutional regulation function of religion, it was probably no coincidence that ultimately three world religions emerged from the very same area of the Near or Middle East, where seemingly severe, dilemmatic contribution–distribution problems over certain, scarce resources had raged since ancient times. However, how far religious belief systems can possibly solve interaction conflicts of agents who subscribe to different sets of religious belief (that means, where value pluralism, moral disagreement and even value decay were present) has to be critically examined.

As discussed in the following section, the prevalence of pluralism as an interaction condition sets the scene for an economic reinterpretation of societal contracting in the Old Testament.

Egypt's economic policies under Joseph's reign

Through the figure of Joseph, the Old Testament depicted one of the first cases of the professional manager and industrial economist. He held substantial decision-making rights regarding rule change and managerial intervention at the top of Egypt's industrial hierarchy (Genesis 39: 4–6, 22–3; 41: 40–5; 42: 8; 45: 8–9, 26; also Gordon 1989: 7). This in effect implied a co-determination scheme between Israel and Egypt. His management and economic policies organized interactions in a way that ensured the emergence and maintenance of mutual gains as interaction outcome. In general, Joseph developed policies independent of ethnic origin and personal values. Specifically, Joseph masterminded Egypt's economic policies, which included, firstly, active fiscal policy, secondly, the hierarchical organization of capital utilization, thirdly, the economic transfer of property rights and fourthly, the utilization and management of human capital, asset specificity and performance-related reward systems. These four elements are now discussed in turn.

A first key element of Joseph's economic policies was the introduction of active fiscal policy. Biblical Egypt was affected by economic upturns and downturns, by cycles of 'seven years of abundance' followed by 'seven years of famine' (Genesis 41: 27–30, 48–9; see also Keller 1989: 91–3). The 'political economist' Joseph (Gordon 1994: 21, 1989: 7) buffered Egypt against such cyclical developments by introducing new incentive structures, namely an anti-cyclical tax policy. Pirson (2002: 91) very briefly touched upon this issue, as did Davidson (1979: 246) when speaking of a 'commonsense scheme to store, during the years of plenty, food for distribution during the years of famine'. Indirectly, the tax policy also buffered other neighbouring tribes which worked for or traded with Egypt (Genesis 47: 13). In times of boom, a 20-per cent income tax, in the form of a barter tax, was administered on crop production (Genesis 41: 34; 47: 24, 26). Located at the lower end of the Laffer curve, the tax was modest enough not to stifle individual striving: The resulting tax system was still incentive-compatible. Thus, in times of boom, tax revenues of crop were taken out of the economy, reducing income and demand. This also had an anti-inflationary impact. Crop was then stored and released back into the economy only in downturns. This, again, was handled economically: Crop was not distributed through rationing by plan or queuing schemes but by paying for crop (Genesis 47: 13, 17, 19). Auctioning or bidding would have been even more sophisticated, economic techniques. Keller (1989: 94) is here imprecise, claiming that only foreigners had to pay when asking for corn from the pharaoh's stockpiling system. As Genesis (47: 13–17) clearly points out, 'all Egypt' had to pay for corn.

An economic approach to crop redistribution helped to ensure that crop was more effectively and efficiently consumed for eating and used for farming than by allocating it on a per head/per day basis. The redistributor did not have to make costly and difficult assessments of neediness. The system also forced choice makers to save money in boom times, which again had an anti-inflationary impact on boom cycles. Overall the system seems to have been well capable of ensuring mutual gains as interaction outcome. Modern principles of fiscal policy are here clearly apparent in the Old Testament's depiction of the barter tax system: Tax proceeds were spent productively and tax largely became an 'instrument by which the consumption of one type of good (public) came to be substituted for another (private)', as Buchanan (1960: 29) characterized modern fiscal policy. As noted, the way the redistribution of the barter-tax crop back into the economy was organized reflected a system that was meant to benefit society as a whole, but it was comparatively individualistically, 'privately' set up: Societal members who had to pay for the allocation of the barter-tax crop.

Being a barter tax, the state could not spend tax revenue instantly, as is the case with monetary tax income. Indeed, the barter tax system only generated monetary income for the state during the recession, when crop was sold back to the people. This income could then be spent in an anti-cyclical manner on large-scale state projects. In the absence of sophisticated banking and capital markets, such an anti-cyclically geared barter tax system was a rather efficient and effective institutional mechanism to buffer a society against upturns and downturns. Interestingly, Joseph's anti-cyclical tax policy can be theoretically backed up by both Keynes' and Friedman's recommendations on tax policy, which was one of the few agreements between Keynes and Friedman on fiscal policy.

A second crucial element of Joseph's economic policies was the introduction of the hierarchical organization of capital utilization. In biblical Egypt, work was hierarchically organized in administrative and managerial bureaucracies. The institutional problem shows up as the organizational problem. In the specific interaction setting that the large and complex Egyptian society found itself, such a hierarchical set-up is likely to have been more transaction-cost efficient and production-cost efficient than less hierarchical structures. Coase's (1937) and Williamson's (1985, 1975) works provide the theoretical underpinning for this argument. Factors that contributed to size and complexity were progressing industrialization, rising demand because of immigration, a growing labour force, etc.

One of the best illustrations of Egypt's hierarchical work organization is Joseph's career development. After having been sold to Egypt by his brothers, he quickly moved up to the top of Egypt's industrial hierarchy. Starting out as a servant in household administration, he moved on to become the household administrator, then to administrator of agricultural projects, then to head of the security department, to head of prison department (Genesis 39: 4–6, 22–3; 41: 40–5), to ultimately become the top manager, the 'governor', 'lord of all Egypt', 'ruler of all Egypt' who only reported to the pharaoh (Genesis 41: 40–5; 42: 8; 45: 8–9, 26, see also Gordon 1989: 7). Once he occupied this position, his very ethnic origin as an Israelite yielded an element of interest equilibration between Egypt and Israel. It provided stability in the interactions of the two nations, stabilizing the kind of societal contracting they can be said to have been involved in.

A third element of Joseph's economic policies was the economic transfer of property rights. As far as Joseph acquired property in production capital for the pharaoh (Genesis 47: 13–19), this was economically organized. Genesis here subscribed to the concept of private property and rejected confiscation. Property was bought and sold and this happened independent of nationality and ethnic discrimination (Genesis 47: 21, 27; Exodus 12: 32, also Genesis 12: 16). In the specific context described in Genesis, this had a positive effect on wealth creation for all interacting choice makers. It benefited both Egypt and Israel (Genesis 47: 27; see also Paris 1998: 80–1). In degrees, such a concentration of property rights can be compared to the switch from the contractor system to functional foremanship and subsequently to the functional hierarchy in the late nineteenth-century and early twentieth-century USA (Wagner-Tsukamoto 2008e, 2007a, 2003: 168–77, 185–6). Then, property rights in production capital were similarly transferred from structurally loosely integrated, independent contractors to an owner–manager who led the hierarchical entity 'firm'. This supposedly occurred for economic reasons, namely the lowering of transaction costs and production costs (Wagner-Tsukamoto 2003: Chapters 4 and 7).

The concentration of property under Joseph's reign did not abolish the concept of property or even promote a communist, feudal or totalitarian set-up for organizing social interactions. If this were the case, then, indeed, the beginning of the Exodus could be traced back to Genesis, in the tradition of Hayek's (1979) critique of communism. Fung (2000: 15) wrongly implied this when he spoke of Joseph setting up an 'incredible scheme of mass enslavement' (see also Fung 2000: 35–43, 137–40, 170, 198–200; similarly argues Meeks 1989: 78–9). However, was this the case? Genesis explicitly stated that Joseph's concentration of property rights yielded mutual gains (see also Exodus 1: 8). Apparently, the idea of serfdom in Genesis is much closer to the idea of employment (without ownership rights) rather than serfdom in a truly communist, socialist, feudal or slavery-like sense, as discussed by Hayek, and implied by so many Old Testament analysts for the Joseph story and, similarly, the Exodus story, for example, Fung (for further examples, see below and the next chapter). Schmidt (1984: 36) makes in this connection the very useful distinction of 'enslavement', 'forced labour' and 'obligation of statute labour'. Glass (2000: 31, 37) discussed, although for Deuteronomy, the fine boundary between rural-based land-worker and debt-slaves as a result of contracts or indebtedness and the economically motivated switch from debt-slave labour to hired free labour. Von Rad (1963: 405) or Davidson (1979: 287–8) pointed out for Genesis that the idea of 'slavery' only entered the Old Testament text in later translations, namely when the so-called Masoretic text of the Hebrew Bible was translated into Greek (resulting in the so-called Septuagint version of the Old Testament, which became the source of many later translations of the Bible). In the original Masoretic text, the later prominent phrase of 'Joseph making slaves of people and reducing them to serfdom' reads differently as 'Joseph removing the people to the cities.' This again implies that the idea of slavery is inappropriate.

In general, despite the property transfer, the concept of private property as such was held up (Genesis 47: 27, also Exodus 12: 32, Genesis 12: 16) as was the concentration of property rights in land strictly economically organized: As indicated, property was acquired independent of nationality and ethnic discrimination (Genesis 47: 21). All people in Egypt, including the Egyptians, had their property transferred, but all retained – apart from the aforementioned barter tax – the right to keep 'fruits' and gains from property they worked with (see also Graves and Patai 1964: 264, Davidson 1979: 286–7). Also, looking back at how Israel's interactions with Egypt had begun, there is little evidence of serfdom to be made out: Israel's homeland was devastated by famine (Jacobs 2003: 334; von Rad 1963: 265) and Egypt and Israel had shared an interest in the Israelites relocating to the Nile delta.

These considerations contradict suggestions in the theological or historical literature, for example, Fung (2000, as quoted above), Valiquette (1999: 50–1), Wildavsky (1994: 48), Neufeld (1993: 50–2),

Meeks (1989: 78–89), Westermann (1987: 175), Rogerson and Davies (1989: 42–3), Noth (1966: 20–1, 32, 52) or Pfeiffer (1948: 20–1) that the leaders of Egypt had turned Israel and the Egyptians into serfs and slaves. (Further authors who promote the idea that the Exodus liberated Israel from slavery are quoted in Chapter 4.)

An important fourth element of Joseph's economic policies was the utilization of human capital, asset specificity and performance-related reward systems. In biblical Egypt, skills specialization reached a high degree. As Gordon (1989: 4) noted, the division of labour was already marked out at the very beginning of Genesis. In the Joseph story, progressing division of labour and human capital deployment could be observed in relation to various skills, specifically manual skills, for example, in brick production (later detailed in Exodus 5: 7–18), agricultural skills (Genesis 39: 5; 41: 2–7, 47; 47: 6, 23), craftsmanship (Genesis 40: 2, also Exodus 35: 25–39: 30), spiritual skills (Genesis 41: 15, 45; 47: 22), administrative skills (Genesis 37: 28, 36; 39: 4–6, 22–3) and managerial and entrepreneurial skills (Genesis 39: 4–6, 22–3; 41: 40–5).

The exchange of human capital in Egypt's operative, administrative and managerial hierarchies was stimulated through economic incentives in relation to skilfulness: 'Special ability' (Genesis 39: 3; 47: 6) determined pay, promotion and fringe benefits. The idea of asset specificity, of unique and difficult-to-replace skills, can be made out, too, especially for those at the top of Egypt's hierarchies. Joseph's career reflected this amply. Because of his specific entrepreneurial and managerial skills, he received special rewards such as land, a mansion and other riches (Genesis 41: 41–51; 47: 6).

These economic policies of Joseph hint at a basic blueprint for handling social problems in institutional and constitutional economic terms. With Joseph, economic societal contracting emerged in force in the Old Testament. His economic policies anticipate, in considerable degrees, suggestions of Hayek, Buchanan, Coase, North, Williamson and Vanberg. Joseph can be said to have mastered the – economic – art of 'soothsaying from the hissing of snakes' (Plaut 1981: 278), although Plaut did not make an explicit link between the snake metaphor and the economic approach and the kind of economic policies Joseph was masterminding as he did not interpret the snake as a methodical reference to economic man and the economic approach. In general, theological interpreters of the Joseph story often seem rather uninterested in Joseph's rise in the industrial hierarchy of Egypt and the economic policies invented by Joseph and the kind of economic reorientation this implied regarding the covenant between God and the people. In many theological and philosophical interpretations of the Joseph story, economic aspects of Joseph's success are just missing. The list is nearly endless, for instance, Jacobs (2003: 318, 328), Kaiser (2001: 95–6), Green (1998: 168–9), Kugel (1997: 247–62), Westermann (1987: 92, 97, 173–4), Schmidt (1984: 71–3), Plaut (1981: 270–1), Graves and Patai (1964: 260–3) or Pfeiffer (1948: 29, 169). Similarly, Davidson (1979: 211) argued that the Joseph story is full of psychological insight – but economic insights of this story remained under-explored in his analysis. Another example is Armstrong (1996). In her book, which she claimed analysed Genesis, she spent one sentence on the Joseph story, over-looking all the economically highly interesting issues discussed above, and this one sentence left more unsaid than said: 'Had he [Joseph] not become vizier of Egypt, the whole family [of Jacob] would have died of hunger in Canaan.' Equally disappointing are Eissfeldt (1974) or Gilboa (1998). Both completely overlook the Joseph story. Even Fromm's (1967) humanist, philosophical analysis of the Old Testament overlooked the richness of ethical principles that can be derived from the Joseph story for a universal, humanist ethics in an economic tradition. As far as Fromm interpreted the Israelites' presence in Egypt, he only identified slavery and focused on the Exodus story (e.g. Fromm 1967: 108–9, 187). Childs (1985: 178; similarly Noth 1966: 9) erred in this connection, too, when he questioned that Israel was not a national entity in the book of Genesis. He suggested that Israel had no concept of the state in Genesis. The Joseph story is here the counter-example, as Buber (1982: 126) briefly noted, too. Then, Israel had its own land assigned to in Egypt and in a sense it had its own representative, Joseph, in governmental decision-making.

The next section develops in more detail a critique of the lacking theological and philosophical interpretation of Joseph's economic policies, spelling out a 'hero thesis' for Joseph and a 'climax thesis' for the Joseph story and taking already a glimpse ahead at the book of Exodus and the role Moses played there.

Joseph: Hero by thesis, Moses: Non-hero by anti-thesis

Joseph's policies clearly imply that he favoured an economic approach over a behavioural one to solving institutional problems of societal contracting in a modern context. From here a rather positive image emerges of Joseph as Israel's hero. In relation hereto, various economic theses on institutional ordering and societal contracting can be spelt out. Above all, the Joseph story implies that Israel regained in the last story of Genesis the kind of paradise which it had lost in the first story. The sophisticated techniques of economic ordering applied by Joseph repaired the underlying interaction dilemmas raised by the original sin. Then, Israel was 're-admitted' to paradise. And in the course of this process, a rather liberated form of contract between God and the people evolved, one in which God took a non-interventionist, backseat role, as it was already signalled by the final outcome of the Jacob story when God lost to Jacob. God's role in the Joseph story can even be linked to mere post-constitutional contracting, especially the provision of con-sultancy advise on public-order goods such as an effective and efficient tax system. Only through visions and dreams, God helped Joseph to set up a tax system which ultimately would benefit both Egypt and Israel. Buber (1982: 101) confirmed in this respect: 'Among the Hebrew tribes resident in Egypt the guiding function of the ancient clan God [as encountered by Abraham and Noah and later re-encountered by Moses, too] had been forgotten.' God's role then resembled a post-constitu-tional, productive role of the state, or governing authority in general, as Buchanan (1975: 97) might call it.

The Joseph story solved problems of overcoming the natural distri-bution state, of Hobbesian anarchy and establishing a constitutional contract, firstly, by drawing on an established system of social order, the Egyptian society and its highly developed institutional structures, and secondly, by letting Joseph participate in this system of social order at its highest, hierarchical levels. The latter was supported by God's intervention, namely by providing valuable economic knowledge and insights to Joseph. But as said, such intervention compares more to post-constitutional contracting regarding public-goods exchanges (rather than a government's or sovereign's enforcement role of rule-keeping with respect to the constitutional contract). If one wanted to link God's intervention to constitutional ordering at all, one had to look at a Lockean model rather than a Hobbesian one. In the Hobbesian model, only the government or sovereign (here: 'God') has rights and the individual members of society 'are essentially parties to a continuing slave contract' (Buchanan 1975: 83). The early covenants between God and Noah and between God and Abraham were in this respect much closer to the Hobbesian model than the less autocratic, less controlling, contractual relationship that emerged in the further course of Genesis involving Jacob and Joseph. In the Lockean tradition of a constitutional contract, the government or sovereign 'is, itself, strictly held within the law of the constitutional contract' (Buchanan 1975: 83). This was a fundamental, conceptual achievement of the philosophers of the Enlightenment:

> Man could now think himself into the role as king; in his mind's eye, man could now leap out of his estate or order, and some man or men would surely act out these dreams. Althusius, Spinoza, Locke, and even more emphatically, Rousseau, commenced and continued to talk about a social contract among independent men, not a Hobbesian slave contract between men and a sovereign master.... For the first time, man seemed to be offered a prospect for jumping out of his evolutionary order. Man, in concert with his fellows, might change the very structure of social order.
>
> (Buchanan 1975: 147–8)

In considerable degrees, the stories of the Old Testament that involved Jacob and even Joseph portray the independent, freely spirited human beings Buchanan here refers to. They acted out their dreams, thought themselves into the role of kings and questioned established order which had an absolute (God-)sovereign in place. The underlying economic principles for establishing a societal contract that can be found in this respect in the Old Testament seemingly anticipated, if carefully read from a institutional and constitutional economic position, the ideas and ideals of the Enlightenment.

Key reasons why in Genesis cooperation emerged between Israel and Egypt are Joseph's invention of and intervention with incentive structures that steered interacting agents towards mutual gains in their capital exchange transactions. Through public ordering and private, market-oriented ordering, both within the confines of established constitutional contract, mutual prosperity, the genesis of wealth for a community of nations resulted. And this happened independent of the sharing or non-sharing of social and moral values among agents. Pluralism, ethnic diversity, moral disagreement and even value decay were mastered as interaction conditions. Joseph resolved the potential dilemma of a 'war about goods' (Genesis 14: 16, also Exodus 1:10), as it was first raised in the Paradise story, namely by equilibrating self-interests among agents (ensuring pareto-superior outcomes for all interacting parties) but not by means of value sharing. An economic vision of a societal contract emerged, and this happened, as indicated, more in the tradition of a Lockean constitutional economics rather than a Hobbesian one. Then, the goal and ideal set out by Genesis in the first covenants between God and Noah and between God and Abraham regarding the *universal* applicability of a covenant for mankind was finally realized – in economic terms.

It can be argued that such an economic approach to societal contracting became mandatory at least since the Jacob story, with Jacob symbolizing the condition of modernity: the agent who exhibited weak (pre-)dispositions regarding social and moral values in interaction scenarios like the large city or the multicultural society. Joseph then demonstrated how the institutional problem could still be solved after the birth of Israel – under the condition of encountering 'Jacob', who stood for a modern, potentially opportunistic and predatory person in the context of the emerging, free capitalist society. Joseph's policies ensured the effective utilization of human capital and prevented conflict in industrial relations. From here a *hero thesis* emerges for Joseph – Joseph as solver of cooperation problems in a multicultural, pluralistic setting and the creator of mutual prosperity. The turn towards Lockean rather than Hobbesian constitutional contracting in the Joseph story underlines this argument too. In consequence, Joseph can easily be characterized as *the hero* of Genesis and of the Old Testament in general. Jacob clearly recognized Joseph as Israel's hero when he praised Joseph as the 'fruitful vine' of the Israelites (Genesis 49: 22–6; this praise was fully quoted above in the motto, at the beginning of this chapter). The praise of Joseph by Jacob has to be linked to Joseph's economic policies, the saving of Israel from famine in its homeland, and his universalistic approach to economically inspired societal contracting. And indeed, it was only in Egypt when Israel developed into one nation, as Buber (1982: 126) confirmed – seemingly in the wake of Joseph's clever economic policies, as this chapter argued. All this strongly supports the hero thesis for Joseph.

As noted, many interpreters of the Old Testament do not discuss such economic themes of Genesis (49: 22–6). Pirson (2002: 129–33), Kugel (1997: 274–5), Westermann (1987: 195) or Plaut (1981: 311) are examples (further were mentioned above). Theology frequently overlooks economic issues of how to successfully organize social interactions in a complex, multicultural setting when addressing the Joseph story. Sarna (1986: 5) even claimed that the 'narratives in Genesis focused upon individuals and the fortunes of a single family.' Or, Eissfeldt (1974: 41) suggested that 'Genesis has no sagas of heroes or leaders.' As already touched upon, equally disappointing is Fromm's (1967) self-claimed 'radical, humanist' interpretation of the Old Testament which basically overlooks the Joseph story and the enlightened, heroic message that emerges from this story. As much as Fromm (1967) hinted at universal interaction principles in the Old Testament (e.g. Fromm 1967: 52–4, 82–5, 187), he did not examine ideas of universalism in the Joseph story. As discussed, this story is likely to be one of the strongest candidates to reveal a universal, humanist and pluralist social philosophy of the Old Testament, a radical economic humanism. Indeed, Fromm (1967: 187) only saw the stay of the Israelites in Egypt as the prelude to their 'liberation' from claimed Egyptian tyranny and slavery. Such claims overlook interaction dynamics and interaction outcomes like mutual gains achieved in Genesis, and how the institutional and organizational problem were solved in Genesis, especially in the Joseph story, when the riches of both Israel and Egypt prospered and friendly relations between the two nations developed.

My analysis disagrees with explicit anti-hero views and even non-hero views on Joseph, which are widespread in the theological and religious economic literature. Wildavsky is a good example. He argued that Joseph 'demonstrated for all to see the path the Hebrew people ought not to take' (Wildavsky 1994: 38, 48). Green is another example. She saw in the Joseph story references to 'an untold story, to an unnamed danger that makes escape even in Egypt a necessity' (Green 1998: 170). Such non-hero views on Joseph are frequently developed by starting out with the Exodus story and a hero thesis for Moses as liberator of Israel from Egypt. In this tradition, Joseph is then frequently assessed as slave master who moved his people from their homeland to Egypt (e.g. Wildavsky 1994: 48; Plaut 1981: 364, 384, 430, 1409; further references are in Chapter 4). The previous discussion indicated that such slavery-related interpretations could not be upheld.

Minor exceptions to the large body of theological literature which ignores hero elements of the Joseph story are Graves and Patai (1964: 275) who spoke of a 'chief-blessing being reserved for Joseph' or Davidson (1979: 308) who referred to Joseph as the 'champion of Jacob' – although they did not further interpret the nature of a 'chief blessing' or 'being a champion' in economic perspective. Kugel's (1997: 252) theological analysis detected hero elements for Joseph, too, but only by focusing on character virtues, such as his resistance to be seduced by Potiphar's wife (Genesis 39: 6–7). As Kugel noted:

> The encounter of Joseph and Potiphar's wife eventually came to be seen by ancient interpreters as *the* central episode in his life. His ability to resist temptation came to be seen as Joseph's great virtue, and many suggested that Joseph's rise to power came as a reward for this virtue.
> (Kugel 1997: 252)

Such a behavioural interpretation sidelines and completely overlooks Joseph's economic wits and skills, as I outlined above, in handling interaction and resource problems and the way he solved the institutional problem in economic terms. Von Rad's (1963: 405–6) reference to an enlightened, awakened period of Old Testament storytelling in the Joseph story hinted at a hero thesis, and the related economically oriented approach to contracting among different nations and between God and the people. Westermann (1987: 29, 98) argued similarly when he spoke of the friendly and positive portrayal of the Egyptian people and the 'peculiarly modern' approach of Joseph to solving the impending problem of famine and economic downturn. But again, like Kugel and the others mentioned above, von Rad and Westermann left more unsaid than said regarding the economic nature of a hero role of Joseph.

As indicated, Joseph's policies implied tolerance, pluralism and the rejection of value fundamentalism. This is reflected by the way the God of Genesis intervened rather indirectly in a non-fundamentalist but constructive manner in interactions between Egypt and Israel: Through visions and dreams he provided intellectual human capital to Joseph which then helped Joseph to economically mastermind policies that would affect the prosperity of Egypt, Israel and other nations. God's role in a covenant with humans then compared to the one of an economic consultant or venture capitalist. God took a 'backseat' role in intervening in societal contracts among humans. In this connection, Gordon linked Joseph's 'wisdom' and 'diplomatic skills' to the 'wisdom of God' (Gordon 1989: 7–8). Institutional economic reconstruction details and abstracts this suggestion for cooperation principles and value principles that are developed, negotiated and implemented through 'human wisdom' (see also Chapter 6). Gordon hinted at such a deconstruction of the idea of God when he attributed Joseph's success to 'human wisdom that can conquer economic difficulties' and the 'economic wisdom schools of Egypt' (Gordon 1989: 8, also Westermann 1987: 251–2; Gordon 1994: 21–3). The present study specified 'human wisdom' through the concepts of dilemma analysis, economic man, incentives management, capital utilization and mutual gains and how these concepts interrelate when it comes to solving social problems in modern, pluralistic settings. Chapter 6 follows up regarding the interpretation of the idea of God with respect to specific cooperation and value principles that govern interactions and contracting relationships among humans. At this stage, it is sufficient to note that a strong economic message emerges from the Joseph story regarding the successful governance of human interactions in a pluralistic setting that anticipates the modern market economy and modern market society.

In relation to the hero thesis for Joseph, I propose a *climax thesis* for the Joseph story in comparison to all the other stories of the Old Testament. Various theses were in this respect already spelled out above, especially the generation of mutual gains for Israel and Egypt and the mastering of pluralism as interaction condition. Thus, I read the Joseph story as the centre of the Torah and the culmination of institutional ordering and societal contracting in Genesis and in the Old Testament. The problem of societal contracting with a *universal* orientation arose as soon as the first covenants between God and humans had been made, namely with Noah and Abraham (Genesis 9: 11; 12: 3; see also Fromm 1967: 24–6). And as Buber (1982: 3) – although without reference to the Joseph story – realized, in the Old Testament 'this people [Israel] is called upon to weld its members into a community that may serve as a model for the so many and so different peoples' (see also Buber 1982: 28, also 35, 86). The Joseph story developed a viable answer to the problem of how to establish, even in pluralistic, nearly global settings, cooperative relationships for *all* mankind and not just for a selected tribe or nation. In this respect, the final story of Genesis provides an ultimate and general – largely economic – answer to the problem of how to include all mankind in a societal contract.

In this connection, Paris is more sophisticated in his analysis than most interpreters of the Old Testament who overlook a hero thesis for Joseph and a climax thesis for the Joseph story. Paris still read the Joseph story by 'coming from' the book of Exodus, viewing Moses as the true hero of biblical storytelling. But Paris also developed a hero thesis for Joseph, namely a cooperation thesis which he refers to as 'hero by anti-thesis' (Paris 1998: 74–5). As noted, his hero by thesis is, of course, Moses and he spells out a related climax thesis for the book of Exodus when he claims Moses to have liberated Israel from slavery (similarly Sarna 1986: 54). On the other hand, Paris detected specific hero elements in Joseph's behaviour regarding the long-term prosperity he generated for Egypt and Israel and his barter tax-crop system (Paris 1998: 78, 81). Besides my disagreement with his 'liberation from slavery' thesis, as discussed above and also in the next chapter, I disagree with some of his other non-hero evaluations of Joseph. Paris (1998: 75) suggested that Joseph's policies and the economic wealth it created led to an increase of the pharaoh's power. In this respect, Paris diagnosed non-hero elements in Joseph's behaviour. This suggestion can be confronted by the wealth sharing arrangements and power sharing arrangements that were in place. I discussed both above; for instance, power sharing was achieved through an institutional arrangement in which the Israelite 'Joseph' occupied the top position in Egypt's industrial hierarchy. And, he was also the 'fruitful vine' for Israel as Jacob praised him (Genesis 49: 22–6), who ensured increases in wealth for the Israelites during their stay in Egypt.

Clearly, the suggestion of a hero thesis for Joseph and climax thesis for the Joseph story contrasts with views that Genesis merely reflected a prologue to what would come in Exodus (e.g. Sarna 1986: 1, 5, 54; Childs 1985: 53; Eissfeldt 1974: 42; Davies 1967: 24, 30; similarly Bruce 1979: 397; Fromm 1967: 187). I interpret the Exodus and what happened in the wake of it rather critically (see also Wagner-Tsukamoto 2008a): social conflict and wars were played out during and after the Exodus and religious fundamentalist rules and governance structures were introduced (see Chapters 4 and 5). Jacob here very outspokenly cursed and condemned the Levites to whom Moses belonged: 'My soul shall not enter their council, my heart shall not enter their company' (Genesis 49: 5–7). Davidson (1979: 303) reckoned that this verdict on the Levites is 'severe' and that hence the tribe of Levi should 'play no part in the developing history of Israel'. However, regarding the latter, Davidson then completely overlooked that Moses came from the very House of Levi. Or similarly, Fromm (1967: 91) reckoned that Moses belonged to the House of Levi but failed to link this insight to Jacob's condemnation of the Levites and he went on to rather uncritically assess, like most theological and philosophical literature, Moses as 'liberator' (e.g. Fromm 1967: 93). In this respect, the critical question arises regarding a widely claimed hero status of Moses in the literature on the Exodus.

The next chapter goes into more details regarding a non-hero thesis of Moses' behaviour. In the present chapter, my analysis strongly suggested that the Joseph story should be read as the preceding economic counter-story to the Exodus story. Of course, the contents of both stories reflect on each other, Egypt and Israel having to solve serious, economic interaction problems as members of one society. This issue links these stories intricately in conceptual terms and the book of Exodus explicitly invokes such conceptual linkages and connections ('junctims') between Genesis and Exodus too (Exodus 1: 8; see also Chapter 4 below and Genesis 40: 23).

3.5 Concluding remarks

The narrative sequence and themes emerging from the stories of Genesis raise the question of how far the oldest stories of the Old Testament already sensed and anticipated the approach of a 'new' institutional and constitutional economics, as it was pioneered by Hayek, Buchanan, Brennan, Coase, North, Williamson and Vanberg. The chapter identified economic concepts, such as capital scarcities, capital contributions and distributions, dilemmatic interest conflict regarding capital contributions and distributions, mutual gains as goal of conflict resolution and economic man-type behaviour, even predation and opportunism. This reconstruction supports the thesis that institutional and constitutional economic themes strongly instruct and guide storytelling in Genesis and that the antecedents of an enlightened, modern political economy go well back in time, definitely much further than modern constitutional and institutional economics.

In relation to invoking the condition of modernity, of value pluralism, moral disagreement and even of value decay, the Old Testament seemed to carefully resist calling upon God, understood in a behavioural, institutional sense, to solve cooperation problems. The stories involving Jacob and Joseph were most indicative in this respect. Genesis apparently realized here that in social arenas like the city, the nation and the international community, behavioural intervention in a theological, sociological, socio-psychological or behavioural economic tradition, as illustrated in the Old Testament through the early covenants between God and Noah, between God and Abraham and between God and Isaac, reflected an inferior strategy for conflict resolution and societal contracting. Increasingly pluralistic interaction contexts define the modern market society. They were already encountered and anticipated by Jacob and Joseph, when Genesis no longer advocated behavioural techniques like value education, or even 'value indoctrination' and 'social conditioning', as behavioural economists suggest (e.g. Sen 1990: 36, Simon 1976: 103, 149–51; also Etzioni 1988; in degrees even Williamson 1998: 15–17). And neither did Genesis then favour a destructive Sodom-and-Gomorrah-type approach for restoring the effectiveness of value contracting. Behavioural institutions like religiosity, reflecting values like compassion, sympathy or benevolence, may only be capable of effectively and efficiently solving the institutional problem and (re-)establishing a stable societal contract when a pre-modern context is encountered or when intragroup interactions in socially highly cohesive and behaviourally strongly bonded social units are met, such as a very close-knit, traditional family or tribe (but even in this respect the Old Testament seemed to be rather critical as, for instance, implied by the Cain–Abel, Esau–Jacob or Joseph—his brothers stories).

The Jacob story and the Joseph story are of critical importance for understanding the intricate relationship between a change in the nature of the societal contract (covenant) between God and the people and the rise of interaction conditions like pluralism and moral disagreement, as encountered in the large city, the multicultural society, the international community and the modern, 'capitalist' market in general (see Figure 3.2). The Jacob story illustrated lengthy tit-for-tat conflict resolution, with cooperation finally emerging through evolutionary, interaction economics. It implied the financial and practical exhaustion of value contracting under the condition of modernity, when meeting a 'Jacob' in social interactions, with Jacob standing for a self-interested, even highly opportunistic and predatory agent. God finally lost to Jacob and a new type of societal contract (covenant) was imposed – largely by 'anarchic' Jacob, Jacob stating his terms for continuing a relationship with God. In the Joseph story, again value pluralism is a huge topic, but this time in macro-perspective. With Israel having relocated to Egypt, value pluralism, ethnic diversity and moral disagreement became unavoidable interaction conditions. In this situation, Joseph's clever economic intervention solved cooperation problems and steered both nations towards long-term, mutual prosperity. I advanced in this respect a hero thesis for Joseph and a climax thesis for the Joseph story in Old Testament storytelling. Joseph created win–win outcomes for Egypt and Israel and he avoided win–loss outcomes of lengthy tit-for-tat approaches to solving social conflict.

The present book thus clearly demonstrated in economic terms that there is much to be learnt from Genesis about conflict resolution and societal contracts that transcend mere principles of justice, revenge and counter-revenge (which became so dominant in the Old Testament from the book of Exodus onwards, as the subsequent discussion demonstrates). It also became clear that in Genesis, and here especially in the Joseph story, the realm of narrow nationalism was left and – economic – principles of supranational universalism were encountered. Such findings give new substance to Fromm's (1967: 4) early critical stance, which he followed up in a liberatory, humanist philosophical tradition, that the Old Testament had much to say beyond revenge principles and narrow nationalism. Although disappointingly, Fromm left out the Joseph story from his humanist analysis of the Old Testament. A key thesis of the present study here is that the concept of God and the concept of the covenant and of related societal contracting matured in the Joseph story into its most modern version in the Old Testament. Institutional ordering was then largely conducted in economic terms and pluralistic, humanist interaction principles were realized. This can be linked to an enlightened political economy in the tradition of Locke. God stopped direct intervention in cooperation problems among people. In certain respects, Fromm's (1967: 25) claim that the development of the covenant throughout the Old Testament culminated in the 'complete freedom of man, even freedom from God' can be traced in the Joseph story in institutional and constitutional economic terms. Ultimately, Fromm (1967: 228–9) stressed that the concept of God may have to be deconstructed for value principles that govern human interactions and mere contracting among humans and nations. Economically enlightened principles can here be deduced from the Joseph story. Chapter 6 follows up on this when the concept of God in the Old Testament is examined in more detail.

By pointing towards economic ordering as a means of solving the institutional problem, Genesis showed more insight and wisdom than the suggestions of many behaviourally oriented social scientists, including behavioural economists, who often analyse and advise to solve cooperation problems under the condition of modernity in a nearly theological tradition, namely by focusing on the individual's value system as institutional regulative. This overlooks social interaction dynamics that cause the 'self-elimination of conscience', of religiosity, of virtues, etc. in a modern context (Wagner-Tsukamoto 2008c, 2003, 2001b, Hardin 1968: 1246; sensed by MacIntyre 1985: 1–3). Such modern contexts, as they also characterize the market economy, were seemingly already anticipated in Genesis. In addition, cost considerations are ignored regarding value contracting and the maintenance of a value consensus when the condition of modernity is encountered (see Figure 3.2).

The Joseph story also reflects what Novak (1993: 26) termed 'democratic capitalism', namely a combination of the three social systems: capitalism, democracy and pluralism. From these three elements, capitalism can be identified most easily in the Old Testament. I interpreted 'capitalism' in this book through the ideas summarized by Figure 1.1. It is encountered throughout the Torah and the book of the Deuteronomic history (as subsequent chapters of the present book will also show). I tracked the modern capitalist society in Genesis in relation to the city metaphor and interaction conditions of pluralism, moral disagreement, ethnic diversity and even value decay. The other two elements are present, too, especially in the Joseph story. Novak interprets pluralism with regard to rights of minorities and the individual, and this interpretation can be reconciled with what I described as value pluralism and moral disagreement, such as incompatible predispositions of individuals, for example religious ones, regarding perceptions of what is right and wrong. Pluralism survived in the Joseph story but was, as I discuss in the next chapters, increasingly lost from the book of Exodus onwards. The idea of democracy is also present in the Joseph story, especially with regard to the power-sharing arrangements that were de facto in place between Israel and Egypt, with Joseph representing Israel at the very top level of Egypt's industrial and political hierarchies. These considerations regarding the enactment of democratic capitalism again underline that the Joseph story reflects a centre or climax of biblical storytelling. Subsequent chapters will demonstrate that both pluralistic and democratic ideals were lost once Israel left Egypt and began its Exodus journey to the Promised Land, which in the end did not turn out to be so promising at all. I then spell out a related non-hero thesis for Moses and a decline thesis for the book of Exodus and subsequent books of the Torah.

4
On the Exodus of the Wealth of Nations

Then a new king, who did not know about Joseph, came to power in Egypt.

(Exodus 1: 8)

Genesis culminated in the Joseph story with successful cooperation emerging between Egypt and Israel. Then, economic cooperation principles helped to resolve potential social conflict and a mutually beneficial societal contract was established. Genesis achieved the vision of a universal brotherhood of humans. This chapter discusses the apparent counter-story in the book of Exodus when cooperation between Egypt and Israel broke down in a dramatic way (see also Wagner-Tsukamoto 2008a). It will become apparent that the Exodus story did not resolve potentially dilemmatic interaction problems and it did not master pluralism as an interaction condition. Seemingly, mutual loss resulted for both parties. The chapter thus reinforces by anti-thesis to the Joseph story that biblical ideals for resolving social conflict mirror institutional economic ideals. I suggest that the key source of conflict in Exodus was the unsuccessful intervention with economic institutions (constitutional contract, governance structures, property rights, reward systems, etc.) and the ignorance of economic cooperation principles, which focus on the idea of the wealth of nations. The book of Exodus very prominently hinted at this right at its outset when it stated that 'a new king, who did not know about Joseph, came to power in Egypt' (Exodus 1: 8). Joseph, of course, stood, in Genesis, for successful institutional economic ordering. Hence, I subsequently do not analyse and praise the Exodus, as conventionally done by theology and religious economics, as the successful resolution of conflict over religious values and the escape of Israel from a claimed system of slavery. As counter thesis to the hero thesis for Joseph, the present chapter develops an anti-hero thesis, better, a non-hero thesis for Moses (and the pharaoh and God of Exodus too). I also advance a decline thesis for the Exodus story. This contrasts with the climax thesis for the Joseph story developed in the previous chapter.

In the following, first, I examine systemic, economic reasons why Egypt and Israel failed, at the outset of the book of Exodus, to resolve cooperation dilemmas (section 4.1). Second, the chapter critically assesses Moses' and the pharaoh's roles in the Exodus interactions (section 4.2). Third, God's special role and intervention tactics are critically reviewed for the Exodus scenario (section 4.3).

4.1 The breakdown of cooperation and rational foolishness as outcome of Moses' and the pharaoh's interactions

In historic perspective, conflict in the Near East and Middle East goes a long way back and it frequently seems to have had a violent tradition. The book of Exodus discusses a legendary, possibly even just a poetic example of such conflict. It tells the story of Egypt and Israel failing to maintain the cooperation that it had developed in such dramatic fashion at the end of Genesis in the Joseph story. The following sections reconstruct the cooperation failure in the Exodus scenario in institutional economic terms, namely as the failure to resolve an economic dilemma structure. This reconstruction implies a secular, rational – institutional and constitutional economic – function of Bible stories for organizing human interactions, as already proposed above for Genesis. Thus, the chapter, by antithesis, reinforces how institutional economic intervention should *not* proceed when the maintenance of mutually beneficial societal contracts are the goal. The section reconstructs decision-making of Moses and the pharaoh as 'economic man-behaviour' in a prisoner's dilemma and commons dilemma. The specific problems discussed in Exodus are problems of population management and industrial relations. The subsequent outlines that Egypt and Israel escalated such problems and ultimately got involved in a futile dilemma game, with mutual loss as the outcome. The following reconstruction suggests that Moses and the pharaoh failed to properly intervene with economic institutions, that is, incentive structures, to resolve interaction conflict. Game-theoretical concepts and rational choice theory are applied in methodical, heuristic perspective only.

The commons dilemma and uncontrolled population growth

Institutional economic theory and practical intervention that is based on institutional economic thought is methodically instructed by heuristic concepts. A key heuristic of institutional economics is the idea of 'dilemma structure' (see element 2 of Figure 1.1). As elaborated on in Chapters 2 and 3, the idea of the dilemma structure suggests that interacting agents simultaneously encounter common interests – to cooperate in order to reap socially desirable outcomes such as mutual gains – and conflicting interests – to organize contributions to and distributions from the interaction to one's own advantage and to the disadvantage of other agents (in detail, Homann 1999a, 1999b, 1994; Brennan and Buchanan 1985; Buchanan 1975). As discussed, institutional economics here models cooperation dilemmas as *interdependence* games and as *nonzero*-sum games, that means it models scenarios in which all agents lose because of self-interested choice, despite the possibility that all could gain if only cooperation succeeded.

Especially under interaction conditions of pluralism, ethnic diversity, moral disagreement and even value decay, it can be suggested that institutional economics which is heuristically grounded in the ideas 'dilemma structure' and 'economic man' is more effective, more efficient and more moral than behavioural approaches (Wagner-Tsukamoto 2008c, 2008e, 2005, 2003: Chapter 8; see also Figure 3.2). The subsequent now spells out this thesis with regard to the story of the Exodus.

At the outset of the book of Exodus, a fundamental cooperation dilemma is depicted. Uncontrolled population growth threatened to exhaust Egypt's natural resources in water, livestock and fertile land: 'The Israelites were fruitful and multiplied greatly and became exceedingly numerous' (Exodus 1: 7; also Genesis 47: 27; see also Paris 1998: 54–5; Gordon 1989: 16). Egypt and Israel encountered a common pool problem with the commons dilemma looming (for general references on common pool problems, see Hardin 1968; also Libecap 1989). The commons 'Nile delta' was under threat. The 'land flowing with milk and honey', as Exodus continuously renews the vision of an economic paradise that had been created and shared by Egypt and Israel in Genesis, was in the process of being destroyed.

Taken as one society, Egypt and Israel had a common interest to cooperate, to restrain population growth and maintain mutually beneficial relations as they had been established in Genesis. This would have benefited both nations regarding the safe and prosperous environment they had been living in since Genesis. However, a potential cooperation problem existed too. Individual Israelites (and Egyptians) had an interest to exercise reproduction rights in a less restrained manner as had Israel and Egypt as subgroups an interest in shifting population balances in their respective favour. In these latter respects, conflicting interests existed. In relation to increasing population imbalances between Egypt and Israel, the pharaoh also feared of being attacked by Israelites or the Israelites siding with a foreign attacker (Exodus 1: 10). This fear further complicated the population management problem. The theological literature on the Exodus does not frequently discuss such economic issues related to common pool problems (e.g. Sarna 1986: 24–6; Noth 1966: 20–4).

Although the book of Exodus is implicit on this, the pharaoh may have considered appeal to resolve the population problem, hoping that Israelites voluntarily constrained reproduction rates once asked to do so (possibly implied by Exodus 1: 8–14). Appeal, however, does not resolve interest conflicts. It leaves the existing incentive logic for reproduction decisions unchanged. It could not make Israelites formulate and implement a constraint on population growth *on grounds of self-interested, rational choice*, as an economic approach to solving population problems would stress. Indeed, appeal is likely to be counter-effective, aggravating existing interest conflicts. Specifically, appeal raises awareness of a looming, unresolved conflict and signals the possibility of forthcoming rule change. Because of appeal, Israelites and Israel as group could be expected to make extended, immediate efforts to reproduce. Hardin (1968: 1246) discussed this process as self-elimination tendencies of non-economic strategies for resolving common pool problems. Knight (1948: li) and Buchanan (1995) indicated this, too, Knight with specific reference to a pharaoh's behaviour as a ruler:

> The more general principles of analytic economics are simply the principles of economic behaviour, of the effective achievement of ends by the use of means, by individuals and groups, irrespective of social and political forms. Even under a 'pharaoh', combining sovereignty with outright ownership of men themselves as well as the lands and goods, much the same choices and decisions would have to be made to make activity effective rather than wasteful and futile; and the abstract principles of economy and organization are the same regardless of who makes the choices or what means and techniques are employed or what ends are pursued
>
> (Knight 1948: li)

Knight here even upholds economic principles for ordering social inter-actions for a pharaoh who enjoys ownership rights of a slave master and he specially referred to the institutional problem in its version as the organizational problem.

After the failure of appeals, the pharaoh could be expected to resort to harsher means. The book of Exodus outlines this. The pharaoh aimed to coerce the Israelites into certain population management policies. In par-ticular, he confiscated reproduction rights and tried to curtail reproduc-tion success by ordering the killing of Israelite baby boys (Exodus 1: 15). Confiscation is likely to be as ineffective as appeal but more so than appeal as confiscation has a high potential to escalate interest conflicts. North's (1993a) ruler-constituent analogy, in which a ruler confiscates property of constituents by reneging promises on wealth distribution, is illustrative. For various reasons, in the specific scenario depicted in Exodus the confiscation order of the pharaoh should instigate rational Israelites to make extended efforts to reproduce. First, the survival chance of an Israelite baby boy had not decreased to zero since institu-tional arrangements of Egyptian society saw Israelite midwives in charge of baby care (Exodus 1: 15–16; also Exodus 2: 5–7). Ineffectiveness could be expected, at least to a degree (see also Noth 1966: 23.). Moses is an example and Exodus (1: 17–19) confirms that the pharaoh's killing order failed to constrain population growth. Second, as far as the pharaoh actually succeeded to kill Israelite baby boys, rational Israelites could be expected to engage in tit-for-tat counter-confiscation. Escalating interaction dynamics of the commons dilemma or prisoner's dilemma illuminate this (Hardin 1968; see also Axelrod 1986). Since child nurs-ing of Egyptian children was also in the hands of Israelite maids, the opportunity for retaliation existed 'already' within the 'moves of the game'. That means for the purpose of counter-defection, the Israelites did not even have to manipulate the existing rules of the game. The plague of the death of Egyptian infants (Exodus 11: 4–7; also Numbers 33: 3–4) can be interpreted as such retaliatory counter-confiscation.

In the population dilemma story of Exodus, counter-defection on an even larger scale could be expected once Israel succeeded to manipu-late the rules of the game (discussed further below). Also, as far as the pharaoh's killing order succeeded, a scarcity in males should make rational Israelites change the organization of their reproduction behaviour, switch-ing from monogamy to polygamy. Genesis hinted at this (Genesis 16: 15; 19: 31–8; 21: 1–2; 25: 1–2, 6; 29: 16–30; see also Kugel 1997: 289). This, again, leaves population problems unresolved.

In degrees, theology sees a retaliatory tit-for-tat rationale; for example, Sarna (1986: 94) stated that the death of the firstborn of the pharaoh reflected 'a kind of measure for measure, as making the punishment fit the crime.' As much as theology hints in this way at tit-for-tat retaliations in the context of the deaths of the Egyptian firstborns, a deeper economic rationale of this escalating process of dilemmatic interactions is not seen. In particular, economic dilemma analysis departs from a theological interpretation of the plagues, especially the deaths of the Egyptian firstborns, as 'godly miracles' (e.g. Sarna 1986: 76–7; Noth 1966: 72–84). Sarna's theological approach (1986: 78, 93) is here explicit: 'The climatic tenth plague [of Egyptian firstborns] must be wholly outside human experience, and must defy any rational explanation. ... It belongs entirely to the category of the supernatural.' The present study here provides a rational scientific, economic explanation along the lines of counter-defection and game-theoretical analysis which involves the Israelites as key agents in executing defection and counter-defection. In the wake of this process, an existing constitutional contract was derailed step-by-step, with Egypt and Israel being thrown back into the anarchic, precontract, natural distribution state. Scarce 'good x' can in this respect be interpreted as reproduction rights.

Theology is well prepared and capable to deconstruct peripheral, claimed miracles in the Old Testament in naturalistic, 'scientific' terms. For example, Sarna (1986: 67–8) did so with regard to a staff turning into a snake (see also Exodus 7: 11–12) or with regard to population figures (Sarna 1986: 95–100). But theology holds back to do so with regard to God and God's intervention principles, such as the plague that caused the death of Egyptian firstborns. A deconstruction of 'God' and his supernatural actions in naturalistic, scientific terms violates the prerogatives and paradigmatic assumptions of theological analysis. It would 'end' the research programme of theology, which is grounded in the idea of the divine. As discussed, an economic reconstruction can here proceed more aggressively and in a more enlightened manner.

Further cooperation dilemmas and unresolved industrial relations problems

In relation to the escalating population problems, Egypt and Israel got involved in conflict that concerned their industrial relations, namely the claimed slavery-like treatment of Israelites by the pharaoh and pay-performance disputes (Exodus 1: 11–14; 6: 9). The organizational problem is here encountered in Exodus. In particular, the pharaoh raised contribution standards while keeping wage distributions constant. He ordered Israelites to provide on own account capital inputs – straw – to brick production: 'You are no longer to supply the people with straw for making bricks; let them go and gather their own straw. But require them to make the same number of bricks as before; don't reduce the quota. They are lazy; that is why they are crying out.' (Exodus 5: 6–8; also Exodus 5: 11, 13–14, 18–19) This rule change implied longer working hours and, if straw had to be paid for, monetary costs too. The pharaoh here broke a previous settlement over wage levels and performance levels, in effect confiscating wealth promised to his workforce. As a result, contribution–distribution arrangements ('the payoff matrix'), which already had been distorted by the pharaoh's population policy, were made further 'incentive-*in*compatible', to use Williamson's (1985: 27–30, 76) terminology. Economic governance structures were as a result increasingly incapable of organizing interactions and resolving interaction problems in a mutually beneficial, pareto-superior way.

Some of the figurative language of the book of Exodus illustrates the seemingly economic escalation of interaction conflict between Egypt and Israel: Moses and the pharaoh's priests were throwing snakes at each other (Genesis 7: 8–12). Of course, since the Paradise scenario, the snake could be interpreted with regard to 'economic man-behaviour' in the context of dilemma structures. Thus, when the staffs of Moses' brother Aaron and the pharaoh's priests turned into snakes this can be read as a reference to economic man and the escalation of interest conflicts, even more so since Aaron's snake-turned staff swallowed the pharaoh's snake-turned staff (see also section 4.2 below.).

The theological, philosophical and religious economic literature on the Exodus generally makes widespread claims on the slavery-like treatment of the Israelites in Exodus (e.g. Jacobs 2003: 310, 330; Fung 2000: 15; Valiquette 1999: 51; Kugel 1997: 325–6, 337; Neufeld 1993: 50–2; Meeks 1989: 82; Rogerson and Davies 1989: 42–3; Sarna 1986: 1, 21; Plaut 1981: 364, 384, 430, 1409; Brams 1980: 81; Davidson 1979: 316; Fromm 1967: 15, 93, 106–7; Noth 1966: 32, 52; Pfeiffer 1948: 20–1). However, not only for the time of Joseph's reign, as already discussed and discounted in Chapter 3, but also for the book of Exodus the slavery hypothesis may be unsustainable. One has to very carefully interpret what Exodus says about 'slavery'. Both in Joseph's time and in later times in Exodus, 'bondage' and the 'obligation to statute labour' were common for non-native *and* native labour in Egypt. As pointed out in Chapter 3, interesting in this connection is the clarification of von Rad (1963: 405) on the original, Masoretic text of the Old Testament.

Von Rad clarified that the later translation of 'made slaves of people', as it can be found in the Greek Septuagint version of the Bible, reads differently in the original, Masoretic text of the Old Testament, namely as 'removed the people to the cities'. This implies a rather different type of relationship between the pharaoh and his labour force than the one we tend to associate with the concept of 'slavery' nowadays and to which many theological interpreters of the Exodus refer, such as:

> What we are dealing with is state slavery, the organized imposition of forced labor upon the male population for long and indefinite terms of service under degrading and brutal conditions. The men so conscripted received no reward for their labours; they enjoyed no civil rights, and their lot was generally much worse than that of a household slave. Organized in large work gangs, they became an anonymous mass, depersonalized, losing all individuality in the eyes of their oppressors.
>
> (Sarna 1986: 21)

Similarly, Meeks (1989: 82) explicitly referred to the Greek translation of the Old Testament when he discussed the issue of slavery for Exodus. In contrast, a reading of 'slavery' along the lines of 'people being removed to the cities' is likely to compare to our understanding of contractual employment. For example, manual work in Egypt's storage cities for grain still came with certain freedoms for the Israelites, such as the right to move around in Egypt. Or, for farming work, only a barter tax had to be paid to the pharaoh. Civil rights were in this respect not as dramatically curtailed as implied by many theological researchers. The relationship between the pharaoh and his labour force did not reflect brutal and inhumane oppression. As also mentioned in the previous chapter in relation to the Joseph story, distinctions of 'slavery', 'forced labour' and 'obligation of statute labour' (Schmidt 1984: 36) are useful in this connection to illustrate the industrial relations between the pharaoh and native and non-native labour. Again, the concept of 'obligation of statute labour' may not be too far away from our understanding of contractual employment labour.

The ten plagues can be read as Israel's retaliatory response to the pharaoh's confiscation policies regarding industrial relations and also the previously mentioned common pool problems regarding population growth. Each of the plagues, not dissimilar to the effects of a retaliatory 'strike', destroyed some of Egypt's wealth. Besides having a retaliation motive, the Israelites had even more opportunity to defect than envisaged by Knight for slaves: They could, while moving around and being in search for straw throughout Egypt, sabotage resources and farming projects. The mere possibility of the Israelites engaging in retaliation, while roaming around in Egypt, also hints that the concept of slavery, understood as the total restriction of civil rights of an individual, does not apply in Exodus. Furthermore, Knight (1948: li) indicated, as fully quoted above, that even under an outright system of brutal and harsh slavery, slaves have still sufficient room to counter-defect and make certain decisions to restrain production output.

It is difficult to imagine that the highly industrialized Egypt described in Genesis and Exodus did not have some biological or other defences in place against naturally occurring plagues like frogs, flies or gnats (Exodus Chapters 7–10). But it was probably quite helpless regarding planned, man-made disasters. This contrasts with an interpretation of the plagues as godly miracles or natural events (e.g. Sarna 1986: 76–8; Tullock 1981: 70–1, Davies 1967: 28). In addition, if the pharaoh of Exodus had scrapped Joseph's system of a barter tax on crop (Genesis 41: 33–7), Egypt would have been ill prepared to survive the disasters caused by the plagues.

Many theological and philosophical interpreters frequently do not make explicit the interrelationships between the population management dilemma and the industrial relations dilemma, on the one hand, and the subsequently occurring plagues and the Exodus of Israel from Egypt, on the other. Sarna (1986: 65–80) or Fromm (1967: 102–4), for instance, analysed the ten plagues without much reference to the preceding unresolved population problem and industrial relations problem and the tit-for-tat retaliations this instigated.

A modern parallel of industrial relations problems in an Exodus-like scenario

Modern examples of comparable industrial relations dilemmas are frequent, with strikes of one kind or another leading to mutual loss as interaction outcome. The works and reports of Taylor (1912, 1911, 1903) here provide an early example. In the Taylorite factory, like in the multicultural interaction setting of Egypt and Israel, institutional ordering through a value consensus and related behavioural, theological, sociological or socio-psychological contracting was not an effective and efficient option. The factory of Taylor's time was characterized by high ethnic inhomogeneity, due to high immigration from Europe to USA (among other factors). We meet again the condition of modernity, with potentially anonymous market interactions here even invading the factory. Taylor's system of 'Scientific Management' then suggested that organization members should be rewarded in economic terms and that reward promises must be permanent (Wagner-Tsukamoto 2008e, 2007a, 2003: Chapter 4). He argued that work contributions should strictly be linked to rewards.

Taylor explicitly related such suggestions to higher normative goals, namely 'mutual prosperity' for both managers and workers. It was the task of the management to install a ' system of management, so that the interests of the workmen and management should be the same, instead of antagonistic.' (Taylor 1911: 53, also Wagner-Tsukamoto 2008e, 2007a, 2003, 2000a; Taylor 1911: 21) Taylor touched here upon an institutional economic rationale, especially regarding the ideas of incentive structures and of the dilemma structure – 'interests systemically being made the same instead of antagonistic.' Similar to Genesis and Exodus, Taylor sensed theoretical and methodical concepts of modern constitutional and institutional economics. However, Taylor's understanding remained incomplete. Especially, he restricted his insights regarding the systemic resolution of a dilemma structure to worker behaviour only, excluding managerial behaviour. Regarding managerial behaviour, he hoped that a behavioural appeal to 'cooperate heartily', in a benevolent manner with workers would be sufficient to resolve the potential dilemma. In this respect, he failed to intervene with incentive structures to handle contribution–distribution conflicts. Rather, and not dissimilar to theology, behavioural economics or socio-economics, he aimed through socio-psychological contracting at the human condition, and values like compassion, sympathy and benevolence but not through economic contracting at a systemic condition. Taylor's behavioural concept of hearty cooperation did not systemically equilibrate managerial interests and worker interests.

Once productivity began to increase because of higher worker performance, 'rational foolishness', as depicted in the prisoner's dilemma, waited to happen in the Taylorite factory. Ultimately managers, not dissimilar to the pharaoh in Exodus, could not consistently resist the temptation to appropriate gains from cooperation that had been promised to workers. Not anticipating counter-confiscation by workers, namely by means of strikes, managerial short-sightedness ultimately 'killed the goose that laid the golden egg', as Taylor (1912: 152) later admitted in his hearing before the US Congress. Instigated by managers who broke wage promises, an Exodus-like wave of national strikes and public unrest occurred across early twentieth-century USA. This led to the abandoning of Scientific Management for the time being and Taylor's questioning and testimonial before the US Congress in 1911/1912. In this connection, the US Congress reprimanded Taylor for his too positive image of human nature and his too cheerful image of social life (Taylor 1912: 151–3; see also Wagner-Tsukamoto 2008e, 2003). Or differently put, he was reprimanded for not modelling all choice behaviour in an organization with the instrumental, heuristic tools 'dilemma structure' and 'economic man'. This holds important lessons for theological research and behavioural research programmes in general, such as sociology, behavioural economics, socio-economics or social psychology, which frequently claim to be alienated by 'economic man' and the 'prisoner's dilemma'.

The failure to intervene with economic institutions in a dilemma structure

In Exodus, the lacking success of appeal, confiscation and counter-confiscation can be related to the failure of these policies to properly intervene with incentive structures. In particular, they failed to equilibrate conflicting interests of Egypt and Israel by means of changing the capital contribution and capital distribution standards that are set by incentive structures. In theoretical perspective, this section attributes the breakdown of cooperation to intervention failures with economic institutions. It suggests that the pharaoh and Moses played out contribution–distribution conflicts in the face of 'defective', incentive-*in*compatible institutional structures. Consequently, I strictly develop practical, normative implications regarding the (re)design of incentive structures. Cooperation problems are not examined as the human condition, as done by religious economics and theology (e.g. Paris 1998; Wildavsky 1994; Gordon 1989; Meeks 1989; Westermann 1987; Brams 1980; Noth 1966). Paris (1998: 50) is a key example here: He advocated the cooperation principle that 'man must honestly cooperate with man and with God.' Or, Brams reconstructed decision-making of Moses, the pharaoh and God in microeconomic terms, advancing the thesis that they were rational, economic game players (Brams 1980: 79–94, 166–8). Such an approach prevents the constructive analysis of social conflict and especially the analysis of incentive structures as a means of social ordering and resolving social conflict. This section analyses the breakdown of cooperation in Exodus through a systemic, methodical application of the idea of a dilemma structure.

It is important to note that not only the pharaoh could intervene with incentive structures but also Moses. Besides each side playing the game (making choices within set rules), both had, albeit in different ways and degrees, competency rights over the rules of the game, especially regarding ad hoc confiscations. Moses held competency rights similar to the ones of a 'union boss' in collective bargaining processes. Besides acting within the rules of the game, he commanded the Israelites and could confiscate through 'wild strikes', sabotage and other defections. He could also use the mere possibility of the Israelites confiscating riches of the pharaoh and defecting from a previous agreement as a bargaining chip in negotiations over rule change. Joseph had shown the way of how to proceed in this respect. His clever policies had equilibrated interests between Egypt and Israel and he had ensured mutual gains for both parties. For this approach, Jacob had praised Joseph as the 'fruitful vine of Israel' (Genesis 49: 22–6). Many interpreters of Jacob's blessings overlook the institutional significance of this 'blessing', even careful ones such as von Rad (1963: 418–19) or Westermann (1987: 195). On the other hand, Jacob had warned to appoint members of the Levites as leaders of Israel because of their violent inclinations to 'solve' social problems. Jacob characterized the House of Levi, to which Moses belonged, in the following way:

> Simeon and Levi are brothers – their swords are weapons of violence. Let me not enter their council, let me not join their assembly, for they have killed men in their anger and hamstrung oxen as they pleased. Cursed be their anger, so fierce, and their fury, so cruel!
>
> (Genesis 49: 5–7)

Davidson (1979: 303) reckoned the severity of this condemnation of the Levites but wrongly implied that as a result of it the House of Levi would 'play no part in the developing political history of Israel.' Moses is the grand counter-example. Similarly, Fromm (1967: 91) was aware that Moses belonged to the House of Levi but failed to link this fact to Jacob's condemnation of the House of Levi. Rather, Fromm went on to uncritically praise Moses as a humanist liberator.

In connection to his warning of the Levites, Jacob expressed the wish to be buried in his homeland once conditions permitted this. Childs (1985: 99–100) here wrongly implied that slavery or bondage of Israel by Egypt prevented Jacob's burial in his homeland. He spoke of the 'deliverance from Egypt' (see also Childs 1985: 218). As discussed in detail in Chapter 3, at the time of Jacob's death at the end of Genesis both Egypt and Israel were involved in mutually beneficial relationships; both nations were prospering and it was natural conditions such as famine (see also von Rad 1963: 265) and droughts which prevented Israel from returning home and burying Jacob in Israel.

The crucial issue for solving industrial conflict and population problems in economic terms is to install structures that equilibrate conflicting interests in a pareto-superior, mutually advantageous manner. At least solutions have to be reached which make rule violations by one party less likely than before. It is very clear form the situation described in Exodus that social order concerning the interactions between Egypt and Israel was highly vulnerable. The status quo at the outset of Exodus had fundamentally changed as compared to the situation described in Genesis. Rules and institutions were now set up in a way that more unfairly distributed wealth between Egypt and Israel than it had been the case in Genesis. Also, Israel had seemingly lost its right to membership in the polity, any collective organs of community, apart from some collective bargaining rights that can be assigned to Moses. But such rights carry much less influence and status than the ones Joseph had enjoyed at the top of Egypt's industrial hierarchies. Such changes in the status quo, as abstractly reviewed by Buchanan (1975: 77) for constitutional contracting in relation to the status quo, clearly play an important role for understanding why the social interactions in Exodus were from the outset on thin ice. Possibly not a '*lack* of freedom', as argued for by Buber (1982: 111), but definitely a *reduced level* of freedom here characterized the interactions between Egypt and Israel when compared to the Genesis scenario. In such a situation, Buchanan (1975) recommended that a constitutional contract has to be renegotiated in order to bring an emerging distance between interacting parties back to acceptable limits. But in Exodus the opposite happened. Rather than reducing a distance between Israel and Egypt regarding unfairly distributed scarce goods ('good x'), Egypt and Israel further escalated the conflict and increased distribution differentials. The pharaoh did not realize that his population management policies and industrial relations policies made the status quo even more vulnerable to violations by the Israelites than it already had been before. Buchanan outlines this argument in abstract terms: 'Violations that remained unpunished in prior periods, whether by government or by persons and groups, make enforcement more difficult and provide an incentive for further violations.' (Buchanan 1975: 85; also Buchanan 1975: 79) In Exodus, violations through the Israelites then happened through their retaliatory response to the pharaoh's population and industrial relations policies, that is, the ten plagues.

The question here is: What would the political economist Joseph have done to solve the problems encountered by Moses and the pharaoh of Exodus? In Exodus, population problems could have been resolved in economic terms through taxing families with many children higher than those with few; through setting out property rights to reproduction, possibly even in intergenerational perspective (see also Wagner-Tsukamoto 2001a); through introducing a state-run pension scheme or a state-run nursing system for the elderly; etc. Such measures would have changed incentives for individual reproduction behaviour and this could have been done independent of ethnic discrimination. Hardin (1968, 1971) argued for similar proposals early on in his analysis of population management problems. Such economic suggestions have little in common with behavioural, theological population management that relies on faith and godly wisdom, as it is also advocated by religious economics (e.g. Paris 1998; Gordon 1989; also Brams 1980).

Similarly, Exodus could have approached industrial relations problems in economic terms, for example, through installing collective bargaining arrangements. Metastructures would have been needed, too, which organized and safeguarded collective bargaining from outside the pharaoh's and Moses' sphere of rights to intervene with rule change. North (1993a: 14) implied in this connection that a ruler has to effectively self-bind himself not to retreat from promises made to constituents regarding contributions and distributions. Or Buchanan (1975) stressed that the role of the 'protective state' regarding the enforcement and negotiation of constitutional contract has to be clearly separated from the role of the 'productive state' regarding its involvement in public goods exchanges and also private goods exchanges. As discussed, both the pharaoh and Moses did not master these challenges. They failed to design economic structures and metastructures that could have resolved (potential) interest conflict. As noted, such metastructures lead directly back to questions of constitutional economic contracting in the tradition of Buchanan.

Of course, population management problems and industrial relations problems, as depicted in Exodus, reflect classic contribution–distribution conflicts. Such problems have been well researched in the institutional economic literature on common pool problems and industrial relations (e.g. Libecap 1989; Williamson 1985, 1975; Buchanan 1975; Hardin 1968). Especially wage and workload disputes have a long history in industrial relations. As indicated above, the studies of Taylor (1912, 1911, 1903), which possibly mark the beginning of research into industrial conflict in modern times, hinted that economic rule change is required to prevent confiscatory behaviour of managers (Wagner-Tsukamoto 2008e, 2007a, 2003) – and of unions and union bosses alike, as Hayek (1960: 270) hinted. Incentive structures need to be intervened with in order to prevent the escalation of conflict. The works of Hayek, Buchanan, North,

Williamson or Vanberg are instructive as is Nyland's (1998, 1996) discussion of the mutual gains strategy for resolving conflict in industrial relations (see also Wagner-Tsukamoto 2008e, 2007a, 2003). Such normative implications regarding the redesign of incentive structures are missing from evolutionary economics, which expects cooperation to emerge through the moves of the game (e.g. Axelrod 1986, 1984). The Exodus story here provides a warning to evolutionary economics.

Mutual loss as interaction outcome

Exodus reports stories of murder and destruction as outcome of unresolved conflict over population management and industrial relations. Seemingly, mutual loss resulted with the 'war of all' breaking out, as Hobbes may have put it. This war was not so much a religious crusade but simply a 'capitalist' war about goods and capital gains, relating to reproduction rights, fertile land, food, water and cooperative industrial relations. Basically the previously fairly balanced system of social interactions between Egypt and Israel, as it had emerged in Genesis, was 'plunged back into anarchy', Egypt and Israel finding themselves in the 'Hobbesian jungle', as Buchanan (1975: 79, 81) may call it. This happened in the wake of the Israelites' response to the discriminatory policies of the pharaoh. The constitutional contract between Egypt and Israel collapsed on a grand scale.

As a result of the Exodus, Egypt lost a considerable amount of human capital and economic benefits from cooperating with the Israelites (Exodus 14: 5). It suffered the costs incurred by the ten plagues (Exodus: Chapter 6–11). It was plundered in the course of the Exodus (Exodus 3: 22; 12: 36–7). And Egypt's army was destroyed when chasing the Israelites into the desert (Exodus 14: 27–8).

However, not only Egypt lost, but also Israel. A constitutional economics would predict this because both parties would find themselves, once their constitutional contract collapses, in the initial, anarchic, natural distribution state where mutual gains from cooperation are forsaken and costly, armament investments regarding the predation and defence of scarce goods x have to be made (Buchanan 1975: 79). In Exodus this can be clearly observed. Not only did Egypt lose as a result of the collapse of a constitutional contract but Israel lost too. Israel was 'liberated' from an affluent society, in a sense from paradise. In this respect, it is difficult to see that 'Moses led Israel into a land of abundance.' (Wilson 1997: 31) The opposite seems to be the case: In the course of the Exodus, Israel lost economic privileges that had come with the emigration to Egypt, such as sharing into wealth creation; being buffered against economic and natural disasters; and being protected by Egypt's legal, judicial and military apparatus against internal civil unrest and against attacks by other nations. In short, during the Exodus, and most of the time ever after (see Chapter 5), Israel relived the consequences of the original sin, losing access to paradise and getting involved in a dilemmatic and futile struggle for survival. Buber (1982: 111) seemed to sense this when he suggested that Moses led the Israelites into a 'problematic freedom' when exiting from the Egyptian society.

To further detail this: After the Exodus from Egypt, Israel had to go through a costly resettlement process (see Chapter 5 for details). Exodus (16: 35) and Numbers (33: 38) speak of the Exodus journey lasting 40 years. During this journey, the Israelites were plagued by thirst, famine, poverty, disease and the natural conditions of the desert (Exodus 14: 3, 20; 15: 22–6; 16: 3, 10; 17: 2–3; 19: 9, 16; Numbers 33: 14). They were exposed to the attack of foreign armies (Exodus 13: 18; 17: 8; 23: 27–30) and they had to recoup their homeland which, during their emigration to Egypt, had been lost to other nations (Numbers 33: 40, 51–5; Deuteronomy 7: 1–6; see also Chapter 5). Israel also had to bear the costs of setting up new judicial and legal institutions for maintaining social order (Exodus Chapters 20–31). Israel had to 'evolve and stress its own distinctive autonomous culture, devise its own structures of national existence, and forge its own institutions.' (Sarna 1986: 81) This was anything than a straightforward, painless process for Israel. In the initial stages of the Exodus, Israel was torn apart by civil unrest and an anti-pluralistic war for a value consensus, as, for instance, reflected by the golden calf story. This led to mass executions within the Israelites own ranks (Exodus 14: 11–12; 16: 1–2, 8; 17: 4; 32: 27–9). This can be interpreted as a first attempt of the liberated Israel to come to terms with the institutional problem and societal contracting (Exodus 14: 11–2; 16: 1–2, 8; 17: 4; 32: 27–9). More constructive albeit still behavioural routes were taken regarding constitutional law-making when the Ten Commandments and their regulatory derivatives were issued. Various chapters of the book of Exodus and various books of the Old Testament that followed Exodus deal with this type of law-making. This illustrates well the costliness of institutional ordering and nation-building for Israel in the wake of the Exodus when Israel struggled to overcome an anarchic, precontract order to set up a new, constitutional order.

Regarding these outcomes of the Exodus, theology, philosophy and religious economics take a too naïve and too optimistic view. The huge losses occurred for Israel as a result of the Exodus are not properly acknowledged. For example, the Exodus and Moses' behaviour are interpreted as 'heroic' (Brams 1980: 174; similarly Kugel 1997: 290,

329; Sarna 1986: 29), as 'liberation' (Meeks 1989: 82; Fromm 1967: 93), as 'solution by faith' (Gordon 1989: 9–10, similarly Paris 1998: 55; Kugel 1997: 287; Noth 1966: 68) or as a 'holy event' and 'deliverance' (Buber 1982: 66–7). Moses is viewed as the 'most powerful hero in biblical history (Plaut 1981: 391), as a nearly 'holy man' (Davies 1967: 52). However, since both nations were made worse off, the present study disapproves and is more critical of these interpretations. I economically reconstruct and more critically interpret Fromm's (1967: 107) insight that 'two powerful blocs of mankind [were] attempting to find a solution to the threat of weapons [the ten plagues].' I here interpret the Exodus story as a nonzero-sum game that went badly wrong and yielded loss/loss outcomes for the two parties involved. Gordon (1989: 10) seemingly hinted at this when commenting that there was 'no soil' and 'no city' in the desert, in which Israel found itself after the Exodus for 40 years. Sarna (1986: 116) spoke of the 'harsh realities of life in the wilderness'. Or, Pfeiffer (1948: 178) noted with a look to the future of the people of Israel, once they had separated from Egypt, that 'the expectations of a continued, uninterrupted prosperity and power for the kingdoms of Judah and Israel … were not fulfilled'. As in the prisoner's dilemma and the commons dilemma, no win–win solutions were generated. In a sense, both Egypt and Israel self-evicted from paradise. A common interest in cooperation and mutual gains was violated. Both parties lost because of rational, self-interested choice, despite the possibility that both could have won if only cooperation had succeeded. The tragedy Israel and Egypt encountered in Exodus is anything but synonymous with irrationality. As Brams (1994: 44) noted for literary analysis (of Shakespeare's *Richard III*): 'The tragic fall is made more, not less, poignant when characters are driven by an inexorable rationality towards some terrible end.' This applies in my discussion of the Exodus, too, although it has to be very carefully analysed, as done below, why this tragedy occurred at all and who possibly could be blamed for it. I here critically examine God's interfering role.

These insights also imply that from an economic point of view, Joseph and the pharaoh of Genesis better reflect true heroes in the Old Testament, who solved problems to the mutual advantage of Egypt and Israel. Right at the beginning, Exodus (1: 8) clearly hinted at this when it stated that a new pharaoh came to power 'who did not know about Joseph'. The same 'not knowing about Joseph' applies for Moses. Hence, as a counter-thesis to the hero thesis and the climax thesis, which I proposed for the Joseph story, I advance a *non-hero thesis* and a *decline thesis* for Moses and the Exodus story and for the events that followed the Exodus. This contrasts with a climax thesis proposed by theology and religious economics for the book of Exodus, for example, Sarna (1986: 54) or similarly Bruce (1979: 397). (Chapter 5 goes into more details regarding events that followed the Exodus of the Israelites from Egypt.)

4.2   Economic man in the Exodus scenario

It has to be asked *why* institutional ordering and societal contracting between Israel and Egypt went so badly wrong in the Exodus. The previous section has already prepared the ground by describing what happened in systemic perspective regarding ill-devised incentives management in a dilemma structure. The subsequent explores reasons for cooperation failures with regard to economic man-behaviour of Moses and the pharaoh. (Section 4.3 addresses the same question of why interactions went so badly wrong in Exodus but with respect to God's role and intervention in the Exodus interactions.) The following examines in more detail how economic man showed up in the Exodus interactions and how this derailed cooperation and a previously mutually beneficial societal contract between Egypt and Israel. A non-hero thesis for Moses was already touched upon above. It is further questioned in this section whether Moses was indeed a heroic 'game player', as for example suggested by Brams (1980: 174) or similarly by Gordon (1989: 8–9) and Plaut (1981: 391).

Moses and the pharaoh acting like economic men

It appears that in Exodus Moses and the pharaoh actually acted like economic men but did not instrumentally, methodically test out their behaviour for detrimental effects of economic man-behaviour in a dilemma structure. This reflects lacking knowledge and problem solving skills to engage in constructive, institutional economic analysis and intervention. As noted, for the pharaoh this is explicitly mentioned at the very outset of Exodus (1: 8), when Exodus stated that 'a new king came to power who did not know about Joseph'. Joseph epitomized like no other biblical figure the skilful political economist, who created mutual gains, even under interaction conditions of pluralism. He stood like no other figure in the Old Testament for economic conflict resolution and the related, sound application of economic methods. Early on, Exodus (2: 16–17) indicated the opposite for Moses, too, that he seemingly 'knew little about Joseph', when it illustrated his non-economic, violent handling of social conflict over water usage (see also Exodus 2: 11–12).

Moses' non-economic, violent inclinations are further illuminated when, in the course of the Exodus from Egypt, he resolved the golden calf incident in a radical, fundamentalist way. Theology interprets such violent behaviour, which distorted cooperative interactions, rather positively as Moses' fine character and personality traits, specifically 'his intolerance of oppression and his wholehearted identification with the plight of his people'. (Sarna 1986: 34) Joseph also showed a whole-hearted identification with the plight of his people, then famine, poverty and starvation in Israel's homeland, but still managed to equilibrate interests between his people and Egypt in a non-violent way when he brought Israel to Egypt and ensured mutual gains and benefits for both parties through his clever industrial policies.

The Old Testament referred to Moses' lack of knowledge about skilful institutional economic problem solving in relation to his membership in the House of Levi. The dying Jacob raised this as a crucial issue. As discussed above, Jacob warned not to bestow leadership functions on members of the House of Levi, to which Moses belonged: 'Let me not enter their council, let me not join their assembly ... Cursed be their anger, so fierce, and their fury, so cruel!' (Genesis 49: 6–7; more fully quoted above in the motto) Pirson's (2002: 125) interpretation of Jacob's condemnation of Simeon and Levi does not deal with such institutional references to 'councils' and 'assembly' but only deals with the other elements of the 'blessing'. But from an institutional and constitutional economic point of view, references to 'councils' and 'assemblies' are especially worthwhile noting. They can be interpreted as references to governance structures, such as collective bargaining and co-determination schemes. In order to analyse economic conflict resolution through such structures, the model of economic man and the idea of the dilemma structure are needed as design tools and as Joseph and Genesis had here shown the way.

However, if an institutional economic approach is given up, behavioural institutional ordering can succeed at best in a sporadic, accidental way, being possibly supported by a behavioural economics but not the type of non-behavioural institutional economics outlined in Chapter 1. In Exodus, not dissimilar to interactions in the Paradise scenario in Genesis, the pharaoh and Moses failed to see that in a situation of incentive-*in*compatible institutional structures, self-interested, 'confiscatory' choice in the mould of economic man-behaviour undermined cooperation. Since their economic man-behaviour yielded mutual loss, one might be tempted to criticize the pharaoh and Moses, like Adam & Eve and God, as 'rational fools', condemn the model of economic man and possibly economics in general. Behavioural economics or socio-economics argue this way (e.g. Sen 1990). However, this overlooks that economics only heuristically, instrumentally – methodically – applies the model of economic man to test out incentive structures. In contrast to Joseph and the pharaoh of Genesis, Moses and the pharaoh of Exodus did not know about such an instrumental, methodical 'playing' of the model of economic man. They seemingly lacked institutional economic wisdom in this respect – and for this they can be criticized. Understood as design tools, economic man and dilemma structure fulfil a similar test and quality assurance function as the car crash dummy and car crash test scenario for assuring the safety of structural features of a car (Wagner-Tsukamoto 2003; see also above). As outlined, institutional economics applies economic man and dilemma structure in order to insure the stability inducing, interest-equilibrating and pareto-superiority assuring effects of governance structures.

The snake metaphor in Exodus

Since Genesis and the Paradise story the snake could be read as a reference to economic man. The snake metaphor is explicitly reconnected to in Exodus, namely when Exodus reports that the assistants of the pharaoh and Moses were 'throwing snakes' at each other (Exodus 7: 8–13, also Exodus 4: 3–4, 17). In Exodus, the throwing of snakes can be read as a reference to predatory and confiscatory 'economic man-behaviour' in conflict over population management and industrial relations. Theology or religious economics do not provide such an economic man-interpretation of the snake story (e.g. Sarna 1986: 59; Noth 1966: 71–2). Sarna (1986: 60) interpreted the staff, which turned into a snake, as a 'serpent staff' sometimes held by pharaohs; he claimed it symbolized sovereignty, power and authority of pharaohs. In this respect, Sarna interpreted Moses' capability to turn a simple staff into a snake as Moses being predisposed to effectively handle Egyptian pharaohs. The critical questions, however, which Sarna does not follow up, is how such 'handling' of pharaohs should proceed and what the goal of 'handling' would be. Institutional economics would here reconnect the snake metaphor to the analysis of economic man-behaviour in a dilemma structure and the generation of win/win outcomes for the parties involved in interactions. Joseph here had shown how to proceed from an institutional economic point of view.

Already since the Paradise scenario, the snake could be read in relation to institutional economic intervention that instrumentally applies the model of economic man (in a dilemma structure). So when Moses and Aaron 'throw snakes' at the pharaoh's priests, with Aaron's staff turning into a snake, and the priests throw snakes back at them, this mirrors the figurative 'throwing' of economic man at each other. In this way they (heuristically) tested out each other's behaviour for opportunism and the effects of opportunism on social interactions. Sarna's (1986: 67) theological interpretation of the snake episode unearths to a degree such an instrumental function of the snake: He stated that the snake was not thrown by the pharaoh himself or by Moses himself but rather by 'assistants' of the pharaoh and of Moses, namely Aaron and the pharaoh's magicians. This hints at a *proxy function* not only of the assistant but also of their behaviour, the throwing of snakes – but proxy for what? Sarna leaves this question open. An institutional economic reconstruction of the Old Testament here relates proxy functions of the snake and the assistants who throw the snake to a metaphorical, instrumental test for self-interested behaviour in a dilemma structure (the population management dilemma and the industrial relations dilemma, as discussed above).

In the Exodus scenario, God, however, actively undermined the effectiveness of this test, driving the two parties further into dilemma interactions rather than showing ways out of the dilemma (see section 4.3 below). Hence, one cannot criticize Moses and the pharaoh alone for their 'rationally foolish' behaviour. Rather, one has to look at who installed the dilemma and the rules that governed the dilemma in the first place – which appears to be God. Fromm (1967: 107) touched upon this insight, too, when he stated that 'the irony of the story [of the ten plagues] is that the all-powerful God chose miracles which repeat, or only slightly improve on, Egyptian magic.'

Anyway, a merely empirical, behavioural critique of Moses' and the pharaoh's economic man-behaviour overlooks that (institutional) economics only heuristically, instrumentally 'throws snakes'. The very purpose of applying the model of economic man (as of the idea of the dilemma structure) is to prevent rational foolishness – but these models do not depict an empirical, behavioural model of rational choice (see also Wagner-Tsukamoto 2003). Institutional economics specifies the purpose of 'throwing snakes' in relation to the design of institutional structures that equilibrate interests and create mutual gains. Exodus even hinted at this when it stated that the 'throwing of snakes' was not a 'vice' in itself but could 'perform miraculous signs' (Exodus 4: 17). But of course, in the Exodus scenario it was the very intervention of God that prevented 'miraculous', mutually advantageous, win/win outcomes (see the next section).

4.3 Prisoners and prosecutor: God's intervention in the Exodus

As discussed in Chapter 3, the God of Genesis, especially in the Joseph story, reflected a rather positive, enlightened approach to institutional intervention, 'providing' Joseph with knowledge and insights on how to resolve interaction conflicts in institutional economic terms. In contrast, it can be argued that the God of Exodus played a much darker, much more destructive role. A Hobbesian sovereign, even a Hobbesian despot, rather than a Lockean sovereign here showed up. To a great extent, God drove the pharaoh and Moses into dilemmatic interactions rather than showing them ways out of their predicament. He basically prevented the pharaoh and Moses to cooperate and to engage in successful societal contracting between Egypt and Israel. As a result, Egypt and Israel were thrown back into the pareto-inferior, natural distribution state.

In general, when this book analyses the idea of God it theorizes more parsimoniously than religious economics or theology. I approach the Old Testament as 'text', independent of questions of divine or human authorship or revelation (see Chapters 1 and 6; see also Wagner-Tsukamoto 2001a; Miller 1994: 756). This section reconstructs the idea of God in rational, scientific terms. (This is followed up in detail in Chapter 6.) In the subsequent, I interpret 'God' as an agent who intervened in inter-actions between the pharaoh and Moses. His role is compared to the one of a law enforcement agent, specifically the prosecutor in the pris-oner's dilemma. I question Brams' suggestion that the Exodus reflected a religious power and obedience game that was played by God to raise his image and reveal his omnipotence (Brams 1980: 81–9, 175; also Plaut 1981: 417). In more abstract terms, the subsequent transcends the idea of God for economic and non-economic cooperation principles. The book here departs from the religious economics of Brams (2002, 1980), Gordon (1994, 1989), Meeks (1989) or Paris (1998) and the more so from theology (e.g. Wildavsky 1994, Noth 1966; also Westermann 1987), which subscribes to a metaphysical concept of a personal, omnipotent God and non-economic cooperation principles derived hereof. Chapter 6 further details my rational, largely economic reconstruction of the idea of God in the Old Testament.

Cooperation failures driven by God

The question has to be raised why Moses and the pharaoh so badly failed to cooperate in Exodus, both through behavioural, for example, theo-logical programmes and/or through economic programmes. Behavioural cooperation is normally advocated by a religious economics or theology in order to overcome social problems. Paris' principle that 'man must honestly cooperate with fellow man and God' is a very good example of this tradition (Paris 1998: 43, 50, 55). For religious economics, which aims at cooperation in this behavioural way, the Exodus story has some rather grim implications since the call for 'honest' cooperation was not only undermined by Moses and the pharaoh but especially by God. One indication of this is God's promise to Israel to lead it to a 'good and spacious land, a land flowing with milk and honey' (Exodus 3: 8). Theological interpreters note in this connection that

> strangely, none of God's solemn pledges to the Patriarchs recorded in the Book of Genesis ever mentions the 'land flowing with milk and honey'. Yet hereafter this epithet is reproduced again and again in biblical literature, about twenty times altogether.
>
> (Sarna 1986: 46; also Sarna 1986: 46–7)

As discussed above for Genesis, it may be little surprising that this promise of the 'land flowing with milk and honey' did not show up in Genesis. The key reason is that this aim was *actually* achieved at the end of Genesis when Israel shared Egypt's wealth and welfare. Israel then actually lived in a paradise, in a 'land flowing with milk and honey'. In contrast, the frequent renewal of the promise of the 'land flowing with milk and honey' in Exodus and later books of the Old Testament reflects aspiration – and desperation, too. It reflects that this goal was actually *not* achieved. It remained a promise. The Promised Land which was to become a new paradise for Israel was never really reached. A critical question here is who was to blame for this? Obvious candidates are the pharaoh of Exodus and Moses but possibly, first and foremost, the most obvious candidate may be the God of Exodus since throughout the Exodus story God 'is the sole, effective actor, the single controlling force, manipulating events toward their predetermined climax' (Sarna 1986: 54). In Exodus, regarding economic cooperation, Moses and the pharaoh failed to develop 'economic wisdom' on institutional and constitutional governance. In particular, it has to be asked why they failed to see that their 'economic man-behaviour', as reviewed in section 4.2, was rationally foolish and would, over time, lead to mutual loss. In terms of the prisoner's dilemma analogy, it is important to inquire by whom and how a prisoner's dilemma was installed for Moses and the pharaoh. It appears that divine intervention played a significant role.

In contrast to Genesis, in Exodus, God did not show Egypt and Israel economic options for rule-making and choice behaviour that could have prevented mutual suffering. Egypt and Israel were not welded into a community of nations, as it had been successfully achieved in the Joseph story. And as Kugel (1997: 316) noted, the God of Exodus could have chosen any means to 'free' the Israelites from a claimed system of slavery, even without the plagues and the mutual sufferings that resulted from the Exodus. Figuratively expressed, it was clearly God who did not let Moses and the pharaoh 'know about Joseph'. In theological terms, God caused the 'stubbornness' and 'evil will' of the pharaoh in order to punish Egypt (Noth 1966: 67–8). God here directly intervened in the constitutional contract between Egypt and Israel and he did so in a rather one-sided way which favoured the sub-group of Israel, of the previously integrated society of Egypt and Israel. This reflects despotic, Hobbesian constitutional contracting rather than a Lockean approach. In the latter model, God would have had a very restricted role to play, being controlled, as enforcing agent, by the very parties who closed the constitutional contract (Buchanan 1975: 83). This was in Exodus no longer the case as it had been, at least implicitly, in the final stories of Genesis.

Regarding God's role in the Exodus, Sarna (1986: 63) speaks in this connection of the 'theologically disturbing perplexities of divine causality' that led to the hardening of the pharaoh's heart and consequently to the ten plagues. To a considerable degree, God reinforced the uncooperative behaviour of the pharaoh, 'thereby making him [the pharaoh] a prisoner of his own irrationality' (Sarna: 1986: 65). In game theoretical terms, God's role can be compared in this respect to the one of the prosecutor in the prisoner's dilemma. In the prisoner's dilemma, it is the prosecutor who makes rational economic agents behave as 'rational fools', by separating the prisoners into different rooms and preventing them to consult each other over choice options. This leads to the economically worst (pareto-inferior) outcome for the two prisoners. In Exodus, God acted as a comparable catalyst and source of conflict. He prevented, by means of psychological, 'value fundamentalist' intervention, Moses and the pharaoh from an economically wise cooperation and intervention. God made Moses and the pharaoh retaliate and not get involved in negotiations over social problems and governance structures that could have resolved problems of population management and industrial relations (Exodus 7: 3–4, 13, 22; 8: 15, 19, 32; 9: 7, 12, 34–5; 10: 1–2, 20, 27; 11: 9–10). Thus, God drove 'rationally foolish' outcomes.

This interpretation is still compatible with Brams' (1980: 86–93) suggestion that divine intervention in Exodus reflected a personal power revelation game of God, with the pharaoh and Moses being 'puppets' of God (similarly Plaut 1981: 417). However, there are differences between my interpretation and the one of Brams when the *purpose* of the Exodus is examined. As for the prosecutor in the prisoner's dilemma, the idea of God in Exodus needs to be transcended for cooperative and non-cooperative interaction principles. The idea of the prisoner's dilemma sheds new light on what theology has described as the 'the pharaoh's divinely hardened heart' (Davies 1967: 35; similarly Sarna 1986: 63–5). In this connection, Brams (1980: 88) evaluated, in the tradition of most theological and religious economic research, a claimed power revelation game of God favourably since it seemingly 'liberated' Israel while enhancing at the same time God's reputation. Brams (1994: 47) claimed that God was obsessed with such reputation games in the Torah (see also Brams 2002: 193; 1994: 34). Of course, the idea of liberation and deliverance is widespread in the theological and religious economic literature when it comes to the Exodus story (e.g. Wildavsky 1994; Miller 1993b: 498; Keller 1989: 111; Meeks 1989: 82; Sarna 1986: 45–6, 81; Davies 1967: 29–30, 34, 47; similarly Paris 1998; Gordon 1994, 1989; Brams 1980; see also Childs 1985: 49, 64, 94, 100, 218; further references were quoted above). The present study is here more critical regarding the idea of liberation. 'Liberation' did not solve cooperation problems: The Exodus occurred and, as reviewed above, mutual suffering and huge costs for both parties resulted. And as discussed, too, it can be generally questioned whether slavery was an issue.

For assessing the role of God in Exodus and hereof-derived cooperation principles, a crucial question is why did God not prevent mutual suffering and use his omnipotence constructively as the God of Genesis had done? Also, why was 'economic trauma', as Brams (1980) refers to, necessary at all? And why did God, only *after* the plagues had happened psychologically intervene and make the Egyptians favourably disposed towards cooperation with Israel (Exodus 12: 36)? Could God not have psychologically intervened from the outset and made the pharaoh and Moses cooperate? Brams in this respect proposed that the economic damage caused by the ten plagues was more revealing regarding God's power and reputation than psychological trauma. But why should this be the case? It can be questioned why economic trauma is more revealing than psychological trauma. Furthermore, Brams seemed to overlook that not only Egypt but also Israel was economically traumatized in the wake of the Exodus. Mutual loss occurred. As indicated, what followed after

Israel's Exodus from Egypt is a lengthy, costly, traumatic re-settlement process which never really ended. The subsequent stories of the Old Testament are here tellingly gruesome (see Chapter 5). Such issues of economic trauma are well illuminated by the prisoner's dilemma game and related economic interaction principles which advise on the resolution of this dilemma.

Thus, economics can well shed new light on the issue of divine influence and God's plan when it came to the hardening of the pharaoh's heart. Theology, for instance Jacobs (2003: 319), here frequently resorts to questions of good and evil and God's role in perpetrating good and evil. In economic terms, the nature of divine influence that brought about trauma for the interacting agents can be related to the specific (non-)communication rules that framed this dilemma game.

Godly intervention in Exodus and the failure to master pluralism as interaction condition

From the point of view of pluralism as a cooperation and contracting condition, one has to critically assess the Exodus too. It implied that interactions moved out of contexts that were defined by pluralism as interaction condition. The challenge of living cooperatively and productively together in a multicultural society was not mastered. Miller (1994: 755, 759; 1993b: 477; also Gordon 1989: 10) discussed, for the early stories of Genesis, this issue when relating a breakdown of contracting to a return to 'iron age'. But then Gordon's analysis of Moses' behaviour as 'heroic' and the Exodus as 'solution by faith' (Gordon 1989: 7–9; also Paris 1998: 41–2; Wildavsky 1994: 38, 48; Keller 1989: 111; Noth 1966: 68), as similarly advocated by most theological and religious economic research, seemingly endorsed such a return to a pre-modern, 'iron age' scenario in the wake of the Exodus story.

Also, the idea of conflict resolution by faith leaves conflict handling outside the realm of human wisdom. Theology and religious economics here proceed on metaphysical grounds. This approach is difficult to reconcile with the philosophical and scientific research tradition of the Enlightenment, which aims to reconstruct metaphysical concepts in non-metaphysical terms. I here reconstructed godly intervention in the Exodus events as an economic disequilibration process of interests that was driven by value fundamentalism. In this respect, the story of the Exodus, like the stories of the Tower of Babel and of Sodom and Gomorrah, seemingly outlines principles of how *not* to proceed when socially beneficial governance is desired in pluralistic contexts (Chapter 6 follows up regarding the idea of God and value principles derived hereof).

Thus, the stories of Babel, Sodom and Gomorrah and the Exodus sandwich the Joseph story which so clearly showed a way for population management dilemmas, industrial relations problems and related problems of managing scarce natural and intellectual resources. Only then emerged, grounded in sound constitutional and institutional economic policies, a peaceful and highly productive societal contract between Egypt and Israel. Pluralism was then successfully handled as an interaction condition.

4.4   Concluding remarks

My analysis of the Exodus story differs in methodological, in theoretical and in practical, normative terms from the few existing, religious economic analyses of the Exodus and, of course, the more so from theological interpretations. I reconstructed decision-making of Moses and the pharaoh as economic man-behaviour in a prisoner's dilemma. The chapter demonstrated for the Exodus story that self-interested behaviour in a dilemma structure can yield disastrous outcomes for both parties. The pharaoh and Moses seemingly played out contribution–distribution conflicts in the face of 'defective' incentive-*in*compatible institutional structures. In this respect, this story serves as a warning to opportunistic, self-interested behaviour that is shortsighted and fails to intervene with incentive structures. The Old Testament warns of such dilemmatic outcomes waiting to happen when agents are involved in interactions who are not skilled in institutional economic analysis or who are otherwise prevented from negotiating and changing the rules of the game in economic terms.

I applied game theoretical concepts and rational choice theory in 'heuristic', instrumental – methodical – perspective only but not in theoretical, empirical perspective. This contrasts with Brams, who reconstructed decision-making of Moses, the pharaoh and God in microeconomic terms, advancing the thesis that they were rational, economic game players (Brams 1980: 79–94, 166–8). This chapter questioned whether Moses was a heroic game player (as claimed by Brams 1980: 174; similarly Gordon 1989: 8–9), whether the Exodus reflected a religious power and obedience game that was played by God to raise his image and reveal his omnipotence (as claimed by Brams 1980: 81–9, 175) and whether the Exodus was primarily caused by rebellion against an inhumane system of slavery (as claimed by Brams 1980: 81 and many others).

The book of Exodus clearly outlined the dilemmatic consequences of self-interested choice and rule making that disequilibrated interests.

'Paradise' was lost in a 'rationally foolish' war for goods, which left both Egypt and Israel counting losses. Genesis, and here especially the Joseph story, provided the apparent counter-story. Economic intervention then equilibrated interests of Egypt and Israel and generated mutual wealth and a stable societal contract. In general, the final stories of Genesis and the first stories of Exodus cannot be read separately. Thematically they deal with the same issues, a multicultural interaction context in which Egypt and Israel are confronted with capital exchange problems, social conflict and societal contracts of various kinds. In this connection, the present study succeeded to *conceptually interrelate* the books of Genesis and Exodus through the same analytical approach. This appears absolutely mandatory because there are explicit conceptual linkages – 'junctims' – between both books, in particular Exodus (1: 8) which states that a 'new king came to power who did not know about Joseph'. I analysed such a conceptual link between Genesis and Exodus: Joseph showed up as 'hero by thesis', namely a hero of successful institutional economic problem solving in a multicultural context. And the Joseph story marks in institutional economic perspective the climax of Old Testament storytelling. Moses, in contrast, takes on the role of a 'non-hero by anti-thesis', namely as a leader who failed to intervene with institutional economic structures in a way which could have resolved societal problems in a pluralistic context. The Exodus story and the stories that follow thus reflect a decline of Old Testament storytelling. I developed these theses through applying the same conceptual apparatus to the economic reconstruction of Genesis and Exodus, namely the ideas of incentive structures, capital contributions and distributions, mutual gains as interaction outcome, the models of economic man and dilemma structure and the consideration of interaction conditions like pluralism, ethnic diversity, moral disagreement and even value decay.

Very many theological, philosophical and religious economic researchers do not see any conceptual links, and even less so economic ones, between Genesis and Exodus in relation to Joseph's and Moses' approaches to institutional intervention and to the interactions with their respective Egyptian rulers. For example, Brams (1980) did not discuss the pharaoh's performance-quota increase and any conceptual junctims between Exodus and Genesis. Or, Sarna (1986: 15) did not link Exodus (1: 8) to the economic success story depicted for the interactions between Egypt and Israel in the final chapters of Genesis. This book questions conventionally rosy views on Moses in the Exodus events where he is depicted as liberator of Israel. I suggested that the pharaoh and Moses played out, driven by a value fundamentalist

God, contribution–distribution conflicts in the face of 'defective', incentive-*in*compatible institutional structures. This approach departs from the behavioural analysis of the Exodus in relation to the human condition and the salvation of Israel from a claimed system of slavery, as done by religious economics, philosophy and theology (e.g. Paris 1998; Wildavsky 1994; Gordon 1989; Meeks 1989; Westermann 1987; Brams 1980; Davies 1967; Fromm 1967; Noth 1966; many more references were quoted above). Thus, by spelling out institutional economic rationales for junctims between Genesis and Exodus, I managed to explain the Exodus more critically and more conclusively than done by previous research.

5
Institutional Ordering after the Exodus

> *Then Moses summoned Dathan and Abiram, the sons of*
> *Eliab. But they said: 'We will not come! Isn't it enough that*
> *you have brought us up out of a land flowing with milk and*
> *honey to kill us in the desert?'*
>
> (Numbers 16: 12–13)

The Exodus from Egypt left the Israelites in a state where a new societal contract and new institutional structures were needed. As members of the Egyptian society they had shared into Egypt's institutional governance structures, from jurisdiction to work allocation and wage arrangements, property laws, etc. As a newly independent nation Israel had to address questions of social order, societal contracting and related questions of conflict resolution. Institutional issues of state formation had to be addressed and the Old Testament here holds important lessons on the early history of an economic theory of state formation. An especially critical question for Israel concerning state formation in this connection was whether and, if so, how pluralism as an interaction condition was still mastered after the Exodus.

The following examines the question of economic governance after the Exodus and asks how far pure economic contracting could be observed rather than value contracting in the footsteps of theology, religious economics or behavioural economics. First, I address this question for the Exodus journey and the relevant books of the Pentateuch, namely Exodus, Leviticus, Numbers and Deuteronomy (section 5.1). Second, I analyse the same question for the settlement process once Israel had reached its homeland (section 5.2). Here, the chapter deals with the books of the so-called Deuteronomic history (Kaiser 2001: 24), from Joshua, Samuel, Judges to 2 Kings. The book of Deuteronomy, which presents an overlap between Pentateuch and Deuteronomic history, is primarily dealt with in section 5.1.

5.1   Institutional ordering during the Exodus journey

Nation-building and the establishing of a new societal contact was an all important issue after Israel's Exodus from Egypt. The Ten Commandments formed the religious backbone of new rules issued in the aftermath of the Exodus, which were meant to govern and unite Israel. They reflected a new, behavioural covenant between God and humans (Exodus 34: 28), which was to group together Israel in a spiritual sense (Buber 1982: 109–10). The First Commandment was here of crucial importance. This contracting purpose was highly relevant since the twelve tribes of Israel were not united by a sense of national identity (Plaut 1981: 516; also Genesis 49: 3–27).

Besides their first issuing in the book of Exodus (20: 3–17), the Ten Commandments were specified and reissued in later books (e.g. Leviticus 19; Deuteronomy 4: 13, 5: 7–21). They embodied a strict, fundamentalist religious approach to institutional ordering and theological contracting. Kaiser (2001: 143–4) identified in this connection six elements the Ten Commandments showed as a theological contract. Subsequently, I look for evidence from the books of Exodus, Leviticus, Numbers and Deuteronomy regarding how these books interpreted the Ten Commandments and what conclusions can be drawn regarding institutional economic ordering. In this connection, I examine how far the Ten Commandments actually solved the institutional problem and grouped together the tribes of Israel as one nation and even more importantly, how far the Ten Commandments helped Israel and its neighbouring nations to resolve multicultural, pluralistic interaction problems.

The following focuses on Israel's 40-year-long desert journey to Canaan. This journey gave an additional purpose to the young nation of Israel when it came to nation-building and societal contracting, a purpose which was later lost when this phase was over and each tribe 'retreated' into its own territory. This latter issue is discussed in section 5.2.

Dilemmatic interest conflicts during the Exodus journey and the Levites' economic man-like, opportunistic acquisition of influence

As members of the Egyptian society, the Israelites had shared into Egypt's sophisticated jurisdiction, executive and work organization structures. As an independent nation they had to find their own institutional rules. Having left Egypt, the Israelites had a common interest to re-establish social order and stability in social interactions among themselves. This required institutional law-making, ruling over organizational issues, the setting up of something like a jurisdictional system, etc. In short, a new constitutional contract was needed. All Israelites would benefit from a swift and democratic resolution of these issues and the quick resettlement in a land flowing with milk and honey', as the vision of the paradise was constantly renewed after the Exodus. However, conflicting interests existed too. The decision to leave Egypt and search for Israel's homeland at the Jordan had been anything than a unanimous decision among the Israelites. Interest conflicts had existed before the journey and there was dissent from the outset and throughout the journey. Many wanted to return to Egypt and choose a different leader than Moses, who was not willing to return (Numbers 14: 2–4). As Sarna (1986: 116) noted: 'Food was in short supply [during the Exodus journey], and public dissatisfaction soon surfaced and broke into a clamorous outcry against the leadership of Moses and Aaron.' Many Israelites viewed Egypt as the land where milk and honey were flowing and grumbled over the implication the Exodus had brought on them (Numbers 16: 13, 41; 17: 5; 20: 5; 21: 5). Even once a resettlement solution was nearly reached, dissent did not disappear. And, Deuteronomy (17: 16) forbade a future king of Israel to return to Egypt for as simple matters as trading horses.

A basic dilemma existed in this respect, namely how to re-establish social order and a stable societal contract in the aftermath of the Exodus and to reconcile common and conflicting interests, firstly, among the Israelites, and then also with a view to neighbouring nations, extending a societal contract in universal perspective. A 'problematic freedom' had to be faced after Israel's exit from Egypt, as Buber (1982: 111) noted. A key question was who should lead the issuing of new institutional rules and what kind of principles would guide institutional ordering. As it turned out, a small selective group, namely Moses and his tribe, the Levites, took over the organization of institutional rules regarding legislative, executive and jurisdictional issues but not the first-borns or elders of all tribes. Initially the first-borns and elders of all tribes were in charge of such issues. For example, in Exodus (4: 27–31), it was still the elders of all tribes with whom Moses discussed and decided problems. Similarly, during the Exodus journey, Moses was at the top of an organization structure that set out new institutional rules. Below him was the group of priests, which was engaged in executive, legislative and jurisdictional issues, mainly the operational enactment of rules Moses had issued. Initially, these priests were recruited from all tribes of Israel: The first-borns of each family were thought to belong to God.

This implied that institutional decision-making was split across Israel (for details, see the next section below). With the de-selection of priests from tribes other than the ones from the House of Levi, a common interest in selecting persons in a democratic and capability-related manner for the job, as it was called for in other parts of Exodus (Exodus 18: 20-2, 24: 1), was, at least in degrees, violated. A key principle of constitutional economic contracting, such as 'free relationships among free men' (Buchanan 1975), was not fully acknowledged. The Levites took over institutional decision-making, especially priestly functions, thus depriving the elders and first-borns of all tribes and hence the tribes of Israel from influencing decision-making and the right to become priests (Numbers 3: 12, 39–51; 8: 15–16; 16: 8–10; 18: 1–32). The specific way this transfer of influence was organized even made the other tribes of Israel pay for their loss of decision-making power and of influence over institutional ordering:

> The Lord said to Moses: '... Take the Levites for me in place of all the firstborn of the Israelites ... To redeem the ... firstborn Israelites who exceed the number of the Levites collect five shekels for each one.... Give the money for the redemption of the additional Israelites to Aaron and his sons.
>
> (Numbers 3: 40–1, 46–8; see also Numbers 3: 39–51)

Once made into priests, the Levites became the caretakers of religious symbolizations of Israel's God, namely the tabernacle and the tent of meeting, where offerings were to be made to God through the priests. From the offerings the priests received a certain share. Specifically, as priests, the Levites were to receive special shares from crops, shares from offerings made to God and shares from plunder that was accumulated during war with other tribes. Unclaimed property went to the priests too. This reflects economic man (discussed further below).

The Levites' special influence through their claims towards priesthood was upheld throughout the Exodus journey and, in degrees, afterwards. Especially Deuteronomy repeatedly stressed that it were only the Levites who could become priests (Deuteronomy 17: 9, 18; 18: 1–4; 21: 5; 24: 8; 27: 9; 31: 9; see also Spencer 1995: 392–3). Many interpreters of the Levites' functions and responsibilities during the Exodus journey overlook such potentially opportunistic elements. Mayes (1983: 37) or Spencer (1995) or Sarna (1986: 127) argue that appointments for the new judiciary of Israel must come from 'all the people' – but Sarna, for example, then fails to make explicit the potentially opportunistic role the Levites took on in this respect. This is the more astounding since accusations of favouritism and nepotism are even mentioned in this connection in the Old Testament itself. Korah is here the leading advocate (Numbers 16: 3, 9–10, 15; see also Kugel 1997: 471–3). Such accusations and challenges to authority were harshly dealt with. In Korah's case, retribution came when the earth opened up and swallowed him (Numbers 17: 31–5). Similarly, Valiquette's (1999: 52) interpretation overlooked opportunistic issues when he suggested that the Levites, once made into priests, were merely there to mediate between Israel and other priests.

There are various other issues that reveal a comparatively opportunistic, more than economic man-like, stance of the Levites in the aftermath of the Exodus. During the 40-year-long Exodus journey, Israel was on the move with tents being carried from one destination to another. The specific rules issued by Moses for tent grouping arrangements saw the Levites and the priests in the centre, being grouped in close distance around the tabernacle and the tent of meeting (Numbers 3: 38). The tent grouping problem reflects a distributional problem: In the case Israel was attacked by other warring nations, the tribes grouped at the 'outskirts' of the Israelite camp (Numbers 2: 1–31) were more prone to suffer than the Levites who were grouped on the inside. Since conflicts with other nations and tribes were a major issue during the Exodus journey a tent grouping arrangement that saw the Levites at the centre was clearly a huge advantage to this tribe. The Levites enjoyed the safest place at the inner core of the structure (see Figure 5.1). Plaut (1981: 1026) did not see such a selfish motive when he discussed the location of the priestly families at the centre of the tent grouping arrangement. Similarly, Pfeiffer (1948: 261) only saw a religious, theological purpose in putting Levite priests and the Levites at the centre of the tent grouping arrangement: 'The Levites encamped between the court of the Tabernacle and the secular tribes, as a protective insulation against their contact with the dangerous holy presence of the deity.' Pfeiffer did not discuss a more worldly, mundane and potentially selfish purpose of being at the centre of the camp. Or, Sarna (1986: 204) did not even detail that the Levites occupied a special place in the centre of the camp. Organization structure issues that relate hereto are discussed in more detail below when incentive structures are focused on.

There were a number of redemption arrangements and rules in place for different types of property, from loans and land to servants and houses. There appears to be one element of philanthropy

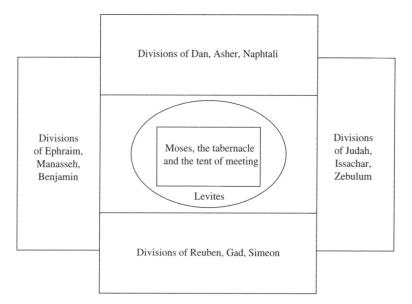

Figure 5.1   Organizing the Exodus journey through a web structure

in Deuteronomy (15: 7–11) when loans to the poor and needy are discussed. The biblical law on debts saw all debts cancelled, following a cycle of seven-year periods. That means unpaid debt was to be forgiven. In general, the redemption rules reflect the model of economic man, the trading and paying for property. At this point it is important to note that it were again the priests, the Levites, who had special arrangements in place. For example regarding redemption arrangements, they could redeem a village house at any time (Leviticus 25: 32–4). This was a right other Israelites did not enjoy. Again, many theological interpreters of the Old Testament do not detect such opportunistic issues. For example, Plaut (1981: 1046, 1078, 1196) discussed the Levites' special influence with regard to priestly functions and the privileges priests and the Levites enjoyed but failed to draw conclusions regarding economic man-behaviour in this respect.

Once the issue of selecting a king for Israel arose, with the Exodus journey coming to an end, Deuteronomy quite explicitly aimed to protect the special position of influence the Levites had acquired. It issued the rule that wealth accumulation of the king is to be restrained by law

(Deuteronomy 17: 16–18). This in effect aimed to protect the position of influence the priests had acquired, especially their wealth.

Incentive structures, biblical laws and new societal contracting

The Ten Commandments provided a summary of biblical laws, which set out institutional structures for a new societal contract. The Ten Commandments and their derivates specified what was to be expected in terms of rules of conduct. They are discussed in great detail throughout Exodus, Leviticus, Numbers and Deuteronomy. Rules and sanctions are spelled out and tit-for-tat regulations are established.

The central rule for societal contracting after the Exodus was a behavioural one: The First Commandment clearly set out that obedience to and faith in God was to be the foundation of social order. Behavioural ideas, such as faith and obedience, were at the heart of the new contract between God and Israel: 'You obey the Lord your God and keep his commands and decrees that are written in this Book of the Law and turn to the Lord your God with all your heart and with all your soul.' (Deuteronomy 30: 10) Thus, in the tradition of Noah and Abraham, a *behavioural* covenant was renewed between God and the Israelites. Although, a universal orientation of societal contracting, as it could be made out for the covenants of Noah and Abraham, is less obvious for the covenant Moses established with God (see also below, when issues of pluralism are discussed). Deuteronomy (30: 9) quite explicitly reconnects the new covenant to earlier covenants: 'The Lord will again delight in you and make you prosperous, just as he delighted in your fathers.' The fathers referred to here are not Jacob and Joseph but above all Noah and Abraham and the kind of behavioural covenants they established with God. Deuteronomy (30: 20) explicitly mentions Abraham, Isaac and Jacob, but as discussed in Chapter 3, a turn away from behavioural contracting towards purer economic contracting could already be made out for Jacob and the more so for Joseph, who was not mentioned by Deuteronomy (30: 20).

In this connection, a critical question regarding the new covenant between God and Moses is whether pure, behavioural contracting was followed or whether behavioural contracting was backed up with economic ideas, as already met for the behavioural covenants of Noah and Abraham. It becomes quickly clear for the covenant Moses reached with God that a behavioural economics was its guiding principle too. Economic ideas are visible regarding both the type of gains Israel was to receive for obeying the Ten Commandments and regarding the sanctioning structures that were established for rule following. With respect to gains, economic promises were made to Israel for upholding the Ten Commandments:

> You will again obey the Lord and follow all his commands I am giving you today. Then the Lord your God will make you most prosperous in all the work of your hands and in the fruit of your womb, the young of your livestock and the crops of your land. The Lord will again delight in you and make you prosperous, just as he delighted in your fathers, if you obey the Lord your God and keep his commands and decrees that are written in this Book of the Law and turn to the Lord your God with all your heart and with all your soul.
>
> (Deuteronomy 30: 8–10)

And, Deuteronomy (30: 15–16):

> See, I set before you today life and prosperity, death and destruction. For I command you today to love the Lord your God, to walk in his ways, and to keep his commands, decrees and laws; then you will live and increase, and the Lord your God will bless you in the land your are entering to possess.

Prosperity in various shades here directs behavioural contracting (see also below, when capital exchange issues are discussed).

A behavioural economics is also visible regarding the sanctions envisioned for violating the Ten Commandments. The Ten Commandments were thought to reflect the Word of God, being issued directly from God to Moses and Israel, but their sanctions were of a comparatively mundane, worldly nature. The Ten Commandments (Exodus 20: 1–17) and other, related biblical laws, such as the covenant code or the ritual decalogue (Exodus 20: 22–3: 33; 34; for an overview, see Eissfeldt 1974: 143–5; Pfeiffer 1948: 210 and his Chapter 7 in general), were embodied in a sophisticated set of economic sanctions. Kaiser (2001: 144) speaks in theological terms of 'stipulations of the covenant' and 'curses and blessings' for obeying and disobeying the stipulations. Or, Plaut (1981) refers to 'retributions and rewards' that came with the Ten Commandments. The sanctions that came with the Ten Commandments mostly enforced rule following on ground of self-interest. Incentive structures can in this respect be clearly made out and the '...legislation [found in Exodus in this connection] has every appearance of serving a settled community, the economic basis of which is agriculture on a small scale, and cattle raising.' (Sarna 1986: 161-2)

Thus, contrary to theological perceptions (e.g. Sarna 1986: 120–1), behavioural, theological contracting in a true sense, through the 'fear of God' that would restrain inhumane, unfaithful behaviour in social interactions, was hardly needed to ensure good social conduct. Economic thinking and the model of economic man drive these rules and their related sanctions. An appeal to be good is not put forward as the foundation of institutional ordering but harsh rules which are armed with severe sanctions are. Tit-for-tat was the guiding principle for most members of the new society but not necessarily for slaves (see Schmidt 1984: 113). The key maxim for institutional ordering was 'an eye for an eye, a tooth for a tooth' (Exodus 21: 24; Leviticus 24: 20 26: 14–46; Deuteronomy 19: 21). Each rule and each rule violation came with a gains-loss calculation, based on the 'soul for a soul' and 'eye for an eye' principle (Kugel 1997: 396–8). If a person suffered a wrongdoing, restitution was to be arranged. This reflects the 'law of equivalence'. (Sarna 1986: 186) This 'law' can be closely linked to economic principles of law enforcement, as discussed by Buchanan's (1975) constitutional economics. Many violations were explicitly regulated in the Old Testament. Tit-for-tat was at times levied with a 20-per cent tax, supposedly to increase deterrence (Numbers 5: 7). If nobody was available to receive a restitution payment for a wrongdoing someone had committed, the priests would take the payment. Inheritance arrangements set out property transfer within tribes (Numbers 27: 8–11).

This all implies that economic ordering regarding sanctions for contract violations strongly supported a behavioural value contract between God and Israel, which subsequently organized societal contracting among the Israelites. A behavioural economics was seemingly the foundation for a new societal contract for the people of Israel. The subsequent discusses in more detail the specific nature of incentive structures that can be found, firstly, for Israel as a group, secondly, for individual Israelites and thirdly, for the Levites.

As a group, Israel was asked by God to celebrate special public holidays, for example, the feast of unleavened bread (Exodus 34: 18, Leviticus 23: 6–8) or most importantly the 'Sabbath' (Exodus 34: 21, Leviticus 23: 3). Also, as a group, Israel was promised rewards for keeping God's rules. Rewards were rather generally specified (e.g. Leviticus 26: 1–13), especially in relation to the ideal of the 'land flowing with milk and honey' (see below). On the other hand, disobedience as a group was cruelly dealt with. If Israel doubted God's rule, terror similar to the plagues that had overcome Egypt would be thrown on Israel (e.g. Leviticus 26: 14–45; Numbers 11: 33, 12: 10; Deuteronomy 28: 15–68, 29: 23). I question in this respect the depth and strength of 'cardinal principles of biblical theology', as referred to by Sarna (1986: 119). The God of the Old Testament did not show in many instances 'divine attributes of ... forbearance under provocation, empathy, magnanimity, and caring for the needy and hungry', as Sarna (1986: 119) attributed to God. Rather, the God depicted in Exodus and later books often appeared as a vengeful and cruel God who severely punished his people for disobedience and moral disagreement, especially when they broke monotheistic rules that had been issued by God (the First Commandment). Even within the group of Israel an anti-pluralistic stance was then taken. And regarding tolerating pluralism, moral disagreement and ethnic diversity, the question of a universal stance of societal contracting arises the more forcefully when the issue of international societal contracting is looked at. With respect to the relationships between Israel and its neighbours, peaceful co-existence was hardly a goal: Israel was reminded that 'the Lord your God will put all these curses on your enemies who hate and persecute you' (Deuteronomy 30: 7).

Various laws were issued at the level of the individual Israelite too. For instance, the Old Testament extensively regulated borrowing and lending. In so-called jubilee years, which came every 50 years, all property in land and Hebrew servants who worked for an 'alien' would fall back to the original owner (Leviticus 25: 8, 47–55; for a review, see Schenker 1998). Specific redemption periods were specified for houses, which were one year (Leviticus 25: 30); or for Hebrew servants the redemption period was seven years (Exodus 21: 2–4; Deuteronomy 15: 12–15; see also Schenker 1998: 35–6). As mentioned above, every seven years, for Hebrew servants, there was a special jubilee year for debt cancellation (Deuteronomy 15: 1–3, 31: 10).

The priests' special role was already mentioned in the previous discussion. Their functions in bringing offerings to God were embodied in a quite complex system of incentive rules that governed payments to the priests. The priests' main tasks related to handing over sacrifices and offerings to God which other people had made (Leviticus Chapters 1–3, Leviticus 7: 31–4); to making economic valuations of houses and animals that were offered to God (Leviticus 27: 12–25); to supervising eating habits; to controlling health issues, for example, 'purification after childbirth' or 'infectious skin diseases' (e.g. Leviticus Chapters 11–13); or to engaging in judicial tasks (Deuteronomy 17: 9–10). Deuteronomy (16: 18–20) mentions here that wise and righteous figures were to be appointed as judges but qualifies that difficult cases were to be handled by the priests, the Levites (Deuteronomy 17: 9–10). For most of these tasks, the priests received certain fixed payments or percentage shares of the task performed, in many cases between one-fifth and one-tenth of the value of the task at hand (e.g. Leviticus 27: 30–1). Also, they received shares from yearly crops and from plunder that was accumulated during wars with other nations (e.g. Numbers 31: 52–5; Deuteronomy 14: 27–9). And in the case property was not redeemed after a certain period, it became the property of the priests (Leviticus 27: 21, Deuteronomy 26: 12). Regarding the distribution of land in Canaan, again the priests took a special role together with heads of clans and Joshua, the appointed successor of Moses (Numbers 34: 16–28). Land was to be split according to clan size (Numbers 33: 54) but special arrangements were made for the Levites. They would receive their own cities and pasture land (Numbers 35: 2–5). This is discussed in more detail in section 5.2.

  This host of incentive structures indicates that the newly independent nation of Israel placed quite some trust into economic rather than pure behavioural ordering and sanctioning when it came to societal contracting and solving the institutional problem. It is apparent that the Levites, once made into priests, acquired some rather special influence during this process. One can in this respect also be rather critical regarding Buber's (1982: 104) observation 'that a seminomadic life [as experienced during the exodus journey] does not encourage a high degree of cult practices and institutions.' Clearly, quite a number of rules regarding 'cult practices' and other issues of institutional governance can already be found during the Exodus journey, but, of course, institutional governance changed in nature and scope once the settlement process began (as discussed below in section 5.2).

Economic organization structures for the Exodus journey

The organization structures implemented by Moses for the Exodus journey deserve some special mentioning. They reflect economic governance, too, similar to the incentive structures discussed above. In considerable degrees, we here encounter the institutional problem in its special variant as the organizational problem. The organization structure chosen by Moses to organize the Exodus journey only loosely reflected a hierarchy. There was Moses at the top, followed by the group of the Levites, the priests, to whom a considerable amount of decision-making was delegated. Comparable to a chief executive that was surrounded by a team of central supporting staff (see Jones 1995: 151), Moses and the Levites had decision-making in their hands.

Geographically and hierarchically the other tribes were grouped around them further outwards (see Figure 5.1).

As discussed, initially such a controlling role of the Levites did not exist when the group of first-borns, the elders and the heads of all clans were involved in decision-making 'below' Moses (Exodus 18: 18–27; also Numbers 10: 4, 30: 1). Then, democratic decision-making and capability seemed to have been the key criteria for selecting persons regarding hierarchical positions (Exodus 18: 25–6). This is, to a degree, reminiscent of Joseph's rise to power in Egypt's hierarchy. However, in the end, Moses developed a rather autocratic, centralized approach to organizing the Exodus journey. This was reflected by setting up the centralized tent grouping arrangement with the Levites at the centre. Childs (1985: 109) spoke in this respect of Moses occupying a unique role which encompassed 'such a rich diversity as to include practically every other office within Israel'. The question has to be asked here why Moses chose such a structure. In this connection, Childs did not review economic reasons for the structure of the tent grouping arrangement. Childs also did not spell out the specific mechanism of nation-building in Exodus. As discussed, the tent grouping arrangement and the structural concentration of functions it reflected for the Levites is here of crucial importance. Organization theory literature details such issues in relation to a centralized, web-like power structure: 'Control is exercised by the centre largely through the selection of key individuals, by occasional forays from the centre or summonses to the centre' (Handy 1985: 189). These organizations 'have the ability to move quickly and can react well to threat or danger. Whether they do move or whether they do move in the right direction will, however, depend on the person or persons in the centre' (Handy 1985: 189). The number of men Moses commanded – Plaut (1981: 1034–5) counted 5,550 – certainly allowed such a clan-based approach. Besides mere opportunism, as reviewed above, there may have been good, organizational economic reasons for organizing the Exodus journey in a clan-based, less hierarchical manner. Moses' task was the organization of an uncertain journey with an unfixed time schedule for relocating his camp. Having priests only recruited from the tribe of the Levites allowed Moses to tightly control decision-making, cut down on information and communication costs and make decisions swiftly without much discussion and disputes to be expected. In this respect, one can agree with Weiser (1961: 13) that Israel grew together into a religious and national unity under Moses, although Weiser's unity thesis can be questioned for the re-settlement phase that followed Moses' departure (as discussed in section 5.2). Also with regard to the external environment, territory, unknown to the Israelites, had to be passed through during the Exodus journey, ranging from deserts, to dangerous mountains and land occupied by belligerent tribes. For this task at hand, with its specific journey attributes and with internal dissent looming, the hypothesis can be put forward that transaction cost and stability advantages arose with a clan-like, family business-like organization structure, as described by Handy. I suggest here a close relationship between task and organization structure and external environment (see also Wagner-Tsukamoto 2003: Chapter 7; Burns 1990; Burns and Stalker 1961).

Especially in relation to the 'small firm-like', web-like organization structure metaphor, a contemporary relevance of tribal organization structures and arrangements during the Exodus journey can be made out. Rogerson (1998: 72) here seemed to underestimate the prevalence of tribal structures in modern society, for example, family-run, clan-based organizations. In the arena of small enterprises they are widespread and parallels can in this respect be drawn between organization structures in Old Testament stories and contemporary management practices.

Capital exchange in social interactions

The new societal contract that was established through the Ten Commandments was embedded in various capital exchange transactions between God and the Israelites. For their spiritual belief into God, the Israelites were to gain prosperity in various ways, as Deuteronomy (30: 9) stressed: prosperity resulting from work (craftsmanship); prosperity resulting from farming (livestock management; harvesting crops); and prosperity resulting from fertility (Israel multiplying as a people). A behavioural societal contract, as outlined by the Ten Commandments and here especially the First Commandment, was thus linked to a capital exchange model.

Societal contracting discussed in the aftermath of the Exodus also reveals in another way some substantial engagement in economic transactions rather than pure religious practices of healing and meditation. This is reflected by the kind of offerings to God the Levites were to make. Offerings were not prayers or mere wishes but they were mostly animals or other types of foods. And from the offerings the priests took their share (Leviticus Chapters 1–8, Numbers 7: 12–88, 18: 21–7, 28: 3–31, 29: 1–39). Capital exchange in a comparatively mundane, economic way manifests itself here.

Equally, the redemption laws discussed above imply capital exchange among the Israelites. For different types of property, different types of capital exchange transactions were spelt out. The capital exchange types mentioned in the Old Testament refer to property in land, houses, persons and debt. This hints at a comparatively high societal development of economic exchange within Israel already during the Exodus journey. Right of passage is another capital transaction that is mentioned for the Exodus journey. For instance, the Israelites had to compensate Esau's descendants and Lot's descendants for crossing their land on the way to Canaan (Deuteronomy 2: 5–6, 9, 19).

Slave trading without the possibility that slaves could be redeemed or redeem themselves are mentioned too (Leviticus 25: 44–6). Apparently, the Old Testament makes a fine distinction between servants or serfs, on the one hand, and slaves, on the other. As discussed, for servants, redemption periods were spelt out (see above), but not necessarily for slaves. This seems to be misstated by Wilson (1997: 29) when he suggested that in jubilee years even slaves were to be freed.

Human capital of a different type is examined in the Old Testament when capabilities of craftsmen and judges become a topic. The selection of craftsmen for the building of religious artefacts is not determined by tribal membership but by capabilities (Exodus 35: 31–5, 36: 1–5). Similarly, judges were to be selected from all tribes of Israel (Exodus 18: 25–6). It appears that especially in the early phase of the Exodus, capabilities rather than tribal membership played a key role in determining the selection of a person for a post at hand. However, as discussed above, once the Exodus journey progressed, the Levites took over most special functions, from craftsmanship relating to the tabernacle and the tent of meeting to religious judgement tasks.

Mutual gains as interaction outcome

Regarding the earnings obtained by the priests, I previously referred to the Levites' economic man-behaviour. The incentive rules governing sacrifices enabled the priests to accumulate wealth beyond what was needed on a daily basis of living and surviving. They clearly occupied a very special position as Moses' and Aaron's 'sons'. This interpretation stresses more worldly purposes of sacrifices. Wealth accumulation by the priests and, on a more positive note, the generation of mutual gains between those who sacrificed and the priests can be diagnosed. Mutual gains arose regarding social purposes and cultural integration by means of sacrifice rituals, which also supported nation-building. This view stresses a worldly and possibly even 'greedy' role played by those who administered sacrifices. This is in contrast to the usual discussion led in the theological literature. For example, the theological literature stresses symbolic meanings of sacrifice, and here especially spiritual ones, such as imitating God by means of sacrifice and maintaining the presence of God through sacrifice rituals (Klawans 2001: 137, 139–40). As far as anti-priestly considerations are made, they refer to concepts of guilt in relation to an interpretation of sacrifice as 'scapegoating'. Klawans (2001: 138) is here critical of some of the theological literature before he outlines his view on the nature and role of sacrifice (namely as means of imitating God and maintaining the presence of God).

The arrangements made in the wake of the Exodus concerning the Levites' roles as priests may not reflect the most democratic solution, but despite that, it seemed to assure mutual gains as interaction outcome, at least to a degree high enough that capital transactions materialized in the first place. The Levites enacted as priests God's commands and this provided stability in social interactions for all Israelites. In this respect, the priests performed a public service: The value contracts they offered linked to a behavioural economics and ensured the solution of critical problems at hand, from health care problems to jurisdictional problems. A new societal contract was thus formed. Then, the nation-building problem was also solved, at least in a rudimentary manner. Israel grouped together. On the other hand, the priests gained, too, through the various taxation and compensation arrangements that were in place for the services they conducted.

The ultimate goal of Israel's Exodus journey, of course, mirrors the vision of the Paradise, the land flowing with milk and honey, a land of peace and abundant prosperity (Leviticus 26: 4–6; Numbers 13: 27; 14: 8; 16: 14; Deuteronomy 6: 3, 24; 11: 9; 27: 3; 28: 11; 30: 5, 9, 15; 31: 20; also 2 Kings 18: 31–2). These goals reflect economic ideals and they guided the Exodus journey throughout. As a group, Israel expected to receive these rewards for believing in their God, ultimately crossing over to the 'good land' at the Jordan, where there was no scarcity (Deuteronomy 4: 21; 8: 7–9, 17–18). A value contract was thus linked to the vision of (re-)entering an economic paradise and in this respect the Old Testament returns again to a behavioural economics, specifically a religious economics, in order to regain the paradise that was lost twice before – first, in the Paradise story, when God confronted Adam and Eve in the context of an ill-devised property rights arrangement regarding the divine trees, and second, in the Exodus story, when, to a considerable degree, a value fundamentalist God did not help Israel and Egypt resolve interaction dilemmas and maintain mutual prosperity.

The loss of pluralism as interaction condition

In their escalating conflict over population management problems and industrial relations problems, Egypt and Israel had lost – driven by a value fundamentalist God – pluralism as an interaction condition.

Moses and the pharaoh had not succeeded to engage in successful societal contracting that could have left Egypt and Israel living in peace and harmony side by side. A critical question for the Exodus journey is whether pluralism as an interaction condition was regained for Israel's in-group interactions and for its interactions with other nations.

Regarding in-group interactions, the outcome of the golden calf incident was a discomforting one for those who supported a pluralistic Israel, which would tolerate diversity and moral disagreement among its members. Once the First Commandment was broken, that there should be only one God, those Israelites involved in the golden calf festival were killed (Exodus 32: 4–8, 28). Religious fundamentalism and severe, deadly sanctions for those who broke the First Commandment were at the heart of the new nation state of Israel and the new societal contract it had closed in the wake of the Exodus journey. Theological interpretations of the golden calf incident, e.g. Kugel (1997: 423–6) or Sarna (1986: 215–20), too easily overlook its anti-pluralistic nature. Another dramatic example of an anti-pluralistic stance for societal contracting among the Israelites is the killing of Aaron's sons, Moses' nephews. God killed them because of a ceremonial mistake they made during an offering ritual (Leviticus 10: 1–2). A further, good example is the earth opening up and swallowing Korah, Dathan and Abiram for being unfaithful to God (Numbers 16: 31–5). Also, an indication of a comparatively anti-pluralistic stance is the aforementioned organization of priestly functions in the hands of the Levites. This deprived the elders and the other tribes' first-borns of their positions of influence (Leviticus 9: 1; Numbers 1: 47–54; see also above).

These anti-pluralistic stances were renewed throughout the books of Exodus, Leviticus, Numbers and Deuteronomy and later books (Leviticus 19: 4, Numbers 33: 52, Deuteronomy 9: 21; 12: 31; 13: 6–11; see also Valiquette 1999: 55, 59). Rebellions against God were cruelly and swiftly dealt with on the Exodus journey (e.g. Numbers 16: 31, 49; 17: 31–5). This is in stark contrast to the intervention of God in the Joseph story, the approach of Joseph to problem solving and his successful handling of pluralism as an interaction condition while being the leader of Egypt's industrial hierarchies. It is more than an understatement of theological interpreters in this respect to say that a violation of the commandment to honour no other gods beside the God of Israel was left to individual conscience (Sarna 1986: 172). The golden calf incident and many other examples demonstrated the opposite.

Israel's religious fundamentalist stance and its value contract with an apparently anti-pluralistic God are further illustrated by the kind of relations it sought with other nations. The 'war of all' was to be fought out with other nations; Hobbesian anarchy reigned; other nations were to be plundered and the Old Testament explicitly forbade Israel to make treaties with other nations. Anarchic, precontract natural distribution states, as abstractly described by Buchanan (1975), would thus rule Israel's social 'exchange' with other nations. No thought is given to 'disarmament contracts' through which a state of anarchy could have been overcome to the mutual advantage of both Israel and the nations and tribes it interacted with. Rather, other nations should be enslaved and if this was not possible, their members should be killed (Exodus 34: 12, 15, Leviticus 25: 44–6, Numbers 31: 3–18; Deuteronomy 7: 1–2, 16; 20: 10–11, 17; 23: 6). On a milder economic note, which hints at the emergence of more democratic societal contracting, Deuteronomy (28: 12) allowed lending to other nations, but still forbade borrowing from them.

In general, this approach to international relations can hardly be a role model for ensuring harmony and peace. Mutual gains here do not result as interaction outcome. Rather win/loss – or loss/loss – games are played. It is safe to conclude they do not provide a sound foundation for cooperative, stable and long-term international relations. Theological interpreters frequently take in this respect a rather naïve and rosy view of the monotheism that was established in the wake of the Exodus. Sarna (1986: 150) spoke in this connection of the monumental achievements of the 'spiritual titan' Moses through whom God communicated his monotheistic rules. As indicated, monotheism, as set out in the Old Testament, implied an anti-pluralistic stance for social ordering within Israel's society as well as for social interactions between Israel and other nations. For resolving social conflict in modern contexts, where pluralism, ethnic diversity and the tolerance of moral disagreement are present or even desirable interaction conditions, this approach quickly runs into problems (see also Wagner-Tsukamoto 2008a, 2008c, 2008e, 2007a and 2003). It is especially from here that the previous chapter developed a non-hero thesis for Moses and a decline thesis for the stories of the Exodus and what followed after.

5.2   Institutional ordering after the Exodus journey

The Exodus journey ended when Israel began to capture land that God had promised to Israel. Then, captured land was divided up among the tribes of Israel. The purpose of institutional ordering and societal contracting changed. It was no longer focused on the organization of an uncertain journey through unknown territory but the distribution of land and the setting up of new institutional structures for establishing and governing a settled society. Issues of state formation arose. The organization of its key institutional structures now seemed to follow a more democratic, more hierarchical pattern as compared to the centralized, clan-based arrangement which just saw the Levites at the centre of decision-making. As long as the various tribes managed to hold on to captured land, some quite sophisticated institutional structures emerged. However, as the following discusses, at other times the 'war of all' broke out regarding scarce, fertile land both among Israelite tribes and between neighbouring nations and the Israelites. This destabilized and even derailed societal contracting, institutional ordering and cooperative interactions.

Dilemmatic interest conflicts after the first settlements: The 'war of all' breaking out

After the Israelites had reached the Promised Land east and west of the Jordan, they began to fight against other nations and tribes who lived there, and as Rogerson and Davies (1989: 63) or Kuan (2001: 142–3) noted there were many powerful neighbouring nations that surrounded Israel. In the Promised Land, the commons dilemma and a population management problem were seemingly encountered: There were too many who wanted to live in a limited area of fertile land. Social conflict erupted and common pool problems were ever-present and interaction conditions of famines and droughts are mentioned throughout the Old Testament (in the settlement phase, e.g. 2 Kings 2: 19; 4: 38).

After Moses' death, Joshua became the leader of the Israelites and under his reign a war for land and water was fully played out. The book of Joshua, but also subsequent books, are filled with violent accounts which illustrate the war-like interactions between Israel and its neighbours (e.g. 2 Kings 2: 19; 3: 5–19, 24–5; Jeremiah 25: 11–14). Here it shows up that Jacob's warning was more than justified not to bestow leadership functions on the Levites because of their belligerent inclinations. One of the most blatant calls for this war, in which even unsuspecting, peaceful tribes and nations were to be slaughtered by the Israelites, is provided in Isaiah, Chapters 20–4. Illustrative is the following quote:

> See, the Lord is going to lay waste the earth and devastate it; he will ruin its face and scatter its inhabitants – it will be the same for priest as for people, for master as for servant, for mistress as for maid, for seller as for buyer, for borrower as for lender, for debtor as for creditor. The earth will be completely laid waste and totally plundered.
>
> (Isaiah 24: 1–3)

In the wake of the resettlement process when Israel tried to regain its claimed homeland, the result was a nearly continuous state of war with games of attack, revenge and counter-revenge being played out. The painful diagnosis has to be made that the book of Joshua offers 'a vision of violence' (Briend 2000: 378). The 'Hobbesian jungle', or the precontract, anarchic, natural distribution state, as Buchanan (1975) also referred to the war of all, is here clearly visible. In the book of Joshua, Israel nearly always succeeded, at least initially, to overpower and evict other nations from their claimed homeland. But time and again overpowered nations fought back and then frequently Israel lost out too (Briend 2000: 371, 376–9; Plaut 1981: 1230, 1381). In such times of extreme warfare, even peaceful gestures were easily misinterpreted as acts of warfare; for example, King David's bearers of a message of sympathy were viewed as spies (2 Samuel 10: 2–5).

At its most extreme, the 'war of all' could be observed as civil war among Israelite clans and tribes (Judges 12: 1–2, 20: 17–47; 1 Samuel 22: 13–14, 18) and warfare even entered families. For example, King David had to flee because one of his sons was plotting against him, or King Solomon got his brother executed (2 Samuel Chapters 15–16; 1 Kings 2: 22–4). We re-encounter here the anarchic, precontract scenario in the aftermath of Adam and Eve's exit from Paradise, as depicted in the Cain-and-Abel story, with even family ties breaking down as institutional regulative.

Besides attacks from the tribes that lived in Israel's homeland, attacks had to be fended off from foreign armies. In terms of geopolitical location described in the Old Testament, Israel was here in a weak position with Lebanon and Assyria in the north, Babylon and Persia to the east and Egypt to the south (Kuan 2001: 142–3, 146; Rogerson and Davies 1989: 63). Once these superpowers formed alliances, for instance, Egypt with Assyria (2 Kings 23: 29), there was little room left for Israel to manoeuvre. Examples of extremely futile outcomes for Israel were here its deportation into exile to Assyria, with Hosea being the last king of the then Israel (2 Kings 17: 6, 8, 23). Or, the deportation of the inhabitants of Judah and Jerusalem and their treasures to Babylon after they lost out to King Nebuchadnezzar (2 Kings 24: 10–14; 25: 11–21). Apparently, all warring parties approached the land distribution problem as a zero-sum game, with crude loss/win games being played out to the bitter end for one side.

Regarding its preparation for war with other nations, the Israelite tribes encountered a dilemma regarding common and conflicting interests: They had a common interest to act as one nation when it came to the defending of newly acquired land since this increased the prospects of success. But there were conflicting interests, too, namely to opt out from helping other Israelite tribes when it became apparent that the attack of a foreign army did not aim at one's own tribe and territory. Constitutional contracts and nation-building arrangements, such as an integrated defence policy and coordinated defence structures, were clearly needed to bridge these interest conflicts. However, one key reason for failures in Israel's warfare was its lacking structural unification of its tribes. In many instances, the Israelites fought as tribal factions rather than as one nation. Childs (1985: 113, 115) correctly identified in this respect the 'loss of a unified leadership … and the collapse of the vision of Joshua for the nation' and the 'tragedy of the nation'. Especially after the settlement process had begun, societal contracting and nation-building took a step back when the so-called twelve-tribe league (Childs 1985: 178) was the governance structure of Israel. Buber (1982: 78) similarly admitted that under Joshua's leadership the continued unity of Israel only partially succeeded. Seemingly, Israel entered a phase of claimed freedom, after its exit from Egypt, which was even more problematic than the kind of already problematic freedom it had experienced under Moses' leadership. I discuss this in more detail below when incentive structures are reviewed.

A contributing factor to the war-like status of affairs with other nations was the failure of Israelite tribes to negotiate peace settlements or strategic alliances with neighbouring tribes. This was largely due to God's command not to make treaties with other nations, especially with those nations that occupied Israel's homeland. In contrast, when Israel built complex institutional structures and formed strategic alliances and trade alliances with neighbouring tribes, seemingly against God's advice, periods of prosperity and peace were enjoyed. King David's and King Solomon's reigns are the best examples. Under Solomon, a strategic alliance existed between Israel and Egypt (1 Kings 3: 1); Solomon made a treaty with Hiram (1 Kings 5: 12, 10: 22); a trade treaty organized the exchange of goods between Solomon and the Queen of Sheba (1 Kings 10: 10, 13) and between Solomon and Arabian kings (1 Kings 10: 14). Kuan (2001: 143, 146, 150) discussed similar examples of trade relations between Israel and the Phoenicians which benefited both sides. Such alliances resolved the institutional problem in international perspective and interactions were stabilized through mutually beneficial, economic exchange. At times, later books mention that war alliances were formed, for example between Israel, Judah and Edom to fight against Moab (2 Kings 3: 9) but this also hints that the then Israel and Judah were no longer one united state as they had been under David and Solomon.

Incentive structures in the resettlement phase

After the Exodus journey, the 'assembly' became a key decision-making tool for Israel as a whole: It comprised the elders, officials, judges and priests (Joshua 8: 33, 9: 14–15, 20: 4, 23: 1–2, 24: 1; Judges 11: 10, 21: 7). It was the assembly which decided the distribution of land, with three men being appointed from each tribe to do a land survey and Joshua, as the then political leader, making final allotments to each tribe (Joshua 18: 1–6). Political leadership rested with the head of the assembly, first so-called judges and later kings (Judges 2: 16, 4: 5, 9: 6; 1 Samuel 7: 15; see also Schmidt 1984: 33–4). Only with the later emergence of the institutional position 'king' was a new suprastructure imposed on the tribes of Israel (see below).

Step by step, the federal nation state is here emerging in the Old Testament, although strong integrative functions and mechanisms at the top were not available for a long time after the Exodus journey. Only with the coming of the monarchy under Saul, David and Solomon this changed. In contrast, the egalitarian, non-hierarchical phase Israel went through after Joshua (Childs 1985: 176) was too federal in a sense.

After Moses' death and after the end of the Exodus journey, societal contracting and nation-building had to be reorganized, moving it from a clan-based power structure of Moses' time to a hierarchical, bureaucratic structure in later times. In the book of Joshua, the new, federal structures that were set up, such as the assembly, still implied that the tribes lacked a suprastructure which could integrate decision-making and make them act quickly as one nation. Undoubtedly, as noted above, there was a need to (self-)organize decision-making as one nation, through calling on the assembly. However, in Joshua, this implied time-consuming and transaction cost-inefficient manoeuvring by the clans when they had to act as one unit. In the book of Joshua, the vision of one nation disintegrated, as it had existed in Genesis and as it had prevailed during the Exodus journey, although in different organizational forms. To a considerable degree, in the book of Joshua, the Israelites deunified. The lacking structural unification of Israel as a newly founded nation state relates to its dissolving power structures once the settlement process began. After the Exodus journey, the organization structures of the Israelite society changed. Land was distributed to the 12 tribes of Israel and in relation hereto each tribe set up its *own* organization structure, a mixture of clan-based and hierarchical structures. There was a leader appointed and a group of elders and judges advised on key decisions. Buber (1982: 78) speaks of a 'tribal amphictyony', Childs (1985: 113, 178) of a 'league of twelve tribes' (see also Buber 1982: 78).

Regarding the integration of the 'league of twelve tribes', its structural set-up was too federalist and not constructive regarding nation-building. Weiser (1961: 155) can rightly claim that in a basic sense the tribal union of Israel existed in some form long before the coming of the kingdom of Solomon and David. This is especially true for the Exodus journey under Moses' reign. However, Weiser's (1961: 13) unity thesis for the people of Israel is more difficult to uphold for the period that followed the Exodus journey. The available coordination mechanisms for constitutional contracting described in the Old Testament after the Exodus journey do not support the idea of a tightly integrated, well functioning nation. The books of Joshua up to Judges and even beyond are illustrative. Israel reflected a collection of tribes, which shared a common history, specifically the Exodus journey, but otherwise acted independently and lacked a federalist metastructure, for example, integrated defence strategies and policies, to hold them together. Insufficient and incomplete constitutional contracting was the major source of this sour state of affairs. Mayes (1983: 59, 68, 81) here suggested that the picture of Israel as a divided nation dominates (the book of Judges): 'The people does not appear as a single whole; tribes and small tribal groups act in their own self-interest' (Mayes 1983: 59). The problematic occurrence of economic man-behaviour is here referred to. Hawk (2003) pointed out in this connection that Israel still underwent a transformation from an old kin-based social order, as it could be found under Moses' leadership, to a new civic, monarchic society, as it would come later under David and Solomon. In the book of Judges, however, 'everyone did as he saw fit' (Judges 21: 25; see also Hawk 2003: 79), with even intertribal warfare being commonplace. This holds important lessons for state formation and the apparent state formation theory that is here advanced in the Old Testament.

In figurative, metaphorical language, the Old Testament illustrates this lacking structural integration of Israel through the story of the cutting up of a concubine into twelve pieces and sending them to the twelve leaders of the tribal areas of Israel (Judges 19: 29, 20: 8). This story reflects a dramatic event. After a Levite's concubine was assaulted, the Levites resorted to this drastic action. This was a call to unite and fight as one unit, in this case even against an 'internal' enemy, the Benjaminites, who had assaulted the Levite's concubine: 'Danger came from within [the tribes of Israel]' (Mayes 1983: 135). In the story of the assaulted concubine, it was a Levite who called upon the assembly to initiate the integration of the tribes. This can be interpreted as a nostalgic reminder of the Levite priests' previous key role (during the Exodus journey) in initiating and communicating action plans to the tribes.

During the Exodus journey, the priests and the Levites had had a stronghold over decision-making and political influence. However, once the settlement process began, the priests' and the Levites' influence was breaking away. In the process of changing governance structures, the priests and Levites were distributed across the territories of all 12 tribes. They got their own cities in each clan's homeland (Joshua Chapter 21; Judges 17: 9–10). This was probably meant to sustain the strong power position they held before and during the Exodus journey and to integrate the 12 clans into one nation. But as it turned out, this distribution of the Levites and priests did not consolidate the power position they had previously enjoyed. Indeed, the distribution dispersed their influence and, as far as power and influence in institutional decision-making and societal contracting are concerned, they are hardly mentioned ever after the book of Exodus. This is not only reflected by the nearly constant lamenting of unfaithfulness of Israel's leaders when it comes to other gods beside Israel's God but also by the very institutional structures that were set up. As mentioned, each of the 12 tribes appointed an own leader (Joshua 4: 4–6, 14: 1, 22: 14, 30).

We can find another metaphorical indication of the (too) loose self-organization of constitutional contracting among the Israelite tribes after the Exodus journey when Saul cuts up two oxen and sends the pieces throughout Israel in order to call upon the tribes of Israel to unite as one army:

> 'This is what will be done to the oxen of anyone who does not follow Saul and Samuel.' Then the terror of the Lord fell on the people, and they turned out as one man. When Saul mustered them at Bezek, the men of Israel numbered three hundred thousand and the men of Judah thirty thousand.
>
> (1 Samuel 11: 7–8)

In this instance, draconic appeal in the tradition of theology or behavioural economics rather than institutional economic integration and hierarchical sanctioning in the tradition of organizational economics made Israel's army unite. The likely ineffectiveness and inefficiency of this self-organizing procedure is hinted at when the tribes of Israel finally ask Samuel to appoint a king, replacing the existing system of judges as leaders of Israel: 'Appoint a king to lead us, such as all the other nations have' (1 Samuel 8: 5).

An obedience element, as it is characteristic for behavioural economics, can be made out too in the story of the cutting up of the oxen. The key role of obedience to God is stressed time and again. Rather than interest equilibration, behavioural intervention is favoured. As noted before, after the Exodus, obedience (to the Ten Commandments) was the key maxim of institutional ordering and interaction between God and man:

> Does the Lord delight in burnt offerings and sacrifices as much as in obeying the voice of the Lord? To obey is better than sacrifice, and to heed is better than the fat of rams.... Because you have rejected the word of the Lord, he has rejected you as king.
>
> (1 Samuel 15: 22–3)

Saul lost as a result his position as king.

Only under the kingdoms of David and more so Solomon a strong executive leadership emerged and a strong nation was built. Then, the king basically had a split function: Besides justice jobs, he was the political leader who would organize warfare (1 Samuel 8: 11–18, 2 Samuel 15: 4–6). Especially Solomon idealized the successful king regarding both judiciary and political functions. Religious leadership was also expected from the king but increasingly with the coming of prophets and seers from the books of the Kings onwards, political and religious functions were split. Especially Solomon imported 'foreign administrative structures' (Childs 1985: 179; see also Schmidt 1984: 35) and his introduction of a standing army and a strong governmental body contributed to the 'social stratification' of society (Childs 1985: 181, 184). Solomon imposed a suprastructure in the form of a non-tribal governmental hierarchy (1 Kings 4: 2–19, 9: 22–3, 10: 5; see also Plaut 1981: 1424). This complemented existing tribal structures (1 Kings 8: 1) but more so shifted an old social order that was based on kinship to a new social order that was based on political and economic institutions, namely the monarchy and the structures that came with it (Hawk 2003: 84–6). In Solomon's hierarchical organization, similarly as in Egypt's industrial hierarchies as met in the Joseph story, personal skilfulness and capabilities rather than tribal affiliation or any other feature determined promotion (1 Kings 11: 28). The tall hierarchy erected by Solomon reflected the great wealth, wide geographical expansion and high political influence Israel gained under his reign. Then, religious functions and the location of priests, which were still supplied by the Levites, were also centralized, being locally concentrated around the temple that housed the ark (Plaut 1981: 1401, 1424).

The implications and hypotheses derived from Figure 3.2 can seemingly, in degrees, be also projected to the phases of the Exodus journey under Moses' leadership, the rebirth of Israel under Joshua, and the political economic advances of Israel under Solomon. One important implication of the development towards the constitutional monarchy under Solomon was:

> Deuteronomy (16: 18 to 18: 22; 19: 1 to 25: 19) then 'aimed not simply at proper establishment of the centralized cult, but rather more comprehensively at the whole religious and social order in Israel: the intention now is to legislate for an integrated and unified society with a constitutional monarchy'.
>
> (Mayes 1999: 70)

Apparently, for administering a huge empire, simple tribal structures were economically inefficient and ineffective. Regarding institutional change, 'the monarchic period was undoubtedly marked by technological and economic development that put considerable strain on traditional social forms' (Mayes 1993: 27). It is fair to say that in the monarchic period described in the Old Testament the economic system then dominated. Worldviews and cultural convictions were relegated to the private level. The monarchy rose as constitutional governance form. This is in contrast to the traditional society, as it had still existed during Israel's Exodus journey and during the early settlement phase. Then, cultural convictions and worldviews had still dominated the economic system (Mayes 1993: 27).

Another important implication of the emerging dominance of the economic system and the related relegation of worldviews to the private level is the rise of pluralism as an interaction condition. This is discussed in more detail below, for example, when King Solomon's open-minded approach towards foreign gods is reviewed.

Although this is not the purpose of my book, in historical perspective, the rise of the monarchy in the highlands of Palestine at the beginning of the Iron Age can be related to specific economic, environmental changes that then occurred:

> The expansion of population made voluntary cooperation more costly than a governmental structure for protecting the incentive to produce and invest from theft. Both for purposes of internal security and to repel external enemies attracted by the agricultural surplus, monarchy arose in the highlands of Palestine.
>
> (Muth 1997: 90)

This historical explanation of the rise of the monarchy is compatible with the historical–textual explanations the present study offers for the kingdoms described in the Old Testament. Issues of internal and external security were frequently raised in the stories of the Old Testament. The story of the concubine reflected an internal problem whereas the story of the cut-up oxen reflected an external security problem. Both stories touch upon societal contracting. Problems of spying behaviour and the secret infiltration of cities, as discussed in many stories, relates to external security problems, too. As Muth (1997: 89), again in historical perspective, hinted, the monarchy here offered a more cost-efficient way for protection than alternative forms of government.

Capital exchange in the resettlement phase

Apart from social order and the institutional integration of society, which can be discussed as social capital (see above), the most valuable asset to be exchanged and distributed after the Exodus was land. After the Exodus journey, the Israelites captured land from tribes who lived in their promised homeland. In Joshua, Chapter 13 spelled out how land was distributed among the tribes of Israel. Specific pieces of land were allocated to specific tribes. Only the Levites, from whom priests were recruited, received no land. Rather, they inherited the offerings the other tribes made to God. In addition, the Levites got plenty of cities allocated in the lands of the other tribes plus pasturelands for their livestock (Joshua Chapter 21). This ensured the distribution of priests across all Israelite tribes.

An altogether different type of capital acquired and distributed reflected plunder. It was in many instances taken when land and cities were conquered by the Israelites (e.g. 2 Samuel 8: 7–8). However, the taking of plunder, which had been deemed unlawful by God, was punished with death (Joshua 7: 19–25). Or, unlawful plundering was punished with the taking away of positional power; for example, Saul lost, for the time being, his position as king (1 Samuel 15: 20); or, the greediness of King David was punished with the death of one of his sons (2 Samuel 12: 1–18). On the other hand, success in warfare was rewarded with great riches. A key example here is the killing of Goliath by David. In return for his brave act, David received great wealth, the king's daughter and tax exemption for his entire family clan (1 Samuel 17: 25). In times of peace, gifts were given to maintain peaceful relations (2 Samuel 7: 9). Most of the plunder and gifts went to the Levites as offerings to God (2 Samuel 8: 11).

Time capital is an issue, too, in the stories after the Exodus journey. It becomes a big topic in relation to the longevity of leaders. Old age is clearly viewed as a reward, mainly one for obeying God's rules. In this respect, God again seems to have shared out, in degrees, the paradisal good x 'eternal life', as it already was the case in Genesis, for instance, for Noah and Abraham. But there were exceptions of highly success-ful leaders, such as Solomon, who lived into old age and who had not obeyed God rules. God did not punish Solomon during his long lifetime for not obeying some of the Ten Commandments, especially the First Commandment.

Under King Solomon 'international' trade bloomed (1 Kings 10: 10-29). This is an indication of peaceful, political and economic relations with other neighbouring nations (see also below). It also reflects a deeply economic approach to capital utilization, namely that asset specificity in skills application rose and that the task at hand determined how the best suitable capital would be drawn upon. For example, skilled human capital was imported from Hiram to build the bronze statues for Solomon's temple because Hiram had the best bronze sculpture makers of the time (1 Kings 7: 14, also 10: 22). Or, the kind of goods exchanged between Solomon and the Queen of Sheba (1 Kings 10: 10, 13) and between Solomon and Arabian kings (1 Kings 10: 14) reflected highly asset specific goods. For instance, for the goods delivered by the Queen of Sheba, the Old Testament mentions that these contained the finest spices then available. This exchange of trade goods is a very dif-ferent type of institutional interaction than the violent acquisition of land after the Exodus journey. It reflects a maturing phase regarding the developmental stage of Israel as a nation state with trade treaties and treaties of friendship increasingly replacing acts of warfare.

Mutual gains: Zero-sum and nonzero-sum games after the Exodus journey

The key game 'played' throughout the Old Testament, and especially after the Exodus journey, is one of conquering foreign land and captur-ing other nations, their kings and people and taking away their riches. This reflects a zero-sum game. Mutual gains can then not be realized. If societal contracting and social interactions are approached in this way, there can only be one winner and one loser, but not two winners or two losers at the same time. In Joshua, Israel frequently won such zero-sum games but in later books the picture changed. At times Israel wins, at other times their opponents win and it is difficult to see one side emerg-ing as the overall winner. If anything, Israel more and more emerged as a loser in these zero-sum approach to handling social conflict and societal contracting, especially once the Assyrian and the Babylonian exiles occurred.

The reason given by the Old Testament for the Israelites ultimately losing these zero-sum games is their lacking commitment to the value contract they made with God under Moses' leadership, especially with regard to the First Commandment. If only Israel had obeyed this commandment of not having other gods beside its God, so the Old Testament argues, it would have been 'blessed' with 'great wealth – with large herds in livestock, with silver, gold, bronze and iron, and a great quantity of clothing' and 'long life' (Joshua 22: 8; 1 Kings 3: 13). But looking back at Joseph and Genesis, it can be critically asked why the Old Testament from the book of Exodus onwards failed to consider economic policies for institutional ordering and societal contracting, especially since this approach had proven to be so successful in Genesis for the transformation of zero-sum games into nonzero-sum ones and the tolerance of value pluralism.

There are a couple of minor exceptions to these zero-sum games. One is the capturing of the ark by the Philistines. A loss/loss outcome can here be observed. Once the Philistines put the ark into their temple, the statue of their god collapsed. A win/win outcome, although not fairly balanced, could be observed when Judah paid off King Hazael of Aram for not attacking Jerusalem. At the price of the temple treasures of King Solomon the city of Jerusalem was so saved from being attacked. A balanced example of a win/win outcome is the sparing of Rahab's life for protecting two Israelite spies (Joshua 2: 17–21, 6: 23, 25). The Gibeonites' deception also yields a win/win outcome, but again a not fairly balanced one: The Gibeonites kept their land (Israel lost this land) but in return the Gibeonites had to serve the Israelites as woodcutters and water-carriers (Joshua Chapter 9).

A major exception to the win/loss games otherwise played after the Exodus journey are the treaties made by King Solomon and the exile treaty offered by the King of Assyria (see also Schmidt 1984: 21, 76). Like under no other king, Solomon's reign created wealth and prosperity for the Israelites and here institutional ordering and societal contracting in the tradition of Joseph and Genesis can be observed. A considerable element of Solomon's success was his ability to transform zero-sum games into nonzero-sum ones. He did so by means of treaties with other nations. King Solomon made an alliance with the pharaoh of Egypt (1 Kings 3: 1); other nations 'listened' to Solomon (1 Kings 4: 31, 34); there was a trade treaty between Solomon and Hiram (1 Kings 5: 12); and goods were exchanged between Solomon and the Queen of Sheba (1 Kings 10: 10, 13). In general, international trade was blooming under Solomon (1 Kings 10: 10–29). Then, Israel achieved the land where milk and honey flowed, and its territory extended to the full size of the Promised Land (see also Plaut 1981: 1239). The ideal of the community of nations and the achievement of mutual gains through economic transactions is touched upon. Besides his conquests, key elements of Solomon's success seem to have been his ability to make treaties with other nations as well as to tolerate value pluralism, specifically foreign religions, under his reign. In this respect, Solomon seemingly broke more fundamentalist biblical laws, especially the First Commandment, as specified in the books of Exodus, Leviticus and Judges.

After King Solomon, international trade collapsed (1 Kings 22: 48) and Israel was thrown back to zero-sum encounters with other nations. It was threatened by exile and then exile in prosperous neighbouring nations appeared the only way to realize the vision of the land where milk and honey flowed (2 Kings 18: 31–2).

Resettlement crusades, institutional ordering and the instrumental role of economic man

The settlement process in Israel's homeland required nation-building and new societal contracts. Predatory, economic man-behaviour is here rather bluntly encountered when other nations are attacked and plundered by Israel. The goal of the resettlement crusades was to conquer the Promised Land by means of a 'holy war', destroy their people and avoid its gods (Mayes 1983: 34, 42–3). Economic man shows up more succinctly when, through warfare, institutional arrangements of other nations were tested out. The Israelites examined how stable and powerful the institutional structures of other nations were. This theme is encountered throughout the resettlement process, which really never ended once the Israelites had entered their promised homeland. Of course, in turn, the Israelites faced the same test for plundering and the testing out of stability of their institutional structures when foreign armies attacked. From here normative implications regarding nation-building can be derived.

The books of Joshua and Judges and most books that follow are full of violent accounts in which opportunistic, predatory economic man shows up in the worst forms. Various examples were given above. Another excellent example is in the book of Judges when the Laish people and their land is attacked:

> Then they [the Israelites] … went on to Laish, against a peaceful and unsuspecting people. They attacked them with the sword and burnt down their city. There was no-one to rescue them because they [the

Laish people] lived a long way from Sidon and had no relationship with anyone else.

(Judges 18: 27–8; see also Judges 18: 7)

The institutional arrangements of the peaceful Laish people were seemingly insufficient to defend themselves as a tribe or nation. They apparently had no army of their own and had not built war alliances with other tribes or nations. In this situation, a self-interested aggressor had easy play. In normative, institutional perspective, this implies that institutional arrangements should be tested out for opportunistic, economic man-behaviour. Social conflict and predation should be expected, as Buchanan's constitutional economics so forcefully stressed. So, whenever stories of plundering are discussed (e.g. Joshua 6: 19, 24, 8: 27; see also above) questions loom in the background regarding institutional ordering and controlling for aggressive 'economic man-behaviour'.

Other stories that told of highly self-interested behaviour similarly tested out spying and deception. In Joshua (2: 17–21; 6: 23, 25), the lives of Rahab and her family were spared because she had helped Israelite spies to survive. Rahab here betrayed her own people and in this respect treason prospered. Another example where treason prospered is the story of the Gibeonites. They lived in an area of Israel's promised homeland and thus were threatened with 'eviction' by Israel. Through deception, they extracted a treaty from Israel, sworn by the oath of Israel's God, not to destroy them (Joshua 9: 6–15). The purpose of these stories can be projected in institutional perspective, namely to carefully test out arrangements for economic man-behaviour before any binding arrangements are made. Such an institutional purpose becomes even clearer in the story when judges and kings, the ultimate leaders of Israel, are suspected and tested out for economic man-behaviour.

The book of Samuel tells the story of Samuel's sons who, in their function as judges, accepted bribes and perverted justice (1 Samuel 8: 1–3). This led to the deselection of Samuel's sons as judges by the assembly of the elders of Israel. In this instance, institutional ordering worked very properly: Samuel did not or could not use personal influence to protect the office of his sons. This hints at a larger institutional purpose of economic modelling when dealing with rulers and their constituents. As North (1993a) pointed out, rulers need to subject themselves to some kind of credible self-binding in order to engage in productive relationships with subordinates – and, I would like to add, the model of economic man as well as the idea of a dilemma structure are here instrumentally useful. The model of economic man was seemingly more constructively applied in the institutional interactions described for the monarchic periods of Solomon and David. Then, win–win outcomes were generated for Israel and its neighbouring nations and trade partners (as reviewed above).

The loss of pluralism as interaction condition

After the Exodus journey, the Old Testament renewed its anti-pluralistic stance, especially in relation to the First Commandment. Moral disagreement and the honouring of other gods were severely punished, as was intermarriage with other tribes (Joshua 23: 12; Judges 3: 5, 9: 56–7; Ezra 9: 1–2). Some of the later prophets were even killed for not strictly obeying God's commandments (1 Kings 18: 40). Anti-pluralism showed up in many ways. Religious crusades against other nations and their religions are constantly reported. Israel is called upon to lead internationalism, religious conversion and slavery over other nations and to take revenge for exiles suffered (Joshua 13: 6–7, 16: 10, 17: 13; Judges 1: 28–35; 2 Samuel 7: 23; Isaiah 14: 1, 60: 5; Jeremiah 25: 11–14; Zechariah 14: 2, 12–14). This fight continues right up to the last pages of the Old Testament when, once again, Israel is asked to enslave Egypt and make the Egyptian people honour the God of Israel (Zechariah 14: 17-18). In this regard, the present book reaffirms a *decline thesis* for what followed after the Exodus. This thesis is complementary to the previously discussed climax thesis for the Joseph story and Genesis. The decline thesis reflects that after the Exodus the institutional problem remained largely unresolved, with feuds and wars being the norm in social interactions, and pluralism as an interaction condition in a multicultural society and in a community of nations being not mastered.

There are exceptions to this anti-pluralistic outlook of the Old Testament after the Exodus journey. To a degree, the Israelites themselves always struggled to keep up with the First Commandment. But then, they were pulled back and punished time and again by God. This was different under King Solomon's reign: Solomon encouraged a high diversity of religions, which can be related to the dominance of the economic system over cultural institutions (Mayes 1993: 27). Figure 3.2 can be projected in this respect, too (see also above). Solomon even built altars and temples for foreign gods (see also Schmidt 1984: 142). He seemingly accepted and endorsed religious pluralism and diversity, which Hick (1985: 34) interpreted as the acceptance that godly salvation and liberation takes place in a plurality of forms. But somewhat surprisingly, Israel's jealous God let Solomon get away with this (1 Kings 11: 4–8) and 'only' took revenge on the next generation (1 Kings 18: 18–21).

Not to punish Solomon reflected an inconsistency on God's behalf in terms of the laws he imposed on Israel, namely not to punish the sons for the sins of the fathers, as Leviticus had stated this issue. It appears that the economic and political success and the religious monuments built by Solomon appeased God, at least for the time of Solomon's reign.

Overall and somewhat disappointingly from an enlightened position, theology seems to take a rather critical stance regarding Solomon's pluralistic dispositions. Childs (1985: 179–80, 184) expressed some rather negative views on Solomon's reign, especially Solomon's openness to innovation, the import of foreign administrative structures of government and the 'folly of the Solomonic rule' regarding different gods and the 'influx of foreign influence'.

Also, once Israel went into exile in Assyria, value pluralism was restored in Samaria. It was filled with different tribes who worshipped different gods (2 Kings 17: 29–32). But then, religious crusades are reported against other gods in Judah at later points in time (2 Kings Chapter 23).

5.3   Concluding remarks

From an institutional point of view, the Exodus journey and the subsequent resettlement phase are highly interesting. Israel left a stable and prosperous institutional environment in Egypt, where societal contracts between Egypt and Israel had been well established, and at least in Genesis to the mutual advantage of both nations. As a result of the Exodus, Israel had to find its own institutional mechanisms to organize social and economic life. The stories following the Exodus from Egypt are full of such accounts. In terms of structural governance mechanisms, a tight, clan-based, web-like structure rather successfully organized the Exodus journey itself. Moses and the Levites (as priests) were at the centre of this structure, with other tribes being aligned to this centre. This ensured quick and effective decision-making. Although there was dissent during the Exodus journey, Moses achieved what he was meant to do: He led the Israelites to their promised homeland. A value fundamentalist approach was the key to this success. During the Exodus journey, punishment for dissent and not obeying God's rules worked comparatively well and was possibly even the most cost-efficient organization structure. Figure 3.2 can be re-examined in this respect, placing Moses close to Noah and Abraham. Still, I do not want to endorse Moses' or Joshua's approach to conflict handling and societal contracting. Under their reigns, pluralism, ethnic diversity and moral disagreement as interaction conditions were generally lost and much suffering resulted because of Moses' and Joshua's policies, not only for other nations and tribes but also for the Israelites. Religion was hotly contested too, not only in relation to the gods of foreign tribes but also within the Israelites' own ranks. Value pluralism was fought against, internally and externally. The golden calf story and the related breach of the First Commandment here tell of civil unrest within the Israelites' own ranks which Moses and the Levites cruelly dealt with. Societal contracting and nation-building was then approached in a rather anti-pluralistic, value fundamentalist way. As a 'state formation theory' the Old Testament here hints how not to proceed if pluralism is to be upheld as a societal interaction condition.

Once the Israelites had reached their homeland, they quickly conquered, with the advantage of surprise on their side, considerable parts of the Promised Land. But then problems seemed to set in. The development of proper institutional structures was aggravated by long periods of warfare which Israel was involved in with neighbouring tribes. Land was hotly contested, especially fertile land. Neighbouring tribes and nations were powerful and aggressive. They included Lebanon, Assyria, Egypt, Babylon and Persia, among others.

This chapter upheld, firstly, a non-hero thesis for Moses and most other leaders of the Israelites after the Exodus. Exceptions, as discussed, are Solomon and David. Secondly, the chapter upheld a decline thesis for the events depicted after the Exodus with Israel most of the time being involved in futile dilemma scenarios. Again, a prominent exception to the decline thesis is David's and Solomon's reigns. They seemingly managed, in the footsteps of Joseph, to successfully lead Israel by means of a largely economic approach to institutional intervention and societal contracting. Figure 3.2 can here be reapplied too, placing David and Solomon close to Joseph.

After the Exodus journey, the Israelites divided up captured land for their tribes in a rather federalist manner but most of the time failed to ensure the institutional integration of political decision-making for shared tasks, such as the defence of land against other nations. During the Exodus journey it was basically the ring of priests, recruited only from the Levites and placed around the tabernacle and the tent of meeting, which had ensured the tight integration of communication lines and the quick communication of decisions from the top downwards. Nothing comparable existed after the Exodus journey (apart from the reign of King Solomon, and, to a degree, the reign of David too).

Once resettlement began, the priests were dispersed across all the Israelite tribes and they could not fulfil a previous, integrative function for institutional ordering. For some time Israel struggled with this issue of nation-building. Over time, hierarchical structures emerged in degrees, led by judges and then by a king, which seemed to close this void. Effectiveness and transaction cost efficiency advantages can be referred to for explaining this development towards the constitutional monarchy under David and Solomon. Theoretical issues of state formation here emerge from the Old Testament. In concrete, practical terms it advises how to proceed and not to proceed in order to generate stable and mutually beneficial outcomes for all involved in the setting up of a new nation state.

In normative perspective, the ideal of the 'land where milk and honey flow' drove the Exodus journey and the subsequent resettlement phase. Israel had lost paradise when they exited from Egypt and they only regained it for a short period, under the reigns of David and Solomon. Especially under Solomon's reign, complex, non-tribal, hierarchical structures emerged and the exchange of capital both inside Israel and with foreign parties bloomed. Israel was then an equal among the powerful nations that surrounded it. Value pluralism, ethnic diversity and moral disagreement were then also mastered as interaction conditions, the organization of social and economic life revolving around non-behavioural issues. Incentive structures rather than value structures organized social life, and capital exchange through contracts and treaties was a considerable element of economic life. The 'war of all' was then resolved and, as indicated, like the Joseph story, the Solomon story provides a role model for organizing social interactions and societal contracting in modern, pluralistic interaction contexts through a liberatory, economic approach. Unfortunately, theology seems to overlook these important insights when it characterizes Solomon's pluralistic, economic approach as the 'folly of the Solomonic rule' (Childs 1985: 179–80, 184).

6
Economic and Non-Economic Interpretations of God in the Old Testament

Then the Lord said to Moses, 'Go down, because your people … have become corrupt. They have been quick to turn away from what I commanded them and have made themselves an idol cast in the shape of a calf.'
(Exodus 32: 7–8)

The very presence of the idea 'God' in the Old Testament does not automatically imply that the Old Testament were a metaphysical, holy or purely religious text. The purpose of the following is to enter an enlightened discussion regarding our understanding of God in the Old Testament, especially regarding secular meanings. In this way, the following reconstructs the idea of God in rational, scientific terms. Here, the present study departs from the religious economics of Brams (2002, 1980), Gordon (1994, 1989), Meeks (1989) or Paris (1998) and more so from theology (e.g. Wildavsky 1994; Noth 1966; also Westermann 1987), which subscribe to a metaphysical concept of a personal, omnipotent God and non-economic cooperation principles. For example, Childs (1985: Chapter 3) interprets 'God' as creator who reveals himself through godly wisdom, through Israel's history and through his very name. In general, the idea of revelation plays a crucial role in theology when the notion of God is discussed.

The previous discussion already touched upon the issue of how to handle the idea of God in an economic, scientific reconstruction of the Old Testament. Understood as an agent, God was heavily involved in different ways in interactions in the Paradise scenario, in the Jacob story, in the Joseph story, in the Exodus story and the stories that followed the Exodus. The subsequent examines in more detail what specific roles the idea of God takes on in these stories. This examination treats the idea

'God' as a mere textual component of the Old Testament and from here it analyses the conceptual role of the idea 'God'. This implies a secular approach to understanding the Old Testament, as argued for by Gilboa (1998: 24): 'God for the purpose of this research, is but a persona in the text and there is no room to assume for him, a priori, qualities or motives that are not written into the very body of the text.' I fully agree that there is 'no one and only perception of God in the Bible ... and that God is perceived as he is exposed in the text' (Gilboa 1998: 44, 261; similarly, Adar 1984: 12; Hirshberg 1964: 84).

By treating the idea of God as a mere textual component of the Old Testament, the present study theorizes more parsimoniously than religious economics and theology. I approach the Bible as 'text', independent of questions of divine or human authorship (in detail, see Chapter 1; also Wagner-Tsukamoto 2001a; Miller 1994: 756). Source-critical theological researchers may find more favour with this approach than literalist researchers (although, if one takes the Bible as the word of God, as done by literalist theological researchers, the previous, successful economic reconstruction of the Old Testament already implies that God 'resembles' an economist, at least a behavioural economist).

The subsequent interprets 'God' at its most concrete as an agent or player who directly interacts with humans (section 6.1). Still rather concrete, I interpret 'God' as a ruler or prosecutor who intervened in interactions among humans (Section 6.2). In these respects, I examine the evolution of different types of societal contracts (covenants) between God and humans. The present study here links God's role as sovereign to the one of an economic ruler, and it analyzes how this role as an economic ruler changed throughout the Old Testament and what kind of contracting principles this reflected. In more abstract terms, the subsequent transcends the idea of God for economic and non-economic cooperation principles as such (section 6.3). It is especially then that I deconstruct the idea of God for moral principles, although, in degrees, such principles are already touched upon when contracting principles and cooperation principles and their changing nature throughout the Old Testament are discussed in previous sections of this chapter. Only at the end of this chapter, in section 6.4, I will reflect on the idea of God in most abstract terms when I reconstruct the idea of God as a meta-principle that refers to the Unexplained in general (section 6.4). Section 6.4 also comments on the potential reduction of schisms between religion and economics which an economic reconstruction of the Old Testament allows for.

6.1 God as player contractor: Economic and non-economic societal contracts with humans

Brams (2002, 1980) outlined in detail how the idea of God can be approached in game theoretical terms as a player. He focused on selected stories of the Bible, such as the Paradise story, to discuss a game theoretical role of God (Brams 1980: 24-32). The subsequent extends such an economic reconstruction of God as a player through institutional economic reconstruction. The section examines various cases in which God showed up as a 'mere' player in stories of the Old Testament.

God as value contractor: Loser in the Paradise story

Chapter 2 analysed in depth how the idea of God can be reconstructed in institutional and game theoretical terms for the Paradise scenario. An important insight then was that God lost as a result of his interactions with Adam and Eve, namely his exclusive access to the tree of knowledge – the 'scarce good x', to pick up Buchanan's (1975) terminology. God could have traded this good through private goods exchange.

In the Paradise scenario, God and Adam & Eve interacted at the same level of players, both 'walking' through the Garden of Eden and enjoying it (Genesis 3: 8). God promised and allocated all fruits to Adam and Eve apart from the ones from the tree of knowledge and the tree of life. God showed in this respect some considerable goodwill. Adam and Eve seemingly accepted this situation and thus the institutional problem and related issues of societal contracting had apparently been solved. However, their societal contract was incomplete regarding credible sanctions not to eat from the forbidden trees. Initially, God placed much trust in a behavioural approach to societal contracting and solving the institutional problem. God implicitly hoped that his trust in Adam and Eve would be rewarded by obedience to the rules set. God only later introduced economic sanctions after the defection of Adam and Eve by placing a cherubim and a sword in front of the tree of life (Genesis 3: 16–19, 24). Costly (re-)armament investments were then made. In this respect, the Paradise story can be interpreted as a parable on master–servant, manager–worker or principal–agent interactions which spells out the problematic nature of regulating incomplete private goods exchanges in the context of unclearly and ambiguously spelled out societal, constitutional order. In the Paradise story, this was especially the case regarding law enforcement. The potential occurrence of opportunism and predation in contracting was not properly dealt with.

Regarding a larger conceptual function in the Old Testament, the Paradise story reflects a 'master heuristic' for examining the institutional problem. I here introduce the idea of the 'research heuristic' for modelling principal-agent relationships in economics and I deal in this respect with the question of how to control potential opportunism in such relationships (see Chapters 1 and 2).

In the Paradise story, opportunism could enter social interactions as a result of the way God created the human being: Humans commanded free will. The underlying principles for organizing social interactions reflect closely on the ones of constitutional economics: The equality principle is not necessarily endorsed but the less assuming principle of 'free relationships among free men' is, as Buchanan (1975) put it. In economic terms, free will can be viewed as an important feature for the effective utilization of human capital since it implies the capability of engaging in self-directed, creative and entrepreneurial problem-solving behaviour. Since human beings were in charge of keeping Paradise cultivated, such a capability was likely to yield productivity gains and it required God to get less involved in supervising and instructing humans, making his job as 'master' and 'principal' more manageable and easier. On the other hand, free will opens up the possibility for opportunistic behaviour.

Many stories that follow the Paradise story analytically reconnect to the manager–worker theme and its implications regarding the institutional problem and societal contracting, famously so the Jacob–Laban stories, the Joseph story or the Exodus story. And the more general theme of handling opportunism in social interactions is a topic in nearly all Old Testament stories that follow the Paradise story. Then, the Old Testament discusses various contractual mechanisms for handling problematic character dispositions in social interactions. New covenants were then meant to prevent mutual loss as interaction outcome. But initially, regarding the image of God, the outcome of the Paradise story reflects a weak God who was raided by Adam and Eve and who had to learn that credible sanctions were needed when incomplete contracting and the potential occurrence of opportunism in social interactions was an issue. This leads back to a reassessment of God's possibly confused double-role in the Paradise scenario, namely as a law enforcement agent at the level of constitutional order and as a potential, albeit unwilling trader of his private goods, the fruits from the divine trees. The important lesson for contracting in a wider sense is already at this early stage that constitutional, post-constitutional, and private contracts have to be tested out for loopholes that can possibly be exploited by opportunistic, economic man. This type of analysis assumes dilemmatic interest conflict between God and humans too – for the purpose of handling and preventing such conflict, as my previous analysis argued. This theme of the Paradise story reflects the economic 'master heuristic' for the analysis of social conflict and incomplete societal contracts that would become a big topic after the Paradise story.

God as value contractor after the Paradise story: New value contracts with humans

A direct result of the Paradise story was that Adam and Eve lost access to Paradise but they did not lose God's interest in societal contracting with them. God apparently owned the entire earth, and in this respect a need for further contracting between the two parties arose. New contracts were meant to re-establish friendly and cooperative relationships between God and humans. The key concept of societal contracting in the Old Testament is then the 'covenant', a contract between God and humans which re-assures the human being of God's friendly intentions and his lasting support. However, after the Paradise story, God does not give away such re-assurances without any paybacks. In a sense, God learnt something form the Eden incident: He now explicitly expects value commitment, love, obedience and faithfulness from the human being, persons being expected to be non-opportunistic. Noah, Abraham and Isaac, and later Moses, too, are the key examples. Lot is another example of a value adhering, good human being. This becomes clear when, through godly intervention, he is saved from the destruction of Sodom and Gomorrah (Genesis 19: 16–29; see also Chapter 3).

God tests out these humans to the extreme regarding their value commitment and the behavioural, societal contracts with them. For instance, Noah is requested to build the ark in order to depart from his unfaithful fellow humans (Genesis 6: 13–21), or Abraham is asked by God to sacrifice his only son Isaac in order to appease God's doubts of Abraham's behavioural, contractual dispositions (Genesis 22: 2). Moses is similarly tested time and again. These instances reflect value commitment tests. The new institutional economics may speak of a hostage model (Williamson 1985: 167–82; 1983) to ensure proper contract fulfilment. Rewards come in the form of blessings and promises of 'fruits', at times even with respect to the one remaining scarce good x 'eternal life'. God then shared it with the faithful, religious patriarchs, at least in degrees, by rewarding them with longevity.

A new type of societal contract emerged in this way, largely developed in religious economic and behavioural economic terms. God and

humans explicitly became contracting partners and through their contracts both parties were bound in one way or another. Fromm (1967: 25)
was clearly aware of this:

> With the conclusion of the covenant, God ceases to be the absolute
> ruler. He and man have become partners in a treaty. God is trans-
> formed from an 'absolute' into a 'constitutional' monarch. He is
> bound, as man is bound, to the conditions of the constitution. God
> has lost his freedom to be arbitrary, and man has gained the freedom
> of being able to challenge God in the name of God's own promises,
> of the principles laid down in the covenant.

Key covenants with Noah were:

> I now establish my covenant with you and with your descendants
> after you and with every living creature that was with you ... I estab-
> lish my covenant with you: Never again will all life be cut off by the
> waters of a flood; never again will there be a flood to destroy the
> earth.
>
> (Genesis 9: 8–11)

And with Abraham:

> I will make you into a great nation and I will bless you; I will make
> your name great, and you will be a blessing. I will bless those, who
> bless you, and whoever curses you I will curse; and all peoples on
> earth will be blessed through you.
>
> (Genesis 12: 2–3)

And also: 'I am your shield, your very great reward.... On that day the
Lord made a covenant with Abraham' (Genesis 15: 1, 18). God established a similar behavioural covenant with Moses (e.g. Deuteronomy
30: 6–20; see Chapter 5). In the cases of Noah and Abraham and later
also of Moses, behavioural value contracting, which was backed up by
economic promises and incentives (see Chapters 3 and 5), dominated
the new covenants. Here, we encounter truly good, righteous, faithful
figures in the Old Testament and because of their character dispositions
a behavioural economics, more precisely a religious economics and the
kind of behavioural economic covenants it inspired, worked very well.
Buber (1982: 34) evoked in this connection the model of a 'faithful
priest' for the patriarchs: 'A faithful priest [Abraham] ... walks before

the anointed of God.... We see the image of the ruler [God] at peace sending a herald.'

Abraham's covenant and blessing was extended in universal and in intergenerational perspective: 'Through your [Abraham's] off-spring all nations on earth will be blessed, because you have obeyed me.' (Genesis 22: 18) A similar blessing and covenant was extended earlier to Noah: 'This is the sign of the covenant I am making between me and you and every living creature with you, a covenant for all generations to come.' (Genesis 9: 12) Such universal and intergenerational contracting among nations was similarly already touched upon when Genesis (9: 12) invoked a 'covenant for all generations to come'. The Table of Nations as listed in Chapter 10 of Genesis has to be read in such intergenerational contracting perspective, too. The accounts of lengthy family trees in other parts of the Bible also reflect a focus on intergenerational contracting (e.g. Genesis 5: 3–32, 11: 10–30, 25: 1–19, 36: 1–40, 46: 8–25).

In these respects, God hosted at this early stage of Genesis universal and intergenerational value contracting. Nation-building and societal contracting was predominantly spiritually oriented, with God 'laying down promises on land and descendants' (Gilboa 1998: 228). This approach to handling cooperation problems in behavioural economic terms worked very well – as long as the faithfulness of humans was assured in social interactions. After the Exodus, God and Moses made a new attempt to resurrect and bring this behavioural approach to societal contracting but anti-pluralism then became quickly an issue too. It shows up for interactions between God and the Israelites, for instance, in the golden calf story, and it also shows up for interactions between the Israelites and their neighbours, who the Israelites frequently tried to eliminate in order to 'solve' the institutional problem (see Chapter 5). In general, a behavioural approach to the institutional problem could be expected to run quickly into problems if another Adam and Eve or 'economic man' showed up, who would break given value promises for personal gain. In the further course of Genesis, this issue is discussed when an opportunistic Jacob enters the scene. Then, new, purer economic principles emerge for societal contracting between God and humans. The next section discusses this in more detail.

God's struggle with Jacob: The value contractor losing to economic man

One could suspect that after God had made new value contracts with Noah, Abraham or Isaac the institutional problem and problems of societal contracting had been finally solved in biblical storytelling. But the opposite is the case. Anarchists, opportunists and militant figures enter the stage who are seemingly not bound and cannot be bound by value-based, behavioural economic contracts. In Genesis, key examples are Jacob or Joseph's brothers.

In Genesis, there is probably no other figure who embodies the darker shades of opportunism and predation better than Jacob. His rather opportunistic interactions with Esau, Isaac or Laban were discussed previously (see Chapter 3). In these stories, the problem of stable, societal contracts is suddenly again as widely unresolved as in the Paradise scenario. Jacob was no Noah or Abraham (or Moses), who were faithful, God-abiding and God-fearing figures. In a sense, the outcome of Jacob's struggle with God symbolises the end of an era in the Old Testament story telling, the end of the good, religious human being and a return to the starting scenario of the Paradise story with anarchy looming and institutional questions of societal contracting rapidly arising. The Jacob stories symbolise both the end of value contracting in Genesis and the end of God as a player contractor in Genesis, who is involved in private goods exchange. In stories that follow, God rather consistently takes on the role of a ruler, mostly a reluctant one and even only a third-party interventionist in interactions among humans. In Genesis, institutional problem solving moves then from the level of value-based, societal contracting to rather pure economic contracting, with God taking a back-seat role. This interpretation is compatible with Gilboa's (1998: 228) view that after the stories involving Jacob a different kind of covenant between God and humans emerged. We then find a different kind of institutional problem solving, nation-building and societal contracting: In contrast to his forefathers, Jacob set the terms of a contract with God and requested certain types of rewards. After his fight with God, Jacob even insisted on being blessed by God before he would let go God:

> Jacob replied, 'I will not let you go unless you bless me.' The man asked him, 'What is your name?', 'Jacob', he answered. Then the man said: 'Your name will no longer be Jacob, but Israel, because you have struggled with God and with men and have overcome.'
> (Genesis 32: 26–8)

God's role in contracting with humans is diminished. Authority and autonomy is in large degrees transferred to humans. A precedent has been set and Buchanan's constitutional economic principle of 'free contractual relationships among free men' has been substantially elevated. A radical, economic humanism emerges in the Old Testament.

Regarding a more liberated, constitutional economic nature of future societal contracting among nations, the Joseph story is then the prime example in Genesis. In this respect, the present study proposed a hero thesis for Joseph and a climax thesis of biblical storytelling for the Joseph story and the kind of societal contracting it promoted. In Exodus and subsequent books, the opposite can be observed, God issuing new behavioural covenants with humans, mainly through Moses and this happened largely in a value-fundamentalist, anti-pluralistic way. Although, as previously discussed for Noah, Abraham and Moses, value-based contracting was supported by certain economic ideas, which make these contracts classify as *behavioural economic* ones rather than pure, moral behavioural or theological ones. However, in these instances, the resolution of the institutional problem was less successful, less efficient and less tolerant of interaction conditions such as pluralism. Figure 3.2 in Chapter 3 provided a summary of the key hypotheses. Comparing Joseph's and Moses' institutional approaches led me to suggest an anti-hero thesis, even a non-hero thesis for Moses and a decline thesis for the Exodus stories and the stories that followed.

If one transcends the role of God for cooperation principles regarding his role as a player contractor, it becomes apparent that it is especially in Genesis that he reflected, at the outset, value principles in a moral behavioural tradition. This tradition relies upon the internalisation of values by human beings in order to ensure successful and cooperative societal interactions. As noted, key ideas are here, faithfulness, love, obedience, etc. However, already the Paradise scenario warned of this approach: It told of a story of the lacking effectiveness of such principles when potentially self-interested human beings were encountered and when effective economic sanctions were absent. Subsequently, Genesis tried to solve this problem by advocating the strengthening of the moral and spiritual profiles of agents. Noah, Abraham, Lot and Isaac were key examples. Societal contracting, hosted by God through covenants made by him with the faithful human being, was then based on religious value principles, which were partly supported by economic means. And this reflects the deeper meaning of the concept of God at this stage of Genesis: God as behavioural (behavioural economic) value contractor. Only in later stories of Genesis, especially from the Jacob stories onwards, the idea of God can be deconstructed for rather different cooperation principles that resembled a purer economic – institutional and constitutional economic – approach to societal contracting. Potential opportunism in societal interactions was then controlled for in economic terms.

6.2   God as rule-maker, interventionist with the moves of the game and source of human capital

The subsequent looks at different stories in the Old Testament in which God intervened as a third party in the moves of the game, changing interaction rules or 'governance structures' for interacting agents and thus the incentives and payouts that were allocated to them. God then performs a different function than the one of a player. He rules over standards which set sanctions and rewards for players. Humans are here mere constituents. Issues of constitutional contracting are then the major topic. As it turns out, the human being is then largely involved in behavioural economic, value contracts that come with drastic sanctions if broken. Section 6.1 already hinted in degrees at such a constitutional, ruler-like role of God in certain stories. The question of governance, or differently put, of 'central authority' plays here a very significant role throughout the Old Testament. Nearly always when God shows up in stories of the Old Testament, the question of ruling in one form or another arises. Hence, in the present book, I acknowledge authority or ruling as a key feature of Old Testament stories. In this respect, my economic reconstruction conceptually departs from evolutionary economics, such as Axelrod (1984), who addressed the question 'under what conditions will cooperation emerge in a world of egoists *without central authority*' (Axelrod 1984: 3, emphasis added; see also North and Taylor 2004: 1). And of course, Axelrod analyzed this question not for the Old Testament.

God as interventionist, ruler and value fundamentalist prosecutor

We encounter early on an interventionist God who intervenes in capital exchange transactions among faithful humans when, for example, Abraham and Lot separate land for their herds. They split up land since their shared grazing grounds could no longer support both herds. Abraham gave Lot first choice and Lot chose the fruitful land near the river Jordan while Abraham was left with less fruitful land (Genesis 13: 10–11). God then intervened and compensated Abraham: He advised him to move his tents and God promised Abraham that he would prosper and that his descendants would be numerous (Genesis 13: 16, 18, also Genesis 19: 29). God did in this instance not act as a player but as sovereign or a supervisory ruler who intervened once one party got seemingly disadvantaged in an unfair manner. Such compensations and rewards can still be linked to a behavioural economic approach of the early stories of Genesis. Wealth was redistributed once a faithful person suffered some injustice. Thus, the goal of mutual gains as outcome of social interactions was preserved. In secular terms, arbitrators or judges of one kind or another can perform such an interventionist function. Value principles reflecting the maintenance of economic justice in societal interactions can here be related to the idea of God. A constitution can enact such arbitration through a societal contract and the Old Testament is inspirational in this respect.

Godly intervention of a different kind and more drastic nature occurs when the great flood happens, when a common language is lost in the Tower of Babel story, when Sodom and Gomorrah are destroyed or when the golden calf incident happened. God then brings destruction on humans for not participating in societal contracting that was based on the faithfulness of humans. Unfaithfulness was punished severely while faithfulness was rewarded by saving the faithful person from these catastrophic incidents. God is here still hosting value contracting that is linked to a behavioural economics. A key example is the saving of Lot from the destruction of Sodom and Gomorrah (Genesis 19: 15, 29). In secular terms, I reconstruct such catastrophic incidents, which wiped out unfaithful humans, as inquisition-like, value-fundamentalist incidents, such as religious crusades or even worse, as terrorist acts, even acts of state terrorism. At a later stage of Old Testament storytelling, when it comes to the Babylonian exile, God similarly punished Israel for being 'challenging' and 'profaning, trivializing, mocking, exploiting' God (Brueggemann 1986: 77). God then even punished Israel with the destruction of Jerusalem and with the subsequent exile in Babylon.

Probably the most famous example of destructive godly intervention in societal contracting among humans is the Exodus story in which God 'solved' cooperation problems by means of dissolving interactions between Egypt and Israel. In this connection, the question arises why leaders like Moses and the pharaoh failed to develop 'economic wisdom' regarding institutional governance, as Joseph had done in Genesis. Why did they give in to value fundamentalist interaction tactics? In particular, why did they fail to see that their predatory, 'economic man-behaviour' was rationally foolish and would over time lead to mutual loss? As previously noted, in terms of the prisoner's dilemma analogy, it is important to inquire by whom and how a prisoner's dilemma was installed for Moses and the pharaoh. It appears that divine intervention here played a significant role (see Chapter 4).

In contrast to Genesis and especially the Joseph story, the God of Exodus did not show Egypt and Israel economic options for rule-making and choice behaviour which could have prevented mutual suffering.

Figuratively expressed, it was God who did not let Moses and the pharaoh 'know about Joseph' (Exodus 1: 8). God's role in this respect compares to the one of the prosecutor in the prisoner's dilemma. In the prisoner's dilemma it is the prosecutor who makes rational economic agents behave as 'rational fools', by separating the prisoners into different rooms and by preventing them to consult each other over choice options. In Exodus, God acted as a comparable catalyst and source of conflict. He prevented, by means of psychological, 'value fundamentalist' intervention, Moses and the pharaoh from economically wise societal contracting. God made Moses and the pharaoh retaliate and not get involved in negotiations over social problems and governance structures (Exodus 7: 3–4, 13, 22; 8: 15, 19, 32; 9: 7, 12, 34–5; 10: 1–2, 20, 27; 11: 9–10). Thus, God at least contributed to 'rationally foolish' outcomes. Anti-pluralistic implications emerge regarding God's role in the Exodus and the kind of governance principles the 'God'-concept stands for. From here, one has to very critically inquire about the intervention rights a ruler should enjoy in constitutional contract. In the Exodus scenario, God seemed to be too unrestrained. A constitutional economics argues in this respect that societal contracts and constitutional order which was set up by subjects should bind rulers and especially law enforcement agents.

After the Exodus, God performed the role of a ruler in an even much more comprehensive manner. The Ten Commandments set out largely in behavioural terms how Israel should organize its social interactions. First issued in the book of Exodus, they were renewed and further detailed in Leviticus and subsequent Books (e.g. Leviticus Chapters 19–20). Through God's rulings, institutional ordering was conducted and societal contracting was organized. And the rules were to be enacted through Israel's leaders, first Moses, then Joshua and later the so-called judges and kings. But as it turned out already under Moses, Israel as a people was often easily swayed to follow other gods. A nearly constant struggle between God and Israel developed regarding the obeying of the Ten Commandments, especially the First Commandment. And this was even more the case under the judges and the kings. Israel was then threatened with cataclysmic events for the disobedience of God's rules. Punishments were plagues, diseases (e.g. Leviticus 26: 14–45, Numbers 11: 33, 12: 10) or a land of burning sulphur that 'will be like the destruction of Sodom and Gomorrah' (Deuteronomy 29: 23; see also Deuteronomy 28: 15–68). Only during the Exodus journey, God's 'army' – the priests, recruited from the Levites – succeeded to tightly enact the Ten Commandments. Then, dissent regarding moral, behavioural precepts was nearly instantly and heavily punished. This included the priests: Disobedient, unfaithful behaviour among the priests, which did not live up to the rules issued by God, was cruelly punished too; for example, Aaron's sons were killed for making unlawful offerings to God (Leviticus 10: 2). As discussed previously (see section 5.1), the success of the priests to enact the First Commandment reflected the then organization structures, with Moses and the priests (Levites) at the centre of a web-like organization structure. This allowed them to tightly control social interactions during the Exodus journey.

In general, a value fundamentalist God is a recurring theme during and after the Exodus, God acting as value prosecutor. For instance, he 'hardens the hearts' of other kings to make peace treaties with the Israelites (Joshua 11: 20) or to let the Israelites pass through their territory (Deuteronomy 2: 27–30; 3: 2). Here, quite intentionally God prevents the two parties to transform a zero-sum game into a mutually beneficial, nonzero-sum game. As for the prosecutor in the prisoner's dilemma, the idea of a prosecuting God in Exodus and in subsequent books needs to be transcended for cooperative and non-cooperative interaction principles. As discussed earlier for the Exodus story (see Chapter 4), the idea of liberation may in this context be difficult to uphold. Much theological and religious economic work on the Exodus proposes this idea, e.g. Brams (1980: 88; many further references were quoted in Chapter 4). Also, once the Exodus had come to an end, Israel's resettlement in regions east and west of the Jordan was anything than straightforward. The Old Testament reports stories of ongoing war and God, time and again, punished Israel with loss of territory for unfaithful behaviour. Another implication of God's enactment of the First Commandment was that interactions moved out of contexts that were defined by pluralism. This was also discussed in some detail in Chapters 4 and 5 (and it is picked up again below). In this respect, the model of a value fundamentalist God and the cooperation principles it reflects can hardly provide a role model for interactions in a modern, pluralistic context.

God as inspirational source of intellectual capital

The Joseph story attributes much of the success of Joseph to his wisdom and intellectual capabilities regarding economic policies. Specifically, it points out his ability for abstract economic thinking and economic explanations: The pharaoh had dreamt about 'seven fat cows' and 'seven ugly cows' (Genesis 41: 2–4, 17–24) and was looking for an explanation. Joseph interprets these dreams with regard to cyclical development of economic upturns and downturns:

> God has shown Pharaoh what he is about to do. Seven years of great abundance are coming throughout the land of Egypt, but seven years

of famine will follow them. Then all the abundance in Egypt will be forgotten.

(Genesis 41: 28–30)

Joseph relates these dreams to spiritual, godly inspirations given to the pharaoh and given to him. In this respect, the idea of God can be interpreted as innovative intellectual capital or 'wisdom'. In secular terms, it can be deconstructed as intellectual human capital about economic development. Gordon (1989), for example, pointed out that Egypt had its own 'economic wisdom schools'. With regard to the preparation for cyclical developments, however, they did not seem to have well-prepared answers. This is indicated by the pharaoh's dreams and the lack of interpretations and conclusions his own people could offer him. Joseph here came up with some careful plans on how to accumulate corn, namely through a 20-per cent barter tax on crop production (for details, see Chapter 3). This and the institutional structures linked to it prepared Egypt well for seven years of economic downturn. Ultimately, Joseph's economic wisdom in interpreting the pharaoh's dreams and fears got him promoted to the position of 'chief economist' of the pharaoh:

> Then Pharaoh said to Joseph, 'Since God has made all this known to you, there is no-one so discerning and wise as you. You shall be in charge of my palace, and all my people are to submit to your orders. Only with respect to the throne will I be greater than you.'
>
> (Genesis 41: 39–40)

The idea of God in the Joseph story can be linked to cooperative, constructive principles of societal contracting, namely God as the provider of intellectual capital that helps to avert economic catastrophes. A specific type of human capital was in this respect created. As indicated, in secular terms, the idea of God can here be deconstructed as clever wisdom and intellectual capital of Joseph and the ability of Joseph to apply his own wits in a highly constructive and effective way. Joseph surpassed in this respect the economic wisdom (human capital) of Egypt's economists. The provision of such wisdom did not lead to the playing of moves within the given set of moves of a game but intervention with the moves. Joseph redesigned the rules of the game, e.g. a tax system. Understood as a persona and comparable to a consultant, God so inspired, in a creative, constructive manner, Joseph and the pharaoh to engage in clever institutional rule-making that could prevent catastrophic events. Therefore, when the book of Genesis closes its discussion of the institutional problem and of societal contracting, rule-making and institutional ordering has been largely delegated to humans; institutional ordering then occurred in a largely economic manner; and God acted truly as a non-behavioural economist and manager who only advised humans to better utilize their own human capital. This explains my suggestion of a radical, economic human-ism emerging in Genesis. This is in comparatively stark contrast to the opening scenario in the Paradise story when God both made rules and played the game with Adam and Eve – and lost to Adam and Eve. In the final stories of Genesis, God took a backseat role in intervening in human interactions and when he intervened, he did so in non-behavioural economic terms. The resulting image of God and the principles it reflects for organizing societal contracting is a rather enlightened and positive one. Paradise is then regained and preserved through the clever, economically inspired organization of interactions among humans. Jacob was here an early predecessor of Joseph – and Jacob, at the end of Genesis, clearly recognized Joseph's economically inspired and highly successful approach to societal contracting, most obviously so when he praised Joseph as the 'fruitful wine of Israel' (Genesis 49: 22–6) while condemning at the same time the House of Levi, from whom Moses would later emerge (Genesis 49: 5–7), with Moses standing for a return to value-fundamentalist, behavioural societal contracting.

6.3 Abstracting the notion of God for economic principles of social ordering

Institutional economic ordering and a normative institutional economics in general are geared towards ethical principles, most directly so aiming the idea of mutuality of gains as interaction outcome. Other ethical principles can be associated with the economic approach, too, such as the self-organizing and democratic ordering of social life, pluralism and the motivational and cognitive autonomy of the individual (Wagner-Tsukamoto 2003: 202–5). The subsequent examines how far the idea of God, as found in the Old Testament, reflects such principles. A so-called Elohist conception of God, which views God as supernatural and tran-scendental entity rather than as a persona (Gordon 1994: 22–3), is here of special interest since it can be related to the idea of principles. Also, a principle-oriented deconstruction of the idea of God for moral coop-eration principles becomes the more necessary if one accepts Fromm's (1967: 228) claim that 'for the contemporary world ... the God-concept [understood in a personal, empirical sense] has lost its philosophical and social basis.' The subsequent abstracts the idea of a personal God for economically inspired principles of institutional intervention and societal contracting.

God as principle of creative social ordering

An abstract meaning of God as a cooperation principle can be associated with the very idea 'God' takes on in certain text passages and translations of the Old Testament. At times, the idea of God is more or less directly related to a principle of social ordering. Hodson (1967: 93) pointed out that the original Hebrew term used for 'God' in Genesis – *Elohim* – refers to 'order of creative, evolutionary intelligence' but not to a personal God as many later translations and interpretations of the Bible imply. If one abstracts an Elohist understanding of God further, it can be linked to principles of organized and self-organizing social order as it permeates the writings of an institutional economics (and institutional studies in general). Hodson's (1967: 95–6, 99, 108, 115–16) discussion of Elohim as 'evolutionary impulse', 'duality of chaos and cosmos' or 'absolute and finite existence' provides abstract examples. Theogonic issues – regarding the origin of god(s) – too arise here. Unless one deconstructs the idea of God in a secular way in line with the idea of Elohim, a more complex and thus more improbable approach to explanation is entered, which relies on the idea of a *personal* God. In the background loom questions on the nature of God and the nature of the universe and the relation of the two to each other. In the literature on the philosophy of religion this is discussed under the headings of the first-cause argument, the cosmological argument and the design argument (Hick 1990: 20–6; see also section 6.4 below).

An Elohist understanding of God as evolutionary intelligence can be related to the contents and structure of the stories of the Old Testament in various ways. In terms of contents, the idea of an interventionist God recedes as the stories of Genesis unfold. Increasingly, humans take over institutional ordering. This is also reflected, as Chapter 3 outlined above, by a switch from a behavioural, religious economics at the outset of Genesis to a much purer, non-behavioural economics at the end of Genesis. And in this process, a normative institutional economics, which directly aims at the rules of the game and is successfully mastered by human beings (at least so in Genesis), increasingly replaced an evolutionary, 'tit-for-tat' economics. The Jacob stories and the Joseph story illustrate this replacement process. This switch from a religious, behavioural economics to a modern, normative institutional economics runs from the stories of Noah and Abraham to the Jacob stories to the Joseph story. The Joseph story reflects the culmination of this process, with God 'only' providing intellectual capital to humans. Chapter 3 spelt out in this connection a climax thesis for Genesis and the Joseph story, and Chapters 4 and 5 a decline thesis for Exodus and the books that follow in the Old Testament. The decline thesis was related to God's less productive, more behavioural economic and more value fundamentalist intervention in social ordering during and after the Exodus.

With regard to Genesis, the Old Testament seemingly culminated in a rich form of democratic capitalism. Even the question can be raised regarding a capitalist ethics and radical, economic humanism as foundation of Old Testament thought (see also section 7.6 below when the Weber thesis is discussed). In this connection, I share Fromm's (1967: 25) and Gilboa's (1998: 237) 'freedom thesis' for the Old Testament, namely that, as events are unfolding in the Old Testament, humans are given increasing freedom, 'even freedom from God.' As my book argues, economic liberation provides this freedom, masterminded by Joseph. And in this connection, Genesis seems to closely endorse principles of an enlightened approach to constitutional economics, based on principles such as Buchanan's 'free relationships among free men'. However, as explained, I do not see freedom and liberation increasing or even occurring in the stories that follow from the book of Exodus onwards, as Fromm and Gilboa and so many others, including religious economists, suggest. Once the idea of a personal, interventionist and value fundamentalist God gains force in the book of Exodus and in the books that follow, humans lose their power over rule-making. The Torah re-enters the realm of a behavioural economics and a largely fundamentalist, religious economics. Then questions of institutional ordering remain widely open, with destructive zero-sum games being played by Israel both within its society and with other tribes and nations. A value fundamentalist, interventionist God drove these games. As indicated in Chapters 4 and 5 above, here a decline thesis emerged for the stories of the Old Testament and the idea of God mirrors intervention principles of how *not* to proceed when stable, efficient, productive, tolerant and pluralistic societal contracting is the goal.

God and the principle of mutuality of gains as interaction outcome

As the previous chapters clearly revealed, many stories of the Old Testament aim at wealth creation and wealth distribution. These ideas are also explicitly invoked by various covenants that were made between God and humans and by God 'blessing' humans with numerous riches, prosperity, longevity, fertility, etc. Distributional justice and socially desirable interaction outcomes are clearly an issue. For example, in the Jacob stories, Jacob made various compensation payments to those who he initially had disadvantaged (Figure 3.1 summarized this in Chapter 3). 'Peace and harmony' in social relations was thus economically worked out. The principle of the wealth of nations looms large here, implying the generation of mutual benefits. Normative institutional economics stresses that this ideal is a prerequisite for peace and harmony to emerge and prevail in economic terms in social interactions.

The Joseph story engineered similar interaction outcomes, which were mutually beneficial to the two nations of Egypt and Israel. More than in the Jacob stories, the Joseph story directly generated mutually advantageous interaction outcomes through clever institutional economic ordering; for example, through Joseph's barter tax system on crop and his reallocation policy on crop to farmers (see section 3.4). The Old Testament here specifically and rather explicitly invoked the ideal of the wealth of nations and the wealth of a community of nations (Genesis 47: 27). Thus, understood in abstract terms, God is here present as a principle of economically inspired sharing that successfully organized societal contracting between Egypt and Israel.

In the Solomon story a similar scenario unfolded. Having made peace treaties and trade treaties with neighbouring nations and tribes, Israel acquired a position of great wealth and power. A key message here seems to be that through economic ordering, peaceful and harmonious relations can be established in international relations. The Solomon story explicitly abandoned principles for societal contracting that reflected the First Commandment, with Solomon honouring different gods and pluralism emerging in Solomon's international relations (see next section).

Such ideas of mutual gains are not far away from Adam Smith's idea of the wealth of nations. The idea of God in the Old Testament can be deconstructed for such normative principles of shared wealth among nations. This type of deconstruction has a high potential to enlighten the debate of wealth in theology, which according to Kaiser (2001: 156) is still in a confused state. The important step to take here, as hinted by Fromm (1967: 228), is a deconstruction of the 'God-concept' for non-personal, social principles – which the present book followed up in economic terms, and in this section with respect to the ideal of mutual gains as interaction outcome.

God as a reflection of the principle of maintaining pluralism as an interaction condition

Pluralism as an interaction condition reflects ethical ideals that concern the motivational and cognitive autonomy of the individual (see also Wagner-Tsukamoto 2003: Chapter 8). Clearly, pluralism can be viewed as an ethically desirable interaction condition since it allows interacting partners with diverse and even incompatible value profiles to peacefully coexist. Ethnic diversity, moral disagreement and even value decay among parties is thus tolerated. In our globalizing and increasingly multicultural world, it appears mandatory to search for solutions to social problems that accommodate pluralism, moral disagreement and possibly even value decay as interaction condition (see also Wagner-Tsukamoto 2008c).

The market economy and its economic approach to institutional ordering and societal contracting require not much regarding harmonious, behavioural pre-dispositions of the individual. Economic analysis and intervention is heuristically based on the model of economic man and the idea of the dilemma structure. And in theoretical and practical perspectives, institutional economics aims at interactions that concern incentive structures, capital exchange and mutual gains (Figure 1.1 summarized this in Chapter 1). This means, as a by-product of an economic approach to social ordering, pluralism and moral disagreement are more or less 'automatically' tolerated as interaction conditions, mainly because they are uncritical, unproblematic conditions or variables for economic analysis and intervention in a capitalist society. This is not the case for behavioural analysis and behavioural intervention, including behavioural economics, religious economics and the more conventional approaches to (Old Testament) theology and moral philosophy. They aim to solve social problems through 'harmonizing' value profiles of interacting agents. In the Old Testament this becomes apparent when a personal, value manifesting and even value fundamentalist God intervenes. This is especially the case in Exodus and the books that follow, but also in some of the early stories of Genesis when Noah and Abraham and Lot undergo various value commitment tests. As noted, the prime example of a value fundamentalist God shows up in the Exodus stories when Egypt is terrorized. On the other hand, stories of Genesis master pluralism as an interaction condition, especially so the Joseph story. Then, we increasingly meet a non-interventionist understanding of God. Especially the Joseph story highlighted this when Israel and Egypt peacefully coexisted. From here some rather positive conclusions can be drawn regarding a deconstruction of the idea of God for pluralistic interaction principles.

6.4 God as a metaprinciple and reference to the Unexplained in general

At the most abstract, the present study deconstructs the idea of God as a metaprinciple and reference to the Unexplained in general. The idea of the Unexplained may loom in many stories of the Old Testament. The subsequent examines in more detail to what extent and what kind of metameanings and references to the Unexplained can be found in the Old Testament regarding the idea of God. Of special interest here is the question how far economic versus non-economic issues dominated the occurrence of metameanings and references to the Unexplained when the idea of God is drawn upon. If it should show up that the Old Testament largely used the idea of God to talk about non-economic questions and problems faced by mankind, then the economic reconstruction of the Old Testament, as pursued in the present book, could be fundamentally questioned. This issue is examined first in the subsequent sections. In a final section, I discuss the question of how far an economic reconstruction of the Old Testament can reduce schisms between economics and religion, especially religion that is supported by Old Testament theology.

The idea of God as a solution for everything?

Genesis draws upon the idea of God in two essential ways, firstly, as the creator of the universe, the world and the human being, and secondly, as problem adviser and problem solver regarding social conflict among humans. The former takes up a mere couple of pages of Genesis (Genesis: Chapters 1–2) whereas the latter makes up more than 99.9 per cent of the Old Testament. This can be interpreted as a reflection of the key interests of the authors of the Old Testament and as a reflection of the kind of problems that were most pressing to mankind then. The institutional problem and related problems of societal contracting seem to be most relevant here.

The idea of God as creator provides a mythical, metaphysical answer to the question of where we come from, and the Old Testament can be said to have accumulated the best knowledge of the time in this respect. More precisely, the Old Testament accumulated here the *lacking* knowledge of the time, providing a largely poetic answer on this issue. Without the advances in modern physics, chemistry, astronomy, biology or anthropology, the God-as-creator-concept was the best available answer the authors of the Old Testament could come up with to satisfy human thirst for learning about the origin of life. Modern theology easily admits this, for instance Gräb says (2002: 284): 'If we were to read the account about God as creator of the world and about his creative actions in Genesis 1 and 2 in any factual, literal sense, we would have to concede that this description is incorrect' (see also Gräb 2002: 279–81, 286, 288).

However, as indicated, it can be suggested that this question concerning the origin of the world and the origin of life was not of too great an interest to the authors of the Old Testament. It just provided a neat opener for discussing other topics: the institutional problem, the problem of social conflict and societal contracting among individuals and nations and within a community of nations. Nation-building was a related big topic too. In these respects, the question of meaning and relevance of the Old Testament needs to focus on the *social* problems and conflicts discussed in the Old Testament. Such problems make up, as indicated, nearly the entire body of the Old Testament. Gräb's recommendation of a necessary dialogue between the *natural* sciences and theology thus needs refocusing on a dialogue between the *social* sciences and theology – and as this book stressed, especially a dialogue between economics and theology.

Regarding questions of social conflict and societal contracting, the authors of the Old Testament developed various answers. They drew on the idea of God in an ambivalent, multifaceted way: God helped to solve social conflict through behavioural, value contracting, namely in the case of Noah, Abraham, Lot and Isaac, and later Moses too. A different, economically oriented understanding of God emerged in the Jacob stories, namely more in the tradition of an evolutionary, interaction economics that moves towards the setting up of a constitutional contract. This hinted at a reorientation of addressing and solving social conflict in the Old Testament. The Joseph story provides a further reorientation, moving the idea of God and the kind of social ordering and institutional problem-solving it implied close to the concepts and principles of normative institutional economics. In Exodus and throughout the remainder of the Old Testament leaving the David story and the Solomon story aside, a return to value fundamentalism and a God that inspires value contracting and value ordering can be observed. Then, at best, a behavioural economics was (re)entered.

Looking at the different types of meaning God takes on in creationist perspective and in social conflict perspective, it can be suggested that the idea of God functioned as a metavariable in the conceptual discussion in the Old Testament. And as outlined, its real significance lies in being a metavariable for conceptualizing and discussing *social conflict*, which is resolved through societal contracting. From here, more specific, economically inspired, ethical principles can be associated with the idea of God. Such principles were discussed in some detail above.

God as a reference to the Unexplained in general

The most general, most abstract understanding of the idea 'God' in the Old Testament can be related to the idea of the 'Unexplained'. Besides issues that concerned the origin of life and the origin of the world, it appears that the Old Testament rationalized natural or human-made catastrophes. Examples are the great flood Noah encountered, the destruction of Sodom and Gomorrah by burning sulphur, the various periods of famine encountered by Israel and by other nations of the Near East or the plagues met by Egypt. For analysing and understanding such issues, I suggest that the authors of the Old Testament drew on 'God' as a general reference and answer to anything that did not make sense to them. For example, literalist Old Testament theology examines the great flood and the destruction of Sodom and Gomorrah as natural events.

Once one begins to break down an understanding of God as a reference to the Unexplained to a more specific issue and related subsets of more concrete variables, questions arise regarding what the idea of God really stands for in the Old Testament. Helpful in this regard is the distinction of Otzen et al. (1980: 13) of *theogonic* issues, which concern the origin and nature of god(s), *cosmogonic* issues, which concern the origin of the world and the establishment of the cosmos, and *cosmological* issues, which concern the explanation of the order of nature. On the one hand, in Genesis 1–2, God basically handles cosmogonic and cosmological issues. God is the master of creation and he controls the natural conditions of the earth. Modern theology, as indicated above, here questions a literalist reading of the Old Testament, especially of Genesis 1–2, invoking instead preconditions of human nature inherent in the Big Bang, or 'the anthropological principle' (Gräb 2002: 279; see also section 6.5 below). However, these matters, as interesting as they are, generally concern a philosophy of religion and are not the key topic of the present book – and neither are they a key topic in the Old Testament as reflected by the very brief coverage of these topics in the Old Testament. The Old Testament is not really about creation in a cosmogonic or cosmological sense.

Theogonic questions, on the other hand, are left wide open in the Old Testament. 'God' is a given concept which is not further questioned.

The question regarding the nature and origin of God can be addressed (for Old Testament studies) by looking at the way God was involved in worldly matters that are depicted in the Old Testament. This chapter provided the answers in sections 6.1–6.3. Thus, as far as theogonic issues regarding the nature of God are concerned, these were economically reconstructed in rational, scientific terms through the various interpretations and principles outlined in the above sections. And the scale of social problems discussed in the Old Testament and the kind of economic principles I unearthed justified such a reconstruction focus on the institutional problem.

Abstracting the *restfrage*: On the reduction of schisms between religion and the sciences

Over the centuries, the realm of religion and theology has become increasingly smaller and the kind of research questions and research problems it advises on has steadily decreased. This process started with the evolution of sciences like physics, chemistry and biology. In this process, religion and theology had to retract step-by-step from subject matter it previously claimed to explain. For example, once the (main) churches accepted Darwin's evolution theory, literalist claims towards the creation of mankind and similarly the creation of the cosmos, as laid out in the Old Testament in Genesis 1–2, had to be given up. Modern theology accepts this, e.g. Gräb (2002: 279) or Hick (1990: 35–6; 1985: 2). As this book hinted, for Old Testament theology this was not too big a sacrifice considering the number of stories and extent of storytelling dedicated to the creation myth in the Old Testament. Kaiser (2001: 81) puts this well by referring to Gilkey (1962: 152–3):

> 'What has happened is clear: because of our modern cosmology, we have stripped what we regard as "the Biblical point of view" of all its wonders and voices.... [W]e have rejected as invalid all the innumerable cases of God's acting and speaking.' I agree not only with Gilkey's analysis but also with his solution; for he went on to conclude that 'first there is the job of stating what the Biblical authors meant to say, a statement couched in the Bible's own terms, cosmological, historical, and theological.'

The intentions of the authors of the Old Testament are critical to understand what they meant to say through the stories of the Old Testament. I have argued here for institutional economic ones, relating to social conflict and societal contracting, and in this respect I would at least add economic categories to, if not replace them for, the ones quoted by Gilkey and supported by Kaiser.

Certainly, over the past centuries the evolution of the natural and social sciences and the accompanying growth of knowledge reduced the number of questions (Old Testament) theology could claim to address and answer: The *restfrage* diminished, that is the interesting and open questions for which we do not have scientifically established answers (see also Hick 1990: 35–7). When asked in the concrete, the *restfrage* got over time increasingly smaller for religion and theology, with sciences deciphering previously godly nature in rational term. In this respect, the very nature of God got smaller when taking account of the fact that, in the case of religion and theology, God tends to be the final, cosmogonic and cosmological answer to the *restfrage*, God creating 'out of nothing' the universe, the earth and humans (Childs 1985: 31). If the idea of God is further abstracted, religious interpretations of creation, such as Childs', may even become compatible with nihilistic ones, such as Hawking (1988: 122–3), who speaks of local irregularities and density fluctuations of matter in space and space-time in order to explain the cosmos and the development of planets and the universe. As mentioned, Hodson's (1967) interpretation of God as 'order of creative intelligence' mediates in this debate, as does Gräb's (2002: 279) which invokes in theological perspective an anthropological principle to be inherent in the Big Bang. A challenge for theological thinking is in this connection to reconcile the idea of God with seemingly theogonic questions of irregularities and fluctuations of physical creation, which potentially can explain the beginning of the cosmos and the ultimate beginning of nature.

As discussed, overall, the kind of explanatory loss the advances in *natural* sciences caused to Old Testament theology may have not been too big a loss considering the extent of discussion the Old Testament dedicated to questions of creation. Possibly of more significance here is to ask how far advances in the *social* sciences affect the *restfrage* for the Old Testament. The book here found that the potential of Old Testament theology to lose out is generally high since most stories of the Old Testament deal with the institutional problem, specifically with issues of social conflict, societal contracting and interaction problems among humans, groups and nations. And these are the kind of problems most commonly addressed in the social sciences too. The book demonstrated that a rational deconstruction and reconstruction of the Old Testament's idea of God in non-behavioural economic terms, especially in relation to principles and ideas like mutual gains as interaction outcome, adds new and high relevance to the Old Testament. However, if this reconstruction is extended to the idea of God, once more religion in general and Old Testament theology in particular tend to lose out regarding the *restfrage,* namely when it comes to the rational reconstruction of concrete, specific questions of how Old Testament stories handled societal contracts, international relations or nation-building. Nevertheless, one thing should not be underestimated: Old Testament *theology* may lose out but not so the Old Testament as such. Following an economic reconstruction, the Old Testament appears to be a highly relevant text for advising on institutional, social problems in modern society.

It seems that both natural and social sciences have contributed in the past to a decrease of the *restfrage* for religion and theology when the *restfrage* is addressed regarding the issue of concrete substance (assuming that religion and theology accept the advances of knowledge made by natural and social sciences). However, such a diminishing of the *restfrage* cannot necessarily be observed for religion and theology when the *restfrage* is addressed in abstract terms. For example, once abstracted in high degrees, economic ideals and religious ones can be reconciled. Similarly, once abstracted in very high degrees, the answers of physics to the questions of the origin of the world can be reconciled with an abstract understanding of God, such as an evolutionary order of intelligence. As discussed, Fromm's (1967: 228) suggestions on the abstraction of the 'God-concept' are here useful too. Such abstraction of the *restfrage* opens up debate between theology and social sciences tremendously, not only regarding the interpretation of Bible stories but in general. In this respect, Old Testament theology has to deconstruct the questions it addresses for abstract meaning and principles, and from here it can salvage, in degrees, the project of Old Testament based religion and theology.

6.5 Concluding remarks

The chapter identified various principles a textual reading of the Old Testament can link to the idea of God. Concrete principles were made out that relate to issues of institutional ordering. God appeared as a player or ruler in the first few stories of Genesis, involving Noah, Abraham, Lot or Isaac. These stories reflected a value fundamentalist God who, supported by a behavioural economics, engaged in rather authoritarian contracting with them. The Jacob stories revealed a much weaker God and an economic reorientation of societal contracting between God and the people, with human beings left to sort out social conflict on their own, mostly in a non-behavioural economic way. And the Joseph stories deal with a God who mirrors ideas and principles of normative institutional economics. A liberatory economic humanism can in these latter respects be identified which demystifies the idea of God in rational, scientific terms. In Exodus, God reappears as a value fundamentalist, retaliatory God, and rather negative, anti-pluralistic value principles emerge for handling social problems. Then, cooperation dilemmas remain unresolved. In addition to these rather concrete roles and principles, God can be related to more abstract functions, such as a principle of social ordering and, most abstractly, a metavariable that relates to the Unexplained in general. Regarding all these principles, variables and functions, the idea of God can be subjected to scientific scrutiny and analysis in an economic reconstruction.

In contrast, religious economics and theology conceptualize the idea of a biblical God in a highly complex, scientifically not testable, metaphysical manner: as an omnipotent person and creator as such, who exhibits multiple and largely incompatible persona in different Bible stories. A lacking coherence regarding the conception of a personal God is a problem for theology and religious economics but less so for institutional economic reconstruction. In an economic reconstruction, different meanings of 'God' are related to the way the Old Testament develops, step-by-step, a critical discussion of the institutional problem and its solution. Here, the present chapter abstracted the understanding of 'God' for being a player within given rules but also for a ruler who can function as cooperation catalyst and worse, as a cooperation saboteur. Hence, the chapter suggested that the moral status of godly intervention and the interaction outcomes and conditions it reflected are ambivalent in Old Testament stories.

In the Jacob stories and in the Joseph stories, God played a constructive, economically inspired role. Here, God successfully worked as an 'economist', largely a non-interventionist, economically inspired ruler. From these stories, a host of economically oriented, enlightened cooperation principles can be deduced regarding the nature of societal contracting among people and interaction conditions that are observed in these stories, especially pluralism. Thus, I deconstructed the idea of God largely as – economically inspired – moral principles and as a reflection of an 'experiential reality', to use a term of Fromm (1967: 229), rather than as a reflection of a persona in any concrete sense. The idea of God then takes on the role of a 'poetic expression of the highest value in humanism [but] not a reality in itself (Fromm 1967: 19)' – a radical, economic humanism, as I argued in the present book.

In contrast, the Tower of Babel story, the Sodom-and-Gomorrah story or the book of Exodus tell stories of a militant, value-fundamentalist God, who prevented cooperation and pluralism. Widespread suffering resulted, also for God's 'own' people; for instance, in the golden calf story when the Israelites were punished for their unfaithfulness. Such suffering relates to God's rather behavioural, value fundamentalist approach to problem solving. I related a set of anti-pluralistic and potentially undemocratic moral principles to these stories and God's intervention strategies as compared to the principles that emerged for the book of Genesis, especially its final stories when the vision of a universal brotherhood of humans was realized.

In his introduction to the philosophy of religion, Capitan (1972: 3) argued that 'the important question about religion today is, not so much which religion one will accept, but whether [one] will accept any at all – whether any religion offers a tenable view of man and the world, and whether a viable way of life follows from it'. Looking at this question under consideration of the various images of God in the Old Testament and the principles of social life it reflects, one can voice both agreement and disagreement. As noted, in particular the Jacob stories and the Joseph stories reflected a rather emancipated and positive image of human nature and social life. For example, God as provider of human capital, which prevents disasters and helps humans to survive periods of famine and starvation, clearly hints at a viable way of life that is based on Old Testament religion. Also, a viable way of life follows from the analysis of God as a principle of social ordering, being related to ideas of creativity in social ordering, mutuality of gains as interaction outcome and pluralism as an interaction condition. However, there are some more sinister issues to ponder about too. God's value-based intervention in the great flood and the even more value-fundamentalist intervention in the Sodom-and-Gomorrah story as well as in the Exodus stories do hardly offer an attractive, normative view of human nature and the world and a viable way of social life. The image of God here is one of a cruel interventionist who meddles in human affairs in a way that prevents favourable, socially acceptable interaction outcomes. In this regard, one has to make up one's mind about which side of Old Testament storytelling and Old Testament religion one wants to use. I have argued for a climax thesis in relation to Genesis and here in particular the Joseph story, and a decline thesis for the book of Exodus and what follows subsequently. Joseph appeared as hero, Moses as the non-hero of Old Testament storytelling. I can follow Fromm's (1967) claimed liberatory, radical humanist views of the Old Testament – but only up to a certain point, namely as far as the book of Genesis is concerned, and in particular the stories involving Jacob and Joseph. In these stories, radical humanist elements, such as the 'final unification of all men and the complete freedom of each individual' (Fromm: 1967: 9), can be observed. In my view, it is above all the final stories of Genesis that offer contemporary relevance and a liberating foundation for an Old Testament-based religion. They are grounded in an economically inspired humanism that can project a tenable view of human nature, of the social world and of a viable way of social life that follows from it. Surprisingly, Fromm did not discuss these final stories of Genesis involving Joseph, Jacob's chief blessing for Joseph, and the condemnation of the Levites. I do not see, as Fromm suggested, an enlightened concept of God and a viable humanist 'global philosophy which emphasizes the oneness of the human race' (1967: 13) emerging from the story of the Exodus and the stories that followed it. The Exodus and the never-ending warfare that came afterwards hardly offer a humanist role model for harmonious, global interactions and peaceful coexistence. After the Exodus, nearly all stories depict anything than the 'final unification of all men and the complete freedom of men' (Fromm 1967: 19) – a maxim which Fromm claimed to uphold for his radical humanist philosophy.

Fromm clearly took an important step in a radical reinterpretation of the Old Testament but he could not make the final step in questioning the potentially anti-humanist, anti-pluralistic and anti-social implications of the Exodus and the role (the idea of) God played in these stories. Being brought up in the Jewish tradition (Fromm 1967: 12–13), he could only in degrees question certain religious precepts of interpreting the Old Testament. In this respect, his interpretations did not fully live up to his own claim that the Old Testament 'can be best understood by those who are least fettered by tradition and most aware of the radical nature of the process of liberation going on at the present time' (Fromm 1967: 7). In considerable degrees, this criticism generally applies to (Old Testament) theology and religious economics too.

Genesis and Exodus and the books that follow essentially document societal contracting and cooperation problems, such as nation-building and managing interactions among nations, under pluralistic conditions where ethnic and cultural diversity and moral disagreement are met. Such interaction conditions have remained a burning issue for the globalizing world of the twenty-first century, especially the multinational firm in a global market economy, the multicultural society and the global community. Genesis, through the figures of Jacob and Joseph, outlines how economic institutions can support conflict resolution in pluralistic contexts and what this implies for our understanding of 'God'. However, pluralism was not mastered as an interaction condition in Exodus and the stories that followed. Then, the 'modern', pluralistic society depicted at the end of Genesis was thrown back into 'iron age'. Indicative is not only the Exodus itself and the endless stories of warfare with other nations that followed but also mass executions within the Israelites' own ranks in the aftermath of the Exodus. Therefore, rosy, conventional views on Moses and the God of Exodus as well as conventional suggestions of an anti-hero thesis or even non-hero thesis for Joseph may need to be qualified (for such conventional views, see Chapters 3 and 4, e.g. Wildavsky 1994; similarly Paris 1998; Gordon 1994, 1989; Brams 1980). God's moral status and the value principles the idea of God reflects have to be critically reviewed too, especially when the question of biblical morality is raised. Rather than asking 'Where is morality 3000 years after Moses?' (Spiegel 1999: 50; similarly Kaiser 2001: 183), the question of biblical morality may be better raised in relation to the God of Genesis and the figure of Joseph in particular (and Jacob too; see also Wagner-Tsukamoto 2001a). These figures reflect economic, ethical ideals which put the project of Old Testament ethics on constructive tracks, especially ethics which are applicable in modern, pluralistic contexts.

Regarding the *restfrage*, the chapter noted that an institutional economic reconstruction of the Old Testament may lead to new adjustments regarding what Old Testament theology can explain and what not. I argued that Old Testament theology and religion which in one way or another draws on the Old Testament can only contribute to a tenable view of human nature and the world and a viable way of life if it accomplishes the abstraction of the *restfrage*. Old Testament theology can here take encouragement from modern theological studies, such as Hick (1985), which have previously abstracted in high degrees rather concrete religious concepts. Otherwise, if such abstraction is not achieved, sciences have 'easy play' in dismantling religious belief and theological debate. This consideration also links back to a discussion of God as a metavariable in general and as a reference to the Unexplained in particular. In these regards, it has to be examined how far Old Testament theology needs to connect to the debate on the *restfrage* and the abstraction of the *restfrage*. Only through increasing abstraction both in natural and social science perspectives, the project of (Old Testament) theology is likely to be salvaged.

7
Conclusions and After thoughts on the Economic Reconstruction of the Old Testament

> *Since this book [the Old Testament] came into being, it has confronted generation after generation. Each generation must struggle with the Bible in its turn, and come to terms with it.*
>
> (Buber 1982: 1)

The economic reconstruction of the Old Testament which I pursued in this book unearthed and stressed, contrary to Pirson's (2002: 10) and Meeks' (1989: 3) pessimism, a high contemporary relevance of the Old Testament. As it became clear throughout this book, the Old Testament contributes much to our understanding and solving of constitutional and institutional problems of the modern world, such as societal contracts and cooperative interactions in the capitalist, multicultural society, in the international community and in pluralistic interaction contexts in general. Such problems permeate and dominate the Old Testament from its very outset. A high influence and social competence, especially with regard to economic principles and concepts, can here be attested to the Old Testament. Seemingly, when projected in institutional economic perspective, the Old Testament has a lot to say about problem-solving for the modern society, especially a world that is ever more involved in globalizing interactions.

The present study provided a new perspective on the Old Testament. The narrative sequence and the message emerging from the stories of Genesis raise the question of how far the Old Testament already sensed and anticipated the approach of modern constitutional and institutional economics, as it was pioneered, for instance, by Hayek, Buchanan, Brennan, Coase, North, Williamson or Vanberg. It became apparent that the history of early economic thought can well be traced to the Old Testament.

The few existing economic interpretations of the Old Testament are either microeconomically oriented, applying the theoretical approach of rational choice theory, or analyse Bible stories through a religious, theologically grounded economics rather than an economics of religion. Institutional economics, as outlined in this book, enables a different, more integrated and more fundamental economic analysis of Old Testament stories: It examined in theoretical and practical perspectives how far the Old Testament positively and normatively handles the institutional problem, especially the problem of societal contracting, as a capital contribution–distribution conflict in relation to incentive structures and methodically grounds such analysis in the idea of conflict-laden interactions (a dilemma structure) and the idea of self-interested choice behaviour (the model of economic man). The book underlined that there is ample room for reconstructing Bible stories in such economic terms. I identified ideas from both a behavioural, religious economics and from a conventional, non-behavioural institutional economics in the Old Testament. In particular, a non-behavioural economic reconstruction of Bible stories has hardly begun. The key question for deciding whether a religious economics or a non-behavioural economics of religion is more relevant for understanding the Old Testament is which of the two approaches better matches the analysis of social conflict and cooperation problems depicted in Old Testament stories, especially problems of international relations and nation-building. This question can be reformulated in normative terms too.

The following summarizes the findings this book made and it outlines some afterthoughts and open questions for future research. First, I review key theses of an economic reconstruction of the Old Testament (section 7.1). The chapter here returns to the climax thesis and the decline thesis as well as the hero thesis and the non-hero thesis as advanced by the book. Second, I discuss the different types of organization structure arrangements that can be found in the Old Testament regarding transaction cost effects (section 7.2). Third, the significance of pluralism as an interaction condition in Old Testament stories is discussed (section 7.3). I relate the Old Testament's apparent switch from behavioural, religious economic contracting to 'pure', non-behavioural economic contracting to the rise of pluralism as an interaction condition in Old Testament stories and the kind of cost implications this had for contracting. Fourth, I stress the instrumental role of the idea of a dilemma structure and of the model of economic man in Old Testament storytelling (section 7.4). The role of the original sin and the snake metaphor are here paid special attention to. Fifth, I briefly comment on the question of authorship of the Old Testament (section 7.5). Sixth, I critically ask how far the findings of the present book support the thesis that the Old Testament is grounded in a capitalist ethics (section 7.6). Max Weber's thesis on the protestant ethics of capitalism is revisited. Finally, I return to the question of whether God, as encountered in the Old Testament, is an economist (section 7.7).

7.1   The Old Testament and economic role models for societal contracting, international relations and nation-building

The Old Testament nearly always addresses interaction problems, although they are frequently not solved, especially when put into the historic-textual perspective that biblical storytelling sets up from Adam and Eve to the very end of the Old Testament. After the Exodus, the Old Testament apparently favoured a value-fundamentalist, religious approach as strategy for 'solving' social conflict – which in many instances left Israel counting losses too. From the book of Exodus onwards, we encounter anti-pluralistic contracting that excluded 'other' nations from the covenant between God and his chosen people. A universal approach to societal contracting, as we found in Genesis for Noah, Abraham, Jacob and Joseph, can then hardly be made out. However, Exodus' value-based approach to solving social conflict ran into problems, not only externally when Israel tried to conquer or wipe out other nations but also internally when the Israelites tried to enact among themselves a tight value consensus, focused on the First Commandment. God acted then at best as a behavioural economist who aimed to defend principles such as faithfulness for establishing social order. In many instances Israel was punished for being unfaithful; for example, it suffered various exiles. Problems of social conflict, nation-building and cooperative international relations then remained unresolved.

Genesis here told a different story. Problems of societal contracting and social conflict were ultimately resolved. Key examples are the stories involving Joseph and also Jacob, and to a lesser degree, outside of Genesis, the Solomon story in the book of Kings. If one looks for role models in the Old Testament regarding international relations and nation-building in a multicultural, pluralistic context, in my view only these stories stand out, the most significant being the Joseph story, but the Jacob story and the Solomon story also offer very valuable insights.

The Joseph story is one of the most intricate and elaborate stories of the Old Testament. It discusses the economics of fiscal policy, hierarchical structures, asset specificity of capital transactions and property rights management. The present book argued that the Joseph story reflects the very centre and climax of Genesis and of the Old Testament in general. Only in this story, Israel solved the two problems which it nearly continuously encounters in the Old Testament: The problem of building its own nation and the problem of coexisting peacefully with other nations in an environment where pluralism and extreme, dilemmatic scarcities in resources such as fertile land and water were met. Joseph's skilful interventions in the footsteps of an institutional economist ensured mutual gains between Egypt and Israel. And while being expatriates in Egypt, Israel had its own land to administer and it solved the nation-building problem by sharing the well-developed institutional structures of Egypt. Also, Joseph's position at the top of Egypt's industrial hierarchies ensured a fine power balance in decision-making that affected both nations. Wealth and prosperity was created for both nations. In the Solomon story, Israel also enjoyed prosperity and stability, this time in its own nation state. Then, Israel made peace treaties and trade treaties with surrounding neighbours. Thus, once again, Israel solved the nation-building problem and the problem of international relations.

In both the Joseph story and the Solomon story, principles of non-behavioural economic ordering shine through, explaining the success of institutional ordering. For the Joseph story and the Solomon story, the question of whether God, as met in the Old Testament, were an economist can be answered in the affirmative, 'God' reflecting non-behavioural, institutional economic intervention and economic cooperation principles (see also section 7.7 below). Because of the mutuality of gains that Joseph's and Solomon's policies generated, interactions were easily sustainable, at least much more so than zero-sum interactions with their win/loss outcomes. As the Old Testament constantly reminds us, the territories Israel tried to conquer and hold on to were among the most hotly contested of the region. In such contexts, the key to successful international relations and the successful building of a nation are the transformation of futile, zero-sum games and prisoner dilemma-type interactions into sustainable, nonzero-sum interactions. Especially Joseph and Genesis here had shown the way out of the dilemma.

Analytically, this problem – and its solution – was already set up in the Paradise scenario and its underlying prisoner's dilemma scenario.

In this respect, outcomes of both the Joseph story and the Solomon story compare in considerable degrees to principles and ideas endorsed by Adam Smith's *Inquiry into the Wealth of Nations* and to reasons why this moral philosopher ultimately switched from a behavioural ethics, which in certain respects is quite close to a religious economics and the theological approach, to a (non-behavioural) economics for investigating social problems of modern society. Such a switch can be observed in Genesis too. At the outset, Genesis pursued a religious, behavioural ethics (linked to a behavioural economics), which in the further course of Genesis was increasingly replaced by an economically oriented, non-behavioural ethics in the footsteps of a constitutional and institutional economics.

In line with these findings, the present study advanced a climax thesis for the final stories of Genesis that involved Joseph. In the Joseph story, Israel regained the kind of paradise that Adam and Eve had lost at the outset of Genesis. At this concluding point, Genesis reflects an enlightened, liberatory and emancipatory approach to institutional problem-solving in complex, pluralistic interaction contexts, such as a multicultural society or a community of nations. This explains my proposal of a hero thesis for Joseph and a climax thesis for the Joseph stories in the Old Testament.

On the other hand, I suggested a non-hero thesis for Moses and I advanced a decline thesis for the books that followed Genesis. Once Israel resorted to nation-building and international relations that was of a belligerent nature, driven by a value-fundamentalist, 'non-economically' oriented God, the outcome were unsustainable, zero-sum interactions. From the beginning of the book of Exodus, futile interactions were played out that involved the conquest and dispersion of other nations. However, success for Israel was then of a short-lived nature, with counterattacks constantly looming and happening. Following the Exodus from Egypt, the Old Testament is filled, right to its final pages, with an endless number of such dismal stories of warfare, killing and dislocation. These interactions hardly depict a role model for cooperative interactions in a modern world which is defined by pluralistic interaction conditions. Here, my analysis attributed anti-social, undemocratic and anti-pluralistic value principles to the stories of the Exodus and most stories that followed. Exodus famously foretold of these dark events to come when it announced in Exodus (1: 8) that a 'new king came to power who did not know about Joseph'. Besides the new king of Egypt, Moses, too, could not live up to Joseph's success. Reasons for this failure have to be related to the anti-pluralistic, value-fundamentalist, intervening role God played in the Exodus stories, and from here the idea of God can be deconstructed for interaction and cooperation principles of how *not* to proceed when stable and successful societal contracts of a universal nature are the goal (see also sections 7.3 and 7.7 below).

Pacifism stood little chance in the Old Testament when, in the wake of the Exodus, the Israelites and other nations engaged in warfare and institutional order was tested out in the extreme. The slaughter of the peaceful Laish people is here the best example. The Laish people were eradicated by the Israelites because of their unsuspecting, peaceful nature, which made them an easy target (see Chapter 5). This also stresses the functional, heuristic purpose of the idea of the dilemma structure and the model of economic man when testing out institutional structures that are meant to order peaceful, social interactions, both internally and externally.

On a comparative note, the New Testament seems to address a rather different institutional problem scenario than the Old Testament. The New Testament's rather pacifist, 'soft', 'social psychological' approach for conflict handling can be related to the specific context in which Christianity emerged. The actual Roman occupation of the territories of the Near or Middle East, as also described in the New Testament, implied the strict rule of Roman law. For instance, Matthew (22: 17–21) hints at such institutional issues when the Pharisees and Herodians ask Jesus: 'Tell us then, what is your opinion? Is it right to pay taxes to Caesar?' and Jesus replied: 'Give to Caesar what is Caesar's, and to God what is God's.' Roman law, of course, frequently and closely mirrors the economic approach and economic ideals. In a sense, a 'hard' economic framework for conflict management and the regulation of social interactions was thus already in place when the New Testament started its 'soft', behavioural analysis of social problems. The scene was then set for the New Testament to focus on comparatively minor, social conflicts and issues that could be settled on a pacifist, goodwill basis. The New Testament largely outlines such behavioural, pacifist principles which, it can be speculated, may have worked well in the specific context described and implied by the New Testament: Then, larger institutional problems of societal contracting had already been settled in predominantly institutional and constitutional economic terms – through Roman institutional structures. This thesis can be advanced in textual perspective, supported by references of the New Testament on Roman institutional structures, and this thesis can also be advanced in actual, historical perspective by looking at Roman laws of the time when the Near or Middle East were occupied. This also implies that from the point of view of understanding economic principles and issues of societal contracting in the Bible, especially ways out of Hobbesian anarchy and the natural distribution state, as Buchanan called it, the New Testament (apart from investigating the principles endorsed by Roman law and how they were perceived in the occupied territories) is comparatively uninteresting whereas the stories of the Old Testament offer fundamental insights in this respect.

7.2   Organization structures, transactions cost efficiencies and environmental conditions

The present study identified different types of governance structures in the tradition of an organizational economics in the Old Testament. The organizational problem showed up as a special variant of the institutional problem. There are the tall, bureaucratic and hierarchical structures of Egypt's pharaohs; there is the web-like, clan-based organization structure that could be observed during the Exodus journey of the Israelites; there is the comparatively loose, federal and non-integrated structure that prevailed after the Exodus journey among Israel's tribes; and there is King Solomon's tall, bureaucratic hierarchy.

Regarding internal conditions and external conditions, the hierarchical structures of Egypt and of King Solomon seemed well matched to the specific purpose of administering a huge empire. They can be viewed as well adapted to their specific, economic environments. They managed to stabilize their environments through governance structures, including trade treaties and peace treaties. I already commented on Joseph's and Egypt's industrial policies in the previous section of this chapter in some detail. I suggested incentive-compatibility advantages and transaction cost efficiencies for these policies: Internal structural features concerning incentive structures and capital exchange were matched with environmental features concerning incentive structures and capital exchange, and here especially cost effects of interaction conditions like pluralism, moral disagreement, value decay, etc. (see also Wagner-Tsukamoto 2008c, 2003: Chapter 7, 2001a).

Also, the tent grouping arrangement during the Exodus journey and the kind of web-like organization structures it reflects appears well adapted to the specific purpose and the environmental conditions of the Exodus journey. The Exodus journey reflected a highly uncertain endeavour. Time frames and the specific route of the journey were decided at short notice. And regarding natural, environmental conditions, deserts and mountains had to be conquered, as had other tribes to be fought against on the journey to the Promised Land. Under these conditions, a web-like, clan-based organization structure appeared economically advantageous. It allowed quick relocation and the quick organization of people when a fight loomed.

The loose, federal structure Israel put in place in the book of Joshua apparently fairly split land among the tribes but it did not ensure the integration of decision-making as it would have been required for a successful confederation of states. When individual Israelite tribes were attacked by other nations it was difficult for Israel to respond as one nation. High communication costs existed since coordination had to be sorted out and negotiated from case to case. Especially the network of priests, which under the tent grouping arrangement had functioned as a tight integration mechanism (see section 5.1), was no longer capable of fulfilling this function since, from the book of Joshua onward, the priests had been dispersed across the territories of all Israelites tribes. Only when judges and kings moved to the top of this federal arrangement, the integration problem was solved. This development can be explained by transaction cost inefficiencies which a previous, too federal arrangement also suffered from.

7.3 The onset of modernity in the Old Testament: Pluralism as interaction condition

In Genesis, the condition of modernity, of value pluralism, even of moral disagreement and of value decay – as it also closely characterizes the modern, capitalist society – was most prominently invoked with the multicultural interaction setting of Israel in Egypt. Then, Genesis carefully resisted calling upon God, understood in a behavioural institutional sense, to solve cooperation problems. Here, the Old Testament realized that in social arenas like the modern city, the multicultural nation, and the international community, religious economic or theological–psychological ordering reflected a too costly ('pareto-inferior') strategy for conflict resolution. At this point, Genesis no longer advocated behavioural techniques for social ordering like value education, or even 'value indoctrination' and 'social conditioning' as behavioural economists and socio-economists also suggest (e.g. Sen 1990: 36, Simon 1976: 103, 149–51; also Etzioni 1988; in degrees even Williamson 1998: 1–2, 10, 15–17, 1985: 6, 30–2, 64–7, 391, 1975: 26–30). Such techniques are likely to be cost-effective only in a small-numbered, socially tightly knit community, where a value consensus can be easily maintained. For Genesis, this approach, linked to a behavioural economics, seemed to succeed in its early stories only, when we meet religious, faithful and God-fearing figures like Noah, Abraham, Lot or Isaac. However, from the Jacob story onwards and also in the Joseph story, Genesis no longer advocated behavioural, religious economic contracts and the related punishment of unfaithful behaviour, such as a destructive Sodom-and-Gomorrah-type approach for restoring the effectiveness of behavioural institutions and value contracting. As indicated, a key thesis of this book is that behavioural institutions like religiosity and related behavioural contracting (including behavioural economic contracting) through value education, etc. may only be capable of effectively and efficiently solving the institutional problem in a premodern context, especially for intragroup interactions within socially highly cohesive and behaviourally strongly bonded social units, such as a traditional family or a small tribe (see Figure 3.2). However, in modern contexts, where pluralism arises as an interaction condition, economic contracting is likely to be more cost-effective than behavioural contracting.

This is not to say that in certain isolated instances, such a premodern, anti-pluralistic context may have survived even in industrial societies today. An example may here be the Amish people in the USA. Still, on the one hand, the Old Testament seemed to be rather critical regarding behavioural institutions, for example, family bonds, as effective institutional regulative, as demonstrated by the breakdown of social order within the family in the Cain-and-Abel story, the Esau-Jacob story or the story of Joseph and his brothers. On the other hand, in the interaction contexts generally described in the Old Testament, a premodern isolation of group interactions, which appears to be a fundamental prerequisite for successful, cost-effective behavioural conditioning through religion, was largely inconceivable: Genesis aimed from the outset at *universal* societal contracts.

Genesis and Exodus and the books that follow essentially document cooperation problems under modern, pluralistic interaction conditions. Of course, such interaction conditions have remained a burning issue for the globalizing world of the twenty-first century and the kind of institutions it entertains in the multinational firm, the multicultural society or the global community. Genesis outlined how economic institutions can support conflict resolution in such pluralistic contexts. The Joseph story and the emigration of Israel to Egypt were here most illustrative. However, pluralism was not mastered as an interaction condition in Exodus and the books that followed (apart from the Solomon story). The condemnation of Exodus (1: 8) is here vindictive when the new pharaoh is characterized as 'not knowing about Joseph'. Then, the modern, pluralistic society depicted at the end of Genesis is thrown back into 'iron age'. Indicative is not only the Exodus itself but also mass executions within the Israelites' own ranks in the aftermath of the Exodus. In this regard, Popper's (1992: 189–90) critical comments on Moses' violent, anti-pluralistic stance in the golden calf story fully apply.

The Pentateuch and the books of the Deuteronomic history seemingly warn behavioural economics, religious economics, theology and behavioural sciences in general not to rely too heavily on 'value contracts' and behavioural institutions for resolving conflict in pluralistic contexts. Although the theological project of a global value contract – a 'world ethos of ethical values' (Küng 1999: 70–3) – outlines, in contrast to Exodus, a constructive, behavioural route to conflict resolution, its viability is in doubt too. It is likely to be less effective and less efficient than economic intervention, especially when we find pluralistic interaction conditions, such as moral disagreement and even value decay. Figure 3.2 implied this as well. Costs for generating a value consensus under pluralistic conditions or for overturning pluralism as an interaction condition are likely to be prohibitively high (see Wagner-Tsukamoto 2008c, 2003, 2001a). Even if a common denominator for a global value consensus could be found, it is difficult to see how a global value contract could be effectively and efficiently enacted without the support of economic institutions. In addition, moral reservations can be raised against this project because of its potentially anti-pluralistic nature. Economics has much to offer in this respect. By methodologically grounding institutional analysis and intervention in the model of economic man and the model of an economic dilemma structure, pluralism presents no obstacle to resolving social conflict. The institutional economic reconstruction of Old Testament stories forcefully underlined this point.

7.4   Encountering dilemma structures and economic man in the Old Testament

Of course, the image of economic man has attracted widespread criticism from behavioural sciences, moral philosophy and theology. They accuse economics in this respect of a dark and dismal image of human nature (for a review, see Wagner-Tsukamoto 2003). Economics, so it is claimed, portrays human nature through the model of economic man as the self-interested agent who aims to maximize own gain. However, such perceptions reflect a misconception of economics. It confuses actual occurrences of merely self-interested behaviour with the economic approach. Of course, at the very heart of economics are the ideas of self-interest (economic man) and dilemma structure but, for one thing, these ideas are mere heuristics, and the wider purpose of these ideas are social, ethical ones – the generation of wealth for a community (mutual gains) and the resolution of the institutional problem. Under the governance structures of the market economy, self-interest is to bloom into socially beneficial outcomes. This is the normative dictum of economics, reflecting its institutional programme. At the level of normative economics, systemic intervention with institutional rules aims to make self-interest socially good. This implies that the economic programme does not doctor with stingy, self-interested behaviour at the level of the individual but merely applies this model of human nature as a methodological, heuristic fiction.

Thus, the present book discounted behavioural criticism of economic man and dilemma structure by tracing the prevalence of these ideas in Old Testament stories, from the Paradise story (and here especially the snake metaphor and the concept of the original sin) to the stories involving Jacob, to the stories of Joseph and Moses and also to David and Solomon. I showed that the Old Testament, when using the figurative language of the Paradise scenario, does not aim to eliminate economic man or the 'snake' and the original sin, but rather examines these ideas for their usefulness to successfully organize social interactions (with regard to the idea of mutuality of gains). I argued in detail that the presence of economic man and dilemma structure in Bible stories does not imply a dark image of human nature or of social life for the Old Testament and for Old Testament economics (and neither does it for Old Testament theology). Rather, I pointed out that the model of economic man and the idea of the dilemma structure only provide methodological fictions – instrumental tools, 'research heuristics', to use Lakatos' terminology – for resolving dilemmatic interaction conflict regarding capital contributions and distributions. Economic man and dilemma structure do so by organizing and directing economic analysis towards situational intervention (with incentive structures, 'economic institutions') in order to ensure mutual gains as interaction outcome. On the basis of this situational, 'non-behavioural' approach, socially desirable interaction outcomes are examined, in particular mutuality of gains (see Figure 1.1). In Genesis, besides Joseph, another key economic hero of a non-behavioural, institutional economic reconstruction was Jacob, while heroes of a behavioural institutional economics were Noah, Abraham, Lot or Isaac. A common feature was that they all had acquired wealth to a high degree in the course of their interactions.

As noted, this book explored descriptions of sinfulness in Old Testament stories and of those who induced sinfulness, such as the snake in the Paradise story, with regard to opportunistic, even predatory, economic man-type behaviour in a dilemma structure. Indeed, theology might easily agree with such an understanding that relates Adam and Eve's behaviour and the original sin to greedy and stingy, economic predispositions at the level of individual behaviour. However, the widespread presence of economic man and dilemma structure in the Old Testament already hints that economic man and dilemma structure do not reflect a bad, immoral *image of human nature* and a dark, immoral *image of social life*. For instance, statements of the Old Testament that 'man's nature is evil from childhood' cannot be taken at empirical, behavioural face value but they should be transcended in methodical, heuristic perspective: Social interactions have to be tested for economic man-behaviour (in a dilemma structure) in order to ensure that cooperation prevails. As Hardin (1968), Buchanan (1975) and similarly Williamson (1975, 1985) noted, otherwise the mere possibility of an economic man 'actually' showing up is sufficient to derail social interactions and yield mutual loss as interaction outcome. The Old Testament's key 'master concepts', or 'meta concepts' or 'research heuristics', to use other terms, were here the original sin and the sinful, greedy behaviour of Adam and Eve. In a sense Adam and Eve can be said to function as non-master heroes for all Old Testament stories to come, of how economic man-behaviour in a dilemma structure develops rather disastrous effects in the face of incentive-*in*compatible institutional structures. Thus, the original sin scenario sets up storytelling that follows after the Paradise story. Then, new societal contracts of different kinds were negotiated between God and humans, more precisely, among humans but 'hosted' by God (whereby the idea of God can be further deconstructed for cooperation principles; see Chapter 6 and section 7.7 below).

The snake poignantly embodied Adam and Eve's behaviour. The snake metaphor and references to sinful behaviour, which seemingly caused cooperation problems, time and again shows up in subsequent Old Testament storytelling. This happens most explicitly so in the Exodus story when the assistants of the pharaoh and of Moses were throwing snakes at each other, driven by a value-fundamentalist God and the non-cooperation principles he then stood for. This subsequently derails interactions because of a lacking knowledge of how to successfully handle 'snake-like', predatory, economic man-type behaviour in a dilemma structure. Joseph, on the other hand, knew well the art of 'soothsaying from the hissing of snakes' (Plaut 1981: 278; see Chapter 3). While Genesis in this way developed various behavioural and non-behavioural approaches to prevent the disastrous effects of 'snake-like', economic man-behaviour in a dilemma structure, as first shown by Adam and Eve, Exodus did the opposite. It showed, as the Paradise scenario had done before, that mutually beneficial interactions quickly come to an end when principles of economic ordering, both heuristic, theoretical and practical ones, are given up.

7.5   A brief note on the question of authorship of the Old Testament

An apparent dialectic in the Old Testament between a behavioural economics and a conventional ('non-behavioural', 'situational') economics can be further explored with regard to questions of authorship of the Old Testament. Such questions are debated in the redactional, theological literature regarding different groups of authors: claimed economically oriented Yahwists and spiritually oriented Elohists (Gordon 1994: 19–21). In this respect, future research can examine whether Elohists were as 'non-economically' oriented as suggested in the literature: They may have pursued 'at least' a behavioural economics, as the stories involving Noah, Abraham, Lot or Isaac hinted early on in this book.

In general, an institutional economic analysis of the Bible sheds new light on questions of authorship by focusing first on the *why* of authorship, asking what basic problems motivated the writing of the Old Testament before the *who* of authorship is re-examined. The present study here hinted that institutional economic problems of societal contracting and of resolving social conflict within a nation and among nations are the key reasons why the Old Testament was written. Possibly, theology has paid in this respect too much attention to the question of authorship of the Old Testament in its own right. In this respect, I share Weiser's (1961: 80) early criticism regarding authorship research. The absence of conclusive findings on questions of authorship despite centuries of theological research underlines this point (see also Mayes 1983: 42–3, 137).

As elaborated on earlier in this book (see section 1.1), the present study intentionally sidelined the question of authorship: The author who had the 'last word' on the writing of the Bible, as reflected by the way the Bible presents itself to us today, provided the implicit reference point for the question of authorship.

7.6 On the capitalist ethics of the Old Testament: Revisiting the Weber thesis

The institutional economic reconstruction pursued in this book gave rise to the question how far world religions that build and draw on the Old Testament in various degrees, such as Judaism, Christianity and Islam, are grounded in a capitalist ethics. Such an examination complements, possibly even revises, Max Weber's analysis and thesis on the relationship of religious – in his case: protestant – ethics and the spirit of capitalism. On a related issue, the spread of certain religions as world religions can be explored in economic terms, as set out in this book.

Weber's key thesis was that Protestantism as a new and spreading theology of the seventeenth and eighteenth centuries gave rise to capitalism as an economic system, mainly because the new theology came with a new spiritual attitude towards profit making (for reviews, see Lehmann 1993; MacKinnon 1993; Nipperdey 1993). Protestantism endorsed, so Weber claimed, a peculiar ethos – a new *Weltanschauung* (worldview), namely a devotion to the calling of making money (Weber 1930: 51, 72). Such an ethos was absent, so Weber claimed, from earlier entrepreneurial and capitalist activity as it could be observed throughout the history of mankind. Weber argued that a distinctively new spirit of capitalism characterized the modern entrepreneur and Weber went on to spell out various features of the modern capitalist firm in this respect: first, the rational industrial organization of free labour; second, a rational bookkeeping system; third, the separation of business from household (the separation of corporate property from private property); and fourth, entrepreneurial activity that was characterized by the spirit of capitalism (Weber 1930: 21–2, 51, 72). Weber claimed that businesses that showed these features were a modern phenomenon that arose in line with the advancement of ascetic Protestantism.

On the basis of the research conducted in my book, it may not be most appropriate to question this thesis of Weber in historical perspective, but I can cast doubt on it in historical-textual perspective, especially in relation to the Jacob stories and the Joseph stories (and also the Solomon stories), which belong to the oldest parts of the Old Testament and emerged many centuries before Christ. In general, it is fair to say that the Old Testament is permeated by a peculiar economic ethos, even an economic humanism. My study amply demonstrated that economic ideas are widely and deeply present in the stories and thought of the Old Testament. In the specific instance of the Joseph story, we find all four of Weber's criteria of a modern capitalist enterprise: First, work in Egypt was organized in tall hierarchies. Skills specification and skills specialization determined the grouping of work activities. And as discussed in Chapter 3, organization members could be characterized as free labour in relation to the rights they enjoyed. Second, references to administration in the Joseph story allow for the conclusion that a bookkeeping system existed. For example, the administration of the discussed 20-per cent barter tax on crop production required measurement techniques and the running of a stockpiling system. Third, especially Joseph's policy of the transfer of ownership in production capital into the hands of the state reflects the separation of household property and business property. Private property, as far as it concerned land, for example, was transferred into the hands of the corporate entrepreneur 'state'. Economic advantages, such as economics of scale, can explain such developments in the Joseph story (and they compare to historic changes in late nineteenth-century USA when so-called independent contractors were organized into the entity 'firm'; see Wagner-Tsukamoto 2008e, 2007a, 2003). Fourth, Joseph's career and his policies amply reflect the 'spirit of capitalism'. Because of his entrepreneurial skills and wits he rapidly advanced in Egypt's industrial hierarchy. He clearly showed economic rationalism and a high propensity to a calling and devotion to labour – features which Weber (1930: 72, 78) identified as the spirit of capitalism. His talent for economic thinking and business matters can be related to his 'Jewish' upbringing as an Israelite. As Jacob's son, he had enjoyed excellent schooling in economic thinking and contracting and it is no coincidence that, with the benefit of hindsight, Jacob praised and 'blessed' Joseph as the 'fruitful vine' of Israel (Genesis 49: 22–6). This reflects a spiritual calling in Weber's terminology, an ethically coloured, economic maxim for the conduct of life, as Weber (1930: 51–2) also characterized the spirit if capitalism.

In these respects, the Joseph story reflects a rather modern story in Weber's terminology. The ideas of the Joseph story are typical of (institutional) economic thinking in the Old Testament. Chapters 2–5 of the present study identified positive and negative examples and proposed a climax thesis for the Joseph story and Genesis and a decline thesis for the Old Testament stories that followed. Besides the Joseph story, there are further positive examples of economic thought in the Old Testament, such as the Jacob story and the Solomon story; negative examples are the Exodus story and most of the stories of warfare that came after the it. MacKinnon's (1993: 218) general assessment of Judaism as lacking a 'this-worldly [economic, capitalistic] direction for salvation' strongly needs to be qualified in this respect. He may have a point for Exodus and the stories that follow (apart from the Solomon story), when Israel was inclined to wait for salvation by God (which ultimately did not materialize). However, MacKinnon may have less a point for Genesis. It was especially Genesis that pointed towards deep-rooted, economic thinking in the Old Testament (and it could even be argued that, by anti-thesis, Exodus did the same).

Besides modifying the Weber thesis in this largely historical-textual way, I want to examine whether it can be reversed in a more fundamental way: whether the Old Testament set the scene for the development of a particular capitalist ethics of religion. It can be speculated that those who listened to and read the stories of prime examples of Old Testament 'economists' like Jacob and Joseph were actually influenced and 'trained' in their worldly (pre)dispositions as businessmen and entrepreneurs. With regard to the specific function, role and motivation of the Old Testament, Weber's claim (1930: 21) can be modified that *only* ascetic Protestantism produced the spirit of capitalism and a capitalist system as demarcated above. In this respect, the present study sides with one of Weber's main critiques of his time, Werner Sombart, who argued, as reviewed by Lehmann (1993), that other religions had contributed to the rise of capitalism too. Sombart himself, however, never clarified how Jewish doctrine, for example, approached this issue. As Lehmann (1993: 200) here pointed out, Sombart (1911: 294) intentionally left this to experts in the field of church history. The present study brought about such clarifications by reconstructing the Old Testament in institutional economic terms and by outlining a normative function of the Old Testament for societal contracting in economic terms. This opens up a fruitful avenue for future, interdisciplinary dialogue between economic research and Old Testament theology.

In general, the present book well demonstrated that economic ideas and principles are widely present throughout the Old Testament. Seemingly, a deeply economic ethos drives the Old Testament. This is likely to have had a deep impact on the upbringing and socio-psychological environment of those who believed in and spiritually followed the concepts and principles of the Old Testament. For example, the Old Testament forms the backbone of Jewish belief and is the most integral element of spiritual Jewish life. It is also a well-known fact that Jewish entrepreneurs are among the most successful ones in the world. This also goes hand in hand with Weber's (1930: 39) observation that immigrants (Jewish ones) often devote their service to industry rather than the service of the state to which they feel not affiliated to (see also

Lehmann 1993: 197, 199; MacKinnon 1993: 213, 230). Clearly, Weber's (1930) observation on Protestantism and its apparent endorsement of economic, business habits as virtues can be projected to the Jewish belief system and the proverbial success of the Jewish businessman. However, and possibly more importantly, the present book affirmed that this spiritual affiliation to economic thought and this calling for making money already emerges from and is endorsed by the Old Testament. This is likely to have considerably influenced the proverbial success of the Jewish capitalist. Thus, the idea of being 'Jewish' and being a successful entrepreneur can be traced to the very, *economic* fabric of the Jewish belief system – the Old Testament (or 'Hebrew Bible'). This is especially true for Genesis and here in particular the stories involving Jacob and Joseph. For Exodus and subsequent books this is less the case (The Solomon story is an exception).

   Therefore, it appears that the Old Testament clearly reflects a capitalist ethics and it appears safe to say that it exerts a considerable normative influence over those who get acquainted with it and believe into these stories. This conclusion and also what I suggested above regarding a historical-textual critique of the Weber thesis give rise to a very different question and thesis than the one envisaged by Weber. The new question would be: How far seemingly religious bodies of thought, like the Old Testament, play a rather earthly role in organizing social interactions in rational, secular, economic terms? In this respect, the thesis can be advanced that religion, as exemplified by Old Testament thought, is grounded in a capitalist, economic ethics *in order to* advise on, and intervene in, worldly problems of – economic – contracting among humans. Future research has to further develop and spell out this thesis and the other theses mentioned on Weber above.

7.7   So, is God an economist?

One thing becomes very clear in the course of this book: that the Old Testament is a deeply economically inspired book. This study comprehensively traced ideas such as capital contributions and distributions, incentive structures, mutual gains, dilemma structure and economic man in Old Testament thinking. For certain stories, a deeply ethical, economic message and economic value principles emerged, especially for successful nation-building and the generation of peaceful international relations, even in difficult environmental contexts, such as extreme scarcities in fertile land and water and pluralism being an interaction condition.

The idea of God showed up in a multifaceted way in the Old Testament and in this respect, the question of whether God is an economist has to be examined in a multifaceted manner too. In rather concrete terms, God entered the scene of Old Testament storytelling as a persona and also as one who performed different institutional economic functions and roles in different stories. In certain stories, he was involved as a player, such as the Paradise story (when Adam and Eve stole from him), the Abraham story (when he tested contract commitment of Abraham through a hostage/sacrifice stipulation) or the Jacob story (when he struggled with Jacob and lost to him). In these examples, when God was actually involved as a player, he was seemingly on a learning curve on what 'good' institutional economic 'playing' and contracting implied. In other stories, God performed more the function of a ruler, basically overseeing 'play' within given 'moves of a game'. I attributed such a ruling function, executed in economic terms, to his dealings in the final events of the Paradise story (when he protected the tree of life with a cherubim and a sword), the Jacob story (when he ordered Laban not to harm Jacob for his misdeeds but to negotiate a new contract) or the Joseph story (when he allocated economic wisdom to Joseph). In these stories, God can be characterized as a successful institutional economist, proceeding in the footsteps of an economically well-trained consultant.

As indicated, the Joseph story was here the prime example, with Israel and Egypt peacefully coexisting and, in a sense, re-entering paradise. This was possible because of clever institutional economic ordering that was inspired by God in this story. I interpret here the idea of God rather concretely with regard to an institutional economist and ruler who provided Joseph with intellectual human capital on institutional economic ordering. In the Jacob story, when God intervened to stop Laban from hurting Jacob, God's involvement is not as straightforward as in the Joseph story but he guides the parties to successful 'peace treaties'. God here shows up more as an evolutionary economist, mainly observing what is going on but not actually intervening in contracting. The Jacob stories and the tit-for-tat web of interactions they spin reflect evolutionary interaction economics – but with a purpose: In the footsteps of Buchanan's constitutional economics, I argued that evolutionary tit-for-tat helped the involved agents to escape from 'Hobessian anarchy', or the natural distribution state, as Buchanan may call it. In this way, step-by-step, a new societal contract emerged that was largely negotiated among humans themselves. Normative institutional economics here follows up: Most clearly principles of normative institutional economics were found in the Joseph story. Such principles actively steered decision-makers towards socially desirable outcomes. I identified here ethical ideas and principles on nation-building and international relations. Thus, following a rather concrete approach to deconstructing the persona of God in the Old Testament in scientific, economic terms, the Old Testament reveals in many shades and colours that God, indeed, showed up as an economist.

We encountered a more uncomforting and non-economic God as ruler in the Exodus stories and the stories that followed the Exodus. The Exodus stories largely reflect value contracting that is coupled with certain economic sanctions. The First Commandment stipulated here faithfulness to God, with other gods being banished. Since Israel broke this commandment time and again, it suffered severe punishments. The message emerging in this respect in the Old Testament is a rather bleak one, with pluralism as an interaction condition not being mastered and ethical, economic ideals being forsaken, such as the mutuality of gains. Nation-building and the building of international relations collapsed too. This was largely because of God's rulings in non-economic terms.

However, what is potentially more important than a concrete deconstruction of the idea of God in the Old Testament as an economically inspired player, contractor and ruler are the very contracting principles and value principles which his actions and interventions, but also his non-interventions, reflected. This enables us to understand what Fromm (1967: 228) referred to as the 'experience to which the concept of God points' – independent of the question whether God in any sense were a persona or were dead or alive. In general, the experience and relevance of value principles cannot be questioned for our contemporary societies. And from here, the question whether the God of the Old Testament is an economist receives some added relevance, namely, first, by spelling out the Old Testament's underlying, economically inspired value principles on contracting among people and societies and, second, by discussing the prevailing interaction conditions which make interactions succeed or fail in Old Testament storytelling. In this way, the present book provided, largely freed from behavioural, theological and philosophical concepts, a modern perspective on the Old Testament as an institutional economic treatise. Especially the value and cooperation principles, which the present study unearthed for Genesis in economic terms, gave new relevance to the Old Testament for our contemporary societies. This questions Meeks' suggestion (1989: 3) that the Bible lacks a modern, scientific, economic theory. The Old Testament clearly showed ways forward of how to establish and maintain cooperative interactions in complex, pluralistic interaction settings. Most of the economic principles discovered for Exodus and subsequent books of the Old Testament provide by anti-thesis additional support to this claim too. From here, the Old Testament gains a high, contemporary relevance for advising modern society on burning problems such as societal contracting among nations and within a nation, as it is encountered in the capitalist, multicultural society or a globalizing, international community. So, an economic reconstruction of the Old Testament showed how 'shivering man' (Buchanan 1975: 130; see also the Introduction to the present book) could solve problems of social order and societal contracting without relying on God in any metaphysical or spiritual sense. In this respect, the book revised Buchanan's scepticism that moral philosophy prior to the Enlightenment could not inform on issues of Hobessian anarchy, social conflict and societal contracting *in a non-metaphysical, enlightened manner*. The Old Testament, as I read and reconstructed it from an economic perspective, here has much to offer, pointing towards a radical, economic humanism.

My economic reconstruction unearthed from many stories of the Old Testament the ever-present interaction conditions of pluralism, ethnic diversity, moral disagreement and even value decay. This, above all, underlines the *modern* approach the Old Testament takes for addressing societal problems. Thus, the present study lives up to calls, such as Buber's, to show modern society how the Bible can be understood anew:

> The man of today has no access to a sure and solid faith, nor can it be made accessible to him. If he examines himself seriously, he knows this and may not delude himself further.... To this end, he must read the ... Bible as though it were something entirely unfamiliar, as though it had not been set before him ready-made, as though he has not been confronted all his life with sham concepts and sham statements that cited the Bible as their authority. He must face the Book with a new attitude as something new.
>
> (Buber 1982: 4–5)

The economic reconstruction of the Old Testament pursued by the present book yielded such a new, modern and enlightened understanding of the Old Testament and the kind of questions and issues it aims to advise on. I achieved this by means of a scientific, economic reconstruction, which was extended to the concept of God too. In this respect, one has to direct critical questions at contemporary theology regarding how it handles the idea of God – in less abstract terms *or* in more abstract terms, as a persona *or* as underlying value principles. A principle-based approach here has potentially the advantage to reconnect (Old Testament) theology to the sciences, especially the social sciences, and strengthen human faith and revive practices of religion. In this respect, we can also outline an answer to Fromm's (1967: 229) question of 'what could take the place of religion in a world in which the concept of God may be dead but in which the experiential reality behind it must live?' The principles of an economic humanism which I unearthed in the present study even for a supposedly religious book like the Old Testament should here encourage theology and behavioural ethical research in general to carefully re-examine the economic approach for moral qualities. Institutional economics and constitutional economics, and economics in general (understood in a conventional, non-behavioural tradition), offer a rational, enlightened humanism, an alternative, modern ethics, that is well capable of solving social conflict in modern, pluralistic and frequently global interaction settings, where moral disagreement and possibly even value decay reign and the harmonization of moral and social values is infeasible or may be even morally undesirable. And as indicated, theology may be well capable of connecting to this kind of radical, economic humanism once it abstracts the concept of God for value principles, especially value principles such as the ones regarding mutual advantages. From here, God can then emerge as a true economist.

Bibliography

Ackroyd, S. and Thompson, P. (1999), *Organizational Misbehaviour*, London: Sage.

Adar, Z. (1984), *God in the Bible*, Tel-Aviv: Publisher n.a.

Alchian, A. A. and Demsetz, H. (1973), 'The Property Rights Paradigm', *Journal of Economic History*, 33, 16–27.

Alexander, P. S. (1992), 'The Fall into Knowledge: The Garden of Eden/Paradise in Gnostic Literature', *Journal for the Study of the Old Testament. Supplement Series*, 136, 91–104.

Anderson, B. W. (1966), *The Living World of the Old Testament*, London: Longman.

Anderson, G. A. (1992), 'The Penitence Narrative in the Life of Adam and Eve', *Hebrew Union College Annual*, 63, 1–38.

Ap-Thomas, D. R. (1972), 'The Context of the Old Testament', in O. J. Lace (ed.), *Understanding the Old Testament*, Cambridge: Cambridge University Press, 11–100.

Armstrong, K. (1996), *In the Beginning. A New Reading of the Book of Genesis*, London: HarperCollins.

Axelrod, R. (1997), *The Complexity of Cooperation*, Princeton, NJ: Princeton University Press.

—— (1986), 'An Evolutionary Approach to Norms', *American Political Science Review*, 80, 1095–111.

—— (1984), *The Evolution of Cooperation*, New York: Basic Books.

Barnard, C. (1938), *The Functions of the Executive*, Cambridge, MA: Harvard University Press.

Barzel, Y. (1989), *Economic Analysis of Property Rights*, Cambridge: Cambridge University Press.

Becker, G. S. (1993), 'The Economic Way of Looking at Behavior', *Journal of Political Economy*, 101, 385–409.

—— (1976), *The Economic Approach to Human Behavior*, Chicago, Ill: The University of Chicago Press.

—— (1965), 'A Theory of the Allocation of Time', *The Economic Journal*, 75, September, 493–517.

Benner, A. (1997), 'Religious Institutions and the Economics of Religion', *Journal of Institutional and Theoretical Economics*, 153, 1: 150–8.

Berle, A. A. Jr. and Means, G. C. (1932), *The Modern Corporation and Private Property*, New York: Macmillan.

Best, T. F. (1983), 'The Sociological Study of the New Testament: Promise and Peril of a New Discipline', *Scottish Journal of Theology*, 36, 181–94.

Bloom, H. (1982), 'Introduction', in M. Buber (ed.), *On the Bible. Eighteen Studies*, New York: Schocken Books, ix–xxxii.

Brams, S. J. (2002), *Biblical Games: Game Theory and the Hebrew Bible*, [extended edition of Brams (1980)], Cambridge, MA: MIT Press.

—— (1994), 'Game Theory and Literature', *Games and Economic Behavior*, 6, 32–54.

—— (1980), *Biblical Games: A Strategic Analysis of Stories of the Old Testament*, Cambridge, MA: MIT Press.

Brennan, G. (1996), 'Selection and the Currency of Reward', in R. E. Goodin (ed.), *The Theory of Institutional Design*, Cambridge: Cambridge University Press, 256–75.

Brennan, G. and Buchanan, J. M. (1985), *The Reason of Rules: Constitutional Political Economy*, Cambridge: Cambridge University Press.

Brennan, H. G. and Waterman, A. M. (1994), 'Introduction: Economics *and* Religion?', in H. G. Brennan and A. M. Waterman (eds), *Economics and Religion: Are They Distinct?*, Boston: Kluwer, 3–15.

Brett, M. G. (2000), 'Reading the Bible in the Context of Methodological Pluralism: The Undermining of Ethnic Exclusivism in Genesis', *Journal for the Study of the Old Testament. Supplement Series*, 299, 48–74.

Briend, J. (2000), 'The Sources of the Deuteronomistic History: Research on Joshua 1–12', *Journal for the Study of the Old Testament. Supplement Series*, 306, 360–86.

Bruce, F. F. (1979), 'The Theology and Interpretation of the Old Testament', in G.W. Anderson (ed.), *Tradition and Interpretation. Essays by Members of the Society for Old Testament Study*, Oxford: Clarendon Press, 385–416.

Brueggemann, W. (1986), *Hopeful Imagination. Prophetic Voices in Exile*, Philadelphia: Fortress Press.

Buber, M. (1982), *On the Bible. Eighteen Studies*, New York: Schocken Books.

Buchanan, J. M. (1995), 'Individual Rights, Emergent Social States, and Behavioral Feasibility', *Rationality and Society*, 7, 2: 141–50.

—— (1994), 'Economic Theory in the Postrevolutionary Moment of the 1990s', in P. A. Klein (ed.), *The Role of Economic Theory*, Boston, Mass.: Kluwer, 47–60.

—— (1987a) *Economics: Between Predictive Science and Moral Philosophy*, College Station: Texas A&M University Press.

—— (1987b), 'The Constitution of Economic Policy', *American Economic Review*, 77, 243–50.

—— (1977), *Freedom in Constitutional Contract. Perspectives of a Political Economist*, College Station and London: Texas A & M University Press.

—— (1975), *The Limits of Liberty. Between Anarchy and Leviathan*, Chicago, Ill: University of Chicago Press.

—— (1960), *Fiscal Theory and Political Economy*, Chapel Hill: The University of North Carolina Press.

Buchanan, J. M. and G. Tullock (1962), *The Calculus of Consent. Logical Foundations of Constitutional Democracy*, Ann Arbor: The University of Michigan Press.

Burns, T. (1990), 'Mechanistic and Organismic Structures', in D. S. Pugh (ed.), *Organization Theory. Selected Readings*, London: Penguin, 64–75.

Burns, T. and Stalker, G. M. (1961), *The Management of Innovation*, London: Tavistock Publications.

Capitan, W. C. (1972), *Philosophy of Religion. An Introduction*, Indianapolis: Pegasus.

Cassirer, E. (1962), *Leibniz' System*, Hildesheim, Germany: Georg Olms.

Cazelles, H. (1979), 'The History of Israel in the Pre-Exilic Period', in G. W. Anderson (ed.), *Tradition and Interpretation. Essays by Members of the Society for Old Testament Study*, Oxford: Clarendon Press, 274–319.

Childs, B. S. (1985), *Old Testament Theology in Canonical Context*, London: SCM Press

Clements, R. E. (1979), 'Pentateuchal Problems', in G. W. Anderson (ed.), *Tradition and Interpretation. Essays by Members of the Society for Old Testament Study,* Oxford: Clarendon Press, 96–124.

Clines, D. J. A. (1998), 'Methods in Old Testament Study', in J. Rogerson (ed.), *Beginning Old Testament Study,* London: SPCK, 25–48.

Coase, R. H. (1984), 'The New Institutional Economics', *Journal of Institutional and Theoretical Economics,* 140, 1: 229–31.

—— (1937), 'The Nature of the Firm', *Economica,* 4, November: 384–405.

Cohn, R. L. (1981), *The Shape of Sacred Space: Four Biblical Studies,* Chico, Cal.: American Academy of Religion (AAR)/Scholars Press.

Coleman, J. S. (1990), *Foundations of Social Theory,* Cambridge, Mass.: Harvard University Press.

Davidson, R. (1979), *Genesis 12–50,* Cambridge: Cambridge University Press.

Davies, G. H. (1967), *Exodus,* London: SCM Press.

Demsetz, H. (1964), 'Toward a Theory of Property Rights', *American Economic Review,* 57, 347–59.

Dragga, S. (1992), 'Genesis 2–3: A Story of Liberation', *Journal for the Study of the Old Testament,* 55, 3–13.

Eissfeldt, O. (1974), *The Old Testament. An Introduction,* Oxford: Blackwell.

Ensminger, J. (1997), 'Transaction Costs and Islam: Explaining Conversion in Africa', *Journal of Theoretical and Institutional Economics,* 153, 1: 4–29.

Etzioni, A. (1988), *The Moral Dimension. Towards a New Economics,* New York: Free Press.

Feinman, P. (1991), 'Drama of the Exodus', *Bible Review,* VII, 1: 26–35.

Friedman, M. (1962), *Capitalism and Freedom,* Chicago: The University of Chicago Press.

—— (1953), *Essays in Positive Economics,* Chicago: The University of Chicago Press.

Fromm, E. (1967), *You Shall Be As Gods. A Radical Interpretation of the Old Testament and Its Tradition,* London: J. Cape.

Fung, Y.-W. (2000), 'Victim and Victimizer. Jospeh's Interpretation of his Destiny', *Journal for the Study of the Old Testament. Supplement Series,* 308, 1–222.

Gerecke, U. (1997), *Soziale Ordnung in der modernen Gesellschaft. Zum Diskurs von Ökonomik, Systemtheorie und Ethik,* Doctoral Dissertation, Wirtschaftswissensch aftliche Fakultät Ingolstadt, Katholische Universität Eichstätt.

Gilboa, R. (1998), *Intercourses in the Book of Genesis,* Lewes: The Book Guild.

Gilkey, L. B. (1962), 'Cosmology, Ontology and the Travail of Biblical Language', *Concordia Theological Monthly,* 33, 143–54.

Glass, Z. G. (2000), 'Land, Slave Labor and Law: Engaging Ancient Israel's Economy', *Journal for the Study of the Old Testament,* 91, 27–39.

Gordon, B. (1994), 'Theological Positions and Economic Perspectives in Ancient Literature', in H. G. Brennan and A. M. Waterman (eds) *Economics and Religion: Are They Distinct?,* Boston: Kluwer, 19–40.

—— (1989), *The Economic Problem in Biblical and Patristic Thought,* Leiden and New York: Brill.

Gottwald , N. K. (1980), *The Tribes of Yahweh,* London: Maryknoll

Gräb, W. (2002), 'Creation or Nature? About Dialogue Between Theology and the Natural Sciences', *Journal for the Study of the Old Testament. Supplement Series,* 319, 277–90.

Graves, R. and Patai, R. (1964), *Hebrew Myths. The Book of Genesis,* London: Cassell.

Green, B. (1998), 'The Determination of Pharaoh: His Characterization in the Joseph Story (Genesis 37–50)', *Journal for the Study of the Old Testament*. *Supplement Series*, 257, 150–71.

Handy, C. B. (1985), *Understanding Organizations*, Harmondsworth: Penguin.

Hardin, G. (1971), 'The History and Future of Birth Control', in J. D. Ray Jr. and G. E. Nelson (eds.), *What a Piece of Work is Man*, Boston: Little, Brown and Company, 286–301.

—— (1968), 'The Tragedy of the Commons', *Science*, 162, 1243–48.

Hardin, R. (1997), 'The Economics of Religious Belief', *Journal of Theoretical and Institutional Economics*, 153, 1: 259–78.

—— (1996), 'Institutional Morality', in R. E. Goodin (ed.), *The Theory of Institutional Design*, Cambridge: Cambridge University Press, 126–53.

Hart, O. (1995), 'An Economist's Perspective on the Theory of the Firm', in O. E. Williamson (ed.), *Organization Theory: From Chester Barnard to the Present and Beyond*, New York: Oxford University Press, 154–71.

Hawk, L. D. (2003), 'Violent Grace: Tragedy and Transformation in the Oresteia and the Deuteronomistic History', *Journal for the Study of the Old Testament*, 28, 1: 73–88.

Hawking, S. W. (1988), *A Brief History of Time*, London: Bantam.

Hayek, F. (1979), *The Road to Serfdom*, London: Routledge & Kegan Paul.

—— (1976), *Law, Legislation and Liberty: The Mirage of Social Justice*, Volume 2, London: Routledge & Kegan Paul.

—— (1960), *The Constitution of Liberty*, London: Routledge & Kegan Paul.

—— (1949), *Individualism and Economic Order*, London: Routledge & Kegan Paul.

Hesterly, W. S., Lieberskind, J. and Zenger, T. R. (1990), 'Organizational Economics: An Impending Revolution in Organization Theory?', *Academy of Management Review*, 15, 402–20.

Hick, J. H. (1990), *Philosophy of Religion*, Englewood Cliffs, NJ: Prentice-Hall.

—— (1985), *Problems of Religious Pluralism*, London: Macmillan.

Hirshberg, H. H. (1964), *Hebrew Humanism*, Los Angeles: California Writers.

Hodson, G. (1967), *The Hidden Wisdom in the Holy Bible*, London: Theosophical Publishing House.

Hodgson, G. M. (2006), 'What are Institutions?', *Journal of Economic Issues*, 40, 1: 1–25.

——(1988), *Economics and Institutions. A Manifesto for a Modern Institutional Economics*, Cambridge: Polity Press.

Hofstadter, D. R. (1979), *Gödel, Escher, Bach. An Eternal Golden Braid*, London Penguin.

Hollis, M. (1994), *The Philosophy of Social Science*, Cambridge: Cambridge University Press.

Holmes, M. W. (1989), 'New Testament Textual Criticism', in S. McKnight (ed.), *Introducing New Testament Interpretation*, Grand Rapids, MI: Baker Book House, 53–74.

Holy Bible, the, New International Version ®. NIV ®. Copyright © 1973, 1978, 1984 by International Bible Society ©. All rights reserved worldwide. London: Hodder & Stoughton Publishers.

Homann, K. (1999a), 'Zur Grundlegung einer modernen Gesellschafts- und Sozialpolitik: Das Problem der Sozialen Ordnung', in U. Blum, W. Esswein, E. Greipl, H. Hereth and S. Müller (eds) *Soziale Marktwirtschaft im nächsten Jahrtausend*, Stuttgart, Germany: Schäffer-Poeschel, 119–48.

—— (1999b), 'Die Bedeuting von Dilemmastrukturen für die Ethik', *Working Paper*, Catholic University of Eichstätt at Ingolstadt, Germany.

—— (1997), 'Sinn und Grenze der ökonomischen Methode in der Wirtschaftsethik', *Volkswirtschaftliche Schriften*, 478, 1–42.

—— (1994), 'Homo Oeconomicus und Dilemmastrukturen', in H. Sautter (ed.) *Wirtschaftspolitik in offenen Volkswirtschaften*, Göttingen, Germany: Vandenhoeck & Ruprecht, 387–411.

—— (1990), 'Ökonomik und Ethik', *Conference Paper*, 5th Symposium 'Kirche heute', 11–13 October 1990, Augsburg, Germany.

Homann, K. and Pies, I. (1991), 'Gefangenendilemma und Wirtschaftsethik', *Wirtschaftswissenschaftliches Studium*, 12, 608–14.

Homann, K. and Suchanek, A. (2000), *Ökonomik. Eine Einführung*, Tübingen: Mohr Siebeck.

—— (1989), 'Methodologische Überlegungen zum ökonomischen Imperialismus', *Analyse & Kritik*, 11, 1: 70–93.

Hopkins, D. (1996), 'Bare Bones: Putting Flesh on the Economics of Ancient Israel', *Journal for the Study of the Old Testament. Supplement Series*, 228, 121–39.

Hurst, L. D. (1989), 'New Testament Theological Analysis', in S. McKnight (ed.), *Introducing New Testament Interpretation*, Grand Rapids, MI: Baker Book House, 133–61.

Iannaccone, L. R. (1998), 'Introduction to the Economics of Religion', *Journal of Economic Literature*, 36, 1465–95.

—— (1995) 'Voodoo Economics? Reviewing the Rational Choice Approach to Religion', *Journal for the Scientific Study of Religion*, 34, 1: 76–89.

Jacobs, M. R. (2003), 'The Conceptual Dynamics of Good and Evil in the Joseph Story: An Exegetical and Hermeneutical Inquiry', *Journal for the Study of the Old Testament*, 27, 3: 309–38.

Jones, G. R. (1995), *Organizational Theory. Text and Cases*, Reading/Mass.: Addison-Wesley.

Kaiser, W. C., Jr. (2001), *The Old Testament Documents. Are They Reliable and Relevant?*, Downers Grove, Ill.: Intervarsity Press

Keller, W. (1989), *The Bible as History*, Oxford: Alion Books

Klawans, J. (2001), 'Pure Violence: Sacrifice and Defilement in Ancient Israel', *Harvard Theological Review*, 94, 2: 133–55.

Knight, F. H. (1948), *Risk, Uncertainty and Profit*, 3rd edition, Boston: Houghton.

Kuan, J. K. (2001), 'Samsi-Ilu and the Realpolitik of Israel and Aram-Damascus in the Eight Century BCE', *Journal for the Study of the Old Testament. Supplement Series*, 343, 135–51.

Kugel, J. L. (1997), *The Bible As It Was*, London: Belknap/Harvard University Press.

Küng, H. (1999), 'Leitplanken für die Moral', *Der Spiegel*, 51, 20.12.1999: 70–3.

Kuran, T. (1994), 'Religious Economics and the Economics of Religion', *Journal of Institutional and Theoretical Economics*, 150, 769–75.

Lace, O. J. (1972), 'The History of Religion in Israel', in O. J. Lace (ed.), *Understanding the Old Testament*, Cambridge: Cambridge University Press, 101–77.

Lakatos, I. (1978), *The Methodology of Scientific Research Programmes*, Cambridge: Cambridge University Press.

—— (1970), 'Falsification and the Methodology of Scientific Research Programmes', in I. Lakatos and A. Musgrave (eds) *Criticism and the Growth of Knowledge*, Cambridge: Cambridge University Press, 91–196.

Lehmann, H. (1993), 'The Rise of Capitalism: Weber versus Sombart', in H. Lehmann and G. Roth (eds), *Weber's Protestant Ethic*, Cambridge: Cambridge University Press, 195–208.

Lemche, N. P. (2005), 'Conservative Scholarship on the Move', *Scandinavian Journal of the Old Testament*, 19, 2: 203–52.

Libecap, G. D. (1989), 'Distributional Issues in Contracting for Property Rights', *Journal of Institutional and Theoretical Economics*, 145, 6–24.

Lohmann, S. (1996), 'The Poverty of Green and Shapiro', in J. Friedman (ed.), *The Rational Choice Controversy: Economic Models of Politics Reconsidered*, New Haven, CT: Yale University Press, 127–54.

Luce, R. D. and Raiffa, H. (1957), *Games and Decision: Introduction and Critical Survey*, New York: J. Wiley.

Machlup, F. (1978), *Methodology of Economics and Other Social Sciences*, New York: Academic Press.

—— (1963), 'Theories of the Firm: Marginalist, Behavioral, Managerial', *American Economic Review*, 57, 1: 1–33.

MacIntyre, A. (1985), *After Virtue*, London: Duckworth.

MacKinnon, M. H. (1993), 'The Longevity of the Thesis: A Critique of the Critics', in H. Lehmann and G. Roth (eds), *Weber's Protestant Ethic*, Cambridge: Cambridge University Press, 211–43.

Margolis, H. (1982), *Selfishness, Altruism and Rationality*, Cambridge: Cambridge University Press.

Maskin, E. S. (1994), 'Conceptual Economic Theory', in P. A. Klein (ed.), *The Role of Economic Theory*, Boston: Kluwer, 187–96.

Mayes, A. D. H. (1999), 'Deuteronomistic Ideology and the Theology of the Old Testament', *Journal for the Study of the Old Testament*, 82, 57–82.

—— (1993), 'On Describing the Purpose of Deuteronomy', *Journal for the Study of the Old Testament*, 58, 13–33.

—— (1983), *The Story of Israel Between Settlement and Exile*, London: SCM Press.

Meeks, M. D. (1989), *God the Economist: The Doctrine of God and Political Economy*, Minneapolis, MN: Fortress Press.

Millard, A. (1984), 'The Etymology of Eden', *Vetus Testamentum*, 34, 103–6.

Miller, G. P. (1994), 'The Legal-Economic Approach to Biblical Interpretation', *Journal of Institutional and Theoretical Economics*, 150, 4: 755–62.

—— (1993a), 'Contracts of Genesis', *Journal of Legal Studies*, 21, 15–45.

—— (1993b), 'Ritual and Regulation: A Legal-Economic Interpretation of Selected Biblical Texts', *Journal of Legal Studies*, 21, 477–501.

Mintz, S. I. (1962), *The Hunting of Leviathan*, Cambridge: Cambridge University Press.

Morschauser, S. (2003), '"Hospitality", Hostiles and Hostages: On the Legal Background to Genesis 19.1–9', *Journal for the Study of the Old Testament*, 27, 461–85.

Muth, R. F. (1997), 'Economic Influences on Early Israel', *Journal for the Study of the Old Testament*, 75, 77–92.

Neufeld, E. (1993), 'The Redemption of Moses', *Judaism: A Quarterly Journal of Jewish Life and Thought*, 42, Winter: 50–9.

Neumann, von, J. and Morgenstern, O. (1947), *Theory of Games and Economic Behavior*, Princeton, NJ: Princeton University Press.

Nipperdey, T. (1993), 'Max Weber, Protestantism, and the Debate around 1900', in H. Lehmann and G. Roth (eds), *Weber's Protestant Ethic*, Cambridge: Cambridge University Press, 73–81.

North, C. M. and Taylor, B. A. (2004), 'The Biblical Underpinnings of Tit-for-Tat: Scriptural Insights into Axelrod's The Evolution of Cooperation', *Faith & Economics*, 44, Fall: 1–25.

North, D. (1993a), 'Institutions and Credible Commitment', *Journal of Institutional and Theoretical Economics*, 149, 1: 11–23.

—— (1993b), 'Institutions and Economic Performance', in U. Mäki, B. Gustafsson and C. Knudsen (eds) *Rationality, Institutions and Economic Methodology*, London: Routledge, 242–61.

—— (1990), *Institutions, Institutional Change, and Economic Performance*, Cambridge: Cambridge University Press.

North, D. C. and Thomas, R. P. (1973), *The Rise of the Western World. A New Economic History*, Cambridge: Cambridge University Press.

Noth, M. (1966), *Exodus. A Commentary*, London: SCM Press.

Novak, M. (1993), 'Eight Arguments about the Morality of the Marketplace', in J. Davies (ed.), *God and the Marketplace. Essays on the Morality of Wealth Creation*, London: IEA Health and Welfare Unit, 8–29.

Nozick, R. (1993), *The Nature of Rationality*, Princeton, New Jersey: Princeton University Press.

Nussbaum, M. C. (1986), *The Fragility of Goodness: Luck and Ethics in Greek Tragedy and Philosophy*, Cambridge: Cambridge University Press.

Nyland, C. (1998), 'Taylorism and the Mutual-Gains Strategy', *Industrial Relations*, 37, 4: 519–42.

—— (1996), 'Taylorism, John R. Commons and the Hoxie Report', *Journal of Economic Issues*, 30, 4: 985–1016.

Otzen, B., Gottlieb, H. and Jeppesen, K. (1980), *Myths in the Old Testament*, London: SCM Press.

Paris, D. (1998), 'An Economic Look at the Old Testament', in S. T. Lowry and B. Gordon (eds) *Ancient and Medieval Economic Ideas and Concepts of Social Justice*, New York: Brill, 39–103.

Parker, K. I. (1999), 'Mirror, Mirror on the Wall, Must We Leave Eden, Once and for All? A Lacanian Pleasure Trip Through the Garden', *Journal for the Study of the Old Testament*, 83, 19–29.

Penrose, R. (1989), *Shadows of the Mind*, Oxford: Oxford University Press.

Persky, J. (1995), 'The Ethology of Homo Economicus', *Journal of Economic Perspective*, 9, 2: 221–31.

Pfeiffer, R. H. (1948), *Introduction to the Old Testament*, London: Adam and Charles Black.

Pirson, R. (2002), 'The Lord of the Dreams. A Semantic and Literary Analysis of Genesis 37–50', *Journal for the Study of the Old Testament. Supplement Series*, 355, 1–168.

Plato (1999), *The Essential Plato*, translated by B. Jowett, Uxbridge: Softback Preview.

Plaut, W. G. (1981), *The Torah. A Modern Commentary*, New York: Union of American Hebrew Congregation.

Popper, K. (1992), *In Search of a Better World*, London: Routledge.

—— (1978), *Conjectures and Refutations: The Growth of Scientific Knowledge*, London: Routledge & Kegan Paul.

Rad, von, G. (1963), *Genesis. A Commentary*, London: SCM Press.

Raskovich, A. (1996), 'You Shall Have No Other Gods Beside Me: A Legal-Economic Approach of the Rise of Yahweh', *Journal of Institutional and Theoretical Economics*, 152, 3: 449–71.

Reventlow, H. G. (1985), *Problems of Old Testament Theology in the Twentieth Century*, London: SCM Press.

Rogerson, J. (1998), 'The World-View of the Old Testament', in J. Rogerson (ed.), *Beginning Old Testament Study*, London: SPCK, 58–76

Rogerson, J. and Davies, P. (1989), *The Old Testament World*, Cambridge: Cambridge University Press.

Sarna, N. M. (1986), *Exploring Exodus. The Heritage of Biblical Israel*, New York: Schocken Books.

Schein, E. (1980), *Organizational Psychology*, London: Prentice-Hall.

Schenker, A. (1998), 'The Biblical Legislation on the Release of Slaves: The Road from Exodus to Leviticus', *Journal for the Study of the Old Testament*, 78, 23–41.

Schmidt, T. E. (1989), 'Sociology and New Testament Exegesis', in S. McKnight (ed.), *Introducing New Testament Interpretation*, Grand Rapids, MI: Baker Book House, 115–32.

Schmidt, W. H. (1984), *Introduction to the Old Testament*, London: SCM Press.

Schotter, A. (1981), *The Economic Theory of Social Institutions*, Cambridge: Cambridge University Press.

Scott, A. (2000), 'Risk Society or Angst Society? Two Views of Risk, Consciousness and Community', in B. Adam, U. Beck and J. Van Loon (eds), *The Risk Society and Beyond: Critical Issues for Social Theory*, London: Sage, 33–46.

Sen, A. K. (1990), 'Rational Fools: A Critique of the Behavioural Foundations of Economic Theory', in J. J. Mansbridge (ed.), *Beyond Self-interest*, Chicago, Ill: University of Chicago Press, 25–43.

Shields, M. E. (2003), '"More Righteous than I": The Comeuppance of the Trickster in Genesis 38', *Journal for the Study of the Old Testament. Supplement Series*, 383, 31–51.

Simon, H. A. (1997), *An Empirically Based Microeconomics*, Cambridge: Cambridge University Press.

—— (1993), 'Altruism and Economics', *The American Economic Review. Papers and Proceedings*, 83, 2: 156–61.

—— (1976), *Administrative Behavior*, 3rd revised edition, New York: Free Press.

—— (1945), *Administrative Behavior*, New York: The Free Press.

Slivniak, D. M. (2003), 'The Garden of Double Messages: Deconstructing Hierarchical Oppositions in the Garden Story', *Journal for the Study of the Old Testament*, 27, 4: 439–60.

Smith, Adam (1976), *An Inquiry into the Nature and Causes of the Wealth of Nations*, 2 Volumes, Oxford: Clarendon.

Smith, I. (1999), 'The Economics of the Apocalypse: Modelling the Biblical Book of Revelation', *Journal of Institutional and Theoretical Economics*, 155, 3: 443–57.

Soggin, J. A. (1993), 'Notes on the Joseph Story', *Journal for the Study of the Old Testament. Supplement Series*, 152, 336–49

Sombart, W. (1911), *Die Juden und das Wirtschaftsleben*, Leipzig: Duncker and Humblot.

Spencer, J. R. (1995), 'Priestly Families (or Factions) in Samuel and Kings', *Journal for the Study of the Old Testament. Supplement Series*, 190, 387–400.

Spiegel (1999), 'Wo ist die Moral 3000 Jahre nach Moses? [Where is Morality 3000 Years After Moses?]', *Der Spiegel*, 20th December 1999, no. 51: 50–73.

Spriggs, D. G. (1974), *Two Old Testament Theologies: A Comparative Evaluation of the Contributions of Eichrodt and von Rad to Our Understanding of the Nature of Old Testament Theology*, London: SCM Press.

Stigler, G. J. and Becker G. S. (1977), 'De Gustibus Non Est Disputandum', *American Economic Review*, 67, 2: 76–90.

Stolz, F. (1974), *Interpreting the Old Testament*, London: SCM Press.

Stratton, B. J. (1995), 'Out of Eden. Reading, Rhetoric, and Ideology in Genesis 2–3', *Journal for the Study of the Old Testament. Supplement Series,* 208, 1–292.

Suchanek, A. (1994), *Ökonomischer Ansatz und theoretische Integration*, Tübingen, Germany: Mohr-Siebeck.

— (1993), 'Der homo oeconomicus als Heuristik', *Working Paper No. 38*, Department of Management and Economics, Catholic University of Eichstaett at Ingolstadt, Germany.

Taylor, F. W. (1912), *Taylor's Testimony Before the Special House Committee*, reprinted in F. W. Taylor (ed.) (1964), *Scientific Management*, London: Harper and Row.

— (1911), *The Principles of Scientific Management*, reprinted in F. W. Taylor (ed.) (1964), *Scientific Management*, London: Harper and Row.

— (1903), *Shop Management*, reprinted in F. W. Taylor (ed.) (1964), *Scientific Management*, London: Harper and Row.

Thompson, T. L. (1974), *The Historicity of the Patriarchal Narratives*, Berlin: de Gruyter.

Tullock, G. (1985), 'Adam Smith and the Prisoners' Dilemma', *Quarterly Journal of Economics*, 100, 1073–81.

Tullock, J. (1981), *The Old Testament Story*, Englewood Cliffs, NJ: Prentice-Hall.

Valiquette, H. P. (1999), 'Exodus–Deuteronomy as Discourse: Models, Distancing, Provocation, Paraenesis', *Journal for the Study of the Old Testament*, 85, 47–70.

Vanberg, V. (1994), *Rules and Choice in Economics*, London: Routledge.

Vanberg, V. J. (2001), *The Constitution of Markets. Essays in Political Economy*, London: Routledge (Taylor & Francis).

— (1986), 'Spontaneous Market Order and Social Rules. A Critical Examination of F. Hayek's Theory of Cultural Evolution', *Economics and Philosophy*, 2, 75–100.

Vanderkam, J. C. (1994), *The Dead Sea Scrolls Today*, London: SPCK.

Wagner, S. A. (1997), *Understanding Green Consumer Behaviour*, London: Routledge.

Wagner-Tsukamoto, S. A. (2008a), 'An Economic Reading of the Exodus: On the Institutional Economic Reconstruction of Biblical Cooperation Failures', *Scandinavian Journal of the Old Testament*, 22, 1: 114–34.

— (2008b), 'Consumer Ethics in Japan: An Economic Reconstruction of Moral Agency of Japanese Firms', *Journal of Business Ethics*, DOI 10.1007/s10551-008-9671-x.

— (2008c), 'Contrasting the Behavioural Business Ethics Approach and the Institutional Economic Approach to Business Ethics: Insights From the Study of Quaker Employers', *Journal of Business Ethics*, DOI 10.1007/s10551-007-9596-9.

— (2008d), 'The Rationality of Ends/Market Structure-Grid: Positioning and Contrasting Different Approaches to Business Ethics', *Business Ethics. A European Review*, 17, 326–46.

—— (2008e), 'Scientific Management Revisited: Did Taylorism Fail Because of a Too Positive Image of Human Nature?', *Journal of Management History*, 14, 4: 348–72.

—— (2007a), 'An Institutional Economic Reconstruction of Scientific Management: On the Lost Theoretical Logic of Taylorism', *Academy of Management Review*, 32, 105–17.

—— (2007b), 'Moral Agency, Profits and the Firm: Economic Revisions to the Friedman Theorem', *Journal of Business Ethics*, 70, 209–20.

—— (2005), 'An Economic Approach to Business Ethics: Moral Agency of the Firm and the Enabling and Constraining Effects of Economic Institutions and Interactions in a market Economy', *Journal of Business Ethics*, 60, 75–89.

—— (2003), *Human Nature and Organization Theory: On the Economic Approach to Institutional Organization*, Cheltenham: Edward Elgar.

—— (2001a), 'Economics of Genesis. On the Institutional Economic Deciphering and Reconstruction of the Legends of Genesis', *Journal of Interdisciplinary Economics*, 12, 3: 249–87.

—— (2001b), 'The Failure of the Quaker Experiments (1900–1940) in Corporate Social Responsibility: Implications for an Economic Approach to Business Ethics', *Conference Paper*, EBEN-Conference, 9–10 April 2001, University of Nottingham, Nottingham, UK.

—— (2000a), 'An Institutional Economic Reconstruction of Scientific Management: On the Lost Theoretical Logic of Taylorism', *Discussion Paper No. 2000/14*, Management Centre/Department of Economics, University of Leicester, UK, December 2000.

—— (2000b), 'The Exodus of the Wealth of Nations: 'Rational Foolishness' and the Disequilibration of Interests in Social Interactions Between Egypt and Israel', *Discussion Paper No. 2000/05*, April 2000, Management Centre/Department of Economics, University of Leicester, UK.

Ward, G. (1995), 'A Postmodern Version of Paradise', *Journal for the Study of the Old Testament*, 65, 3–12.

Weber, M. (1930), *The Protestant Ethic and the Spirit of Capitalism*, London: Unwin.

Weiser, A. (1961), *Introduction to the Old Testament*, London: Darton, Longman and Todd.

Westermann, C. (1987), *Genesis 37–50: A Commentary*, London: SPCK.

—— (1986), *Genesis 12–36. A Commentary*, London: SPCK.

—— (1984), *Genesis 1–11. A Commentary*, London: SPCK.

Wildavsky, A. (1994), 'Survival Must Not Be Gained Through Sin: The Moral of the Joseph Stories Prefigured Through Judah and Tamar', *Journal for the Study of the Old Testament*, 62, 37–48.

Williamson, O. E. (1998), 'Human Actors and Economic Organization', *Conference Paper*, 7th Biannual Meeting of the International Joseph Schumpeter Society, June 1998, Vienna, Austria.

—— (1996), 'Economics and Organization: A Primer', *California Management Review*, 38, 2: 131–46.

—— (1985), *The Economic Institutions of Capitalism*, New York: Free Press.

—— (1983), 'Credible Commitments: Using Hostages to Support Exchange', *American Economic Review*, 73, 519–40.

— (1975), *Markets and Hierarchies. Analysis and Antitrust Implications*, New York: Free Press.

— (1967), *The Economics of Discretionary Behavior: Managerial Objectives in a Theory of the Firm*, London: Kershaw.

Wilson, R. (1997), *Economics, Ethics, and Religion*, Basingstoke, UK: Macmillan.

Wolde, van, E. J. (2003), 'Love and Hatred in a Multiracial Society: The Dinah and Shechem Story in Genesis 34 in the Context of Genesis 28–35', *Journal for the Study of the Old Testament. Supplement Series*, 373, 435–49.

Author Index

266   *Author Index*

Nozick, R., 47
Nussbaum, M., 47, 62
Nyland, C., 154

Otzen, B., 17, 24, 50, 52, 60–1, 65,
    67, 122, 224

Paris, D., 3, 7, 32–8, 42, 44, 52,
    60–1, 120–1, 125, 134, 142,
    150, 153, 156, 161–2, 164–5,
    168, 203, 231
Parker, K. I., 71
Patai, R., 90, 115–16, 126, 128, 132
Penrose, R., 26, 46
Persky, J., 27, 48
Pfeiffer, R. H., 16, 86, 98, 115, 119,
    127–8, 146, 156, 173, 176
Pies, I., 47
Pirson, R., 108, 123, 131, 158, 232
Plato, 76, 102
Plaut, W. G., 13, 51, 65–7, 69, 71,
    86, 90, 110, 112, 115, 127–8,
    131–2, 146, 156–7, 161, 164,
    170, 173–4, 176, 180, 187, 192,
    197, 244
Popper, K., 26, 39, 46, 49, 241

Rad, von, G., 1, 50, 53, 58, 61–2, 65,
    90, 114–16, 118, 126, 133,
    146, 151
Raiffa, H., 23, 26–7, 47, 49, 85
Raskovich, A., 32, 69
Rawls, J., 77
Reventlow, H. G., 30
Rogerson, J., 1, 13, 61, 84, 122, 127,
    146, 181, 186–7
Rousseau, J. J., 130

Sarna, N. M., 121, 131, 134–5, 143,
    145–8, 155–60, 162–4, 167,
    171–3, 177–8, 184–5
Schein, E., 76
Schenker, A., 29–30, 178
Schmidt, T. E., 14, 38, 39, 42
Schmidt, W. H., 119, 126,
    128, 147, 177, 189, 192,
    196, 199
Schotter, A., 47
Scott, A., 47

Sen, A. K., 24, 27–8, 41, 49, 64, 136,
    159, 239
Shakespeare, W., 156
Shields, M. E., 77
Simon, H. A., 25, 28, 41, 49, 64,
    136, 239
Slivniak, D. M., 66–7, 69
Smith, Adam, 24, 41–3, 65, 74, 97–8,
    220, 236
Smith, I., 32
Soggin, J. A., 119
Sombart, W., 247
Spencer, J. R., 172
Spinoza, B., 104, 116, 130
Spriggs, D. G., 1, 37, 75
Stalker, G. M., 181
Stigler, G. J., 23–4, 28
Stolz, F., 39
Stratton, B. J., 50, 58, 71
Suchanek, A., 27, 39, 41, 47–9, 64

Taylor, B. A., 21, 90, 212
Taylor, F. W., 148–50, 153
Thomas, R. P., 86
Thompson, P., 87
Thompson, T. L., 13
Tullock, G., 22–3, 27, 35, 97, 98
Tullock, J., 1, 24, 37, 60–1, 120,
    122, 148

Valiquette, H. P., 16–17, 91, 126, 146,
    173, 184
Vanberg, V., xiii, 3, 11–12, 23, 47–8,
    127, 136, 154, 232
Vanderkam, J. C., 16

Wagner, S. A., 14
Wagner-Tsukamoto, S. A., 6–7, 14,
    20, 23–8, 31, 37, 39, 41–2,
    46–9, 57, 63–5, 68, 86–7, 97,
    99, 101–2, 125, 135, 138, 140,
    142, 149–50, 153–4, 159–60,
    181, 185, 204, 221, 231, 241
Ward, G., 71
Waterman, A. M., 40
Weber, M., 10, 219, 234, 245–8
Weiser, A., 15, 26, 180, 190, 244
Westermann, C., 15, 53, 58, 67, 71,
    85, 90, 95, 100, 102, 113, 115,

Subject Index

Junctim (conceptual) between
  Genesis and Exodus, 74, 135,
  140, 156–7, 163, 167–8, 214,
  236–7, 240

Laban, 63, 84–5, 87–92, 94–6, 1–2–3,
  107, 110, 115–18, 206, 210, 249
  Jacob's mischief, 63, 84, 86–9, 91–2,
    94–6, 115–17, 206
  revenge of Jacob, 87–91, 110, 115
  see also Jacob
Levites, 101, 108, 110, 135, 151, 158,
  170–5,177, 179–84, 186, 190–2,
  194, 200–1, 214, 217, 230
  Jacob's warning against the House
    of Levi, 135, 151, 158, 186,
    217, 230
  Moses as leader of the Levites, 135,
    151, 158, 179–80, 182, 200,
    215, 217
Lot, 36, 63, 75, 77, 79, 81, 83–6, 95,
  100–1, 105, 110, 114, 182, 207,
  211–13, 221, 223, 227, 240,
  242, 244

Modernity, *see* pluralism
Moral diversity, *see* pluralism
Moses, xiv, 3, 9, 26, 67, 128–9, 132,
  134–5, 139, 141, 144, 146,
  150–67, 169, 171–5, 179–80,
  182, 184–6, 188–92, 196,
  200–1, 203, 207–11, 213–15,
  217, 223, 231, 236–7, 241, 243
  acting as economic man, 67, 141,
    146, 157–65, 243
  and decline thesis, xiv, 156–7, 185,
    211, 229, 236
  and the escalation of dilemmas in
    the exodus story, 142–8, 150–4,
    157–65
  Jacob's warning against Levite
    leadership, 135, 151, 158, 186,
    217, 230
  and the loss of pluralism, 165–6,
    157–8, 175, 184–5, 188, 196,
    201, 203, 207, 209, 211, 217,
    231, 237, 241, 243
  non-hero thesis, 139, 141, 156–7,
    185, 211, 229, 236

and slavery thesis, 132, 134, 141,
  145–8, 163–4, 166, 168
  see also Levites
Multi-cultural society, *see* pluralism
Mutual gains
  concept of, 8, 19, 23–6, 41, 46, 48,
    55, 74, 96–7, 110, 160, 195,
    220, 242, 248
  during the exodus journey, 182–3
  in Genesis (prior to the Joseph
    story), 97–8, 11, 117–18, 213
  in the Joseph story, 110, 121, 126,
    130, 133–4, 136, 151, 158, 235
  pareto-superiority, 22–4, 34–5, 41,
    50, 61, 82, 88, 97–8, 100, 102,
    117, 130, 146, 152, 159
  in the Solomon story, 196–7
  compare mutual loss
Mutual loss, 185, 195
  in the exodus story, 110, 154, 156
  in the paradise story, 58–60, 68, 72
  pareto-inferiority, 59, 71, 161,
    163, 239
  in the resettlement phase after the
    exodus journey, 185, 195
  see also rational foolishness
  compare mutual gains

Natural distribution state, *see* anarchy
New Testament, 236–8
Noah, 75–7, 79–80, 86, 99–101, 103,
  105, 107–9, 111–12, 116,
  129–30, 134, 136, 175, 195,
  200, 207–10, 211, 219, 221,
  223–4, 227, 234, 240,
  242, 244
  loss of pluralism, 76, 99–101, 103,
    108, 111–12, 129, 175, 200,
    207, 211, 221
Non-economic humanism, 5–7, 78,
  106, 128, 131–2, 137–8, 151,
  228–30
  value contracts
  compare economic humanism
Non-hero thesis, xiv, 9, 74, 128, 132,
  134–5, 139, 141, 156–7, 185,
  201, 211, 229, 231, 233, 236
  compare anti-hero-thesis
  compare hero-thesis